TANK ACTION

TANK ACTION

An Armoured Troop Commander's War
1944–45

DAVID RENDER
WITH STUART TOOTAL

W&N

WEIDENFELD & NICOLSON

First published in Great Britain in 2016
by Weidenfeld & Nicolson

1 3 5 7 9 10 8 6 4 2

A CIP catalogue record for this book
is available from the British Library.

ISBN 978-1-474-60326-3 (HB)
ISBN 978-1-474-60327-0 (ETPB)

Typeset by Input Data Services Ltd, Bridgwater, Somerset

Printed and bound by CPI Group (UK) Ltd, Croydon, CR0 4YY

Weidenfeld & Nicolson
The Orion Publishing Group Ltd
Carmelite House, 50 Victoria Embankment
London EC4Y 0DZ

An Hachette UK Company

www.orionbooks.co.uk

*In war it is the man that counts, and not only the machine. A good
tank is useless unless the team inside it is well trained, and the men in
the team have stout hearts and enthusiasm for the fight.*

Field Marshal Bernard Montgomery,
'Some Notes on the Conduct of War', written in November 1944

CONTENTS

LIST OF ILLUSTRATIONS

13. A Squadron officers on leave in Brussels in November 1944. (Sherwood Rangers Yeomanry archives)
14. Major Bill Enderby, A Squadron Leader after John Semken. (Sherwood Rangers Yeomanry archives)
15. The Sherwood Rangers Yeomanry parade through German streets. (Sherwood Rangers Yeomanry archives)
16. One of the mass graves at the Sanbostel concentration camp in Germany. (Sherwood Rangers Yeomanry archives)
17. Padre Leslie Skinner, the Sherwood Rangers' chaplain. (Sherwood Rangers Yeomanry archives)
18. Field Marshal Bernard Montgomery with Major General Ivor Thomas. (Sherwood Rangers Yeomanry archives)
19. Lieutenant General Brian Horrocks. (Sherwood Rangers Yeomanry archives)
20. Stanley Christopherson. (Reproduced by kind permission of David Christopherson)
21. An example of German propaganda leaflets. (David Render's private collection)
22. At the French Residency to receive the *Légion d'honneur*. (Benjamin Grafton/French Embassy)

LIST OF MAPS

FOREWORD

Having interviewed and written about numerous veterans from the Second World War, those men that served their country all those years ago constitute a remarkable fraternity. I first met David when I was in 'conversation' with him at the Chalke Valley History Festival, to commemorate the 70th anniversary of the Normandy campaign. His candid, self-effacing and, at times, humorous revelation of his experiences as a young troop commander in 1944 and 1945 held the packed audience in fascination. At the end of it they gave him a standing ovation that lasted for several minutes.

In 1944 the life expectancy of a newly commissioned tank troop officer in Normandy was estimated as being two weeks. David Render was a nineteen-year-old second lieutenant, fresh from Sandhurst, when he was sent to France as a battle casualty replacement to a veteran armoured unit that had already spent years fighting in the deserts of North Africa. Joining the Sherwood Rangers Yeomanry five days after the D-Day landings, the combat-hardened men he was sent to command did not expect him to last long. In the following weeks of ferocious fighting in Normandy, in which over 90 per cent of his fellow tank commanders became casualties, David's ability to survive numerous dangerous encounters and close shaves, led his squadron commander to nickname him the 'inevitable Mr Render' as he won his spurs in the battle and gained the confidence and respect of his men.

David Render remained in the thick of the action throughout the last year of the war. He went on to survive the culmination of the vicious close-quarters tank battles in the bocage country around Caen and to take part in the Allied breakout from Normandy. He led his troop of Sherman tanks in the fast-moving armoured dash into Belgium and the failed attempt to reach the beleaguered British paratroopers at Arnhem, as part of Operation Market Garden. He participated in the bitter winter fighting in the mud and flooded waterways of Holland and his regiment's bloody assault on the Siegfried Line. Despite having two tanks destroyed under him, he then took part in the crossing of the Rhine and numerous actions to clear out pockets of fanatical German resistance during the final advance into the heart of the Third Reich.

What is remarkable about David's story is his willingness to reflect on the contentious issues regarding the nature of the fighting that are so often left out of individual front-line accounts of the Second World War. His story exposes the psychological and physical impact of the stresses and strains of being involved in near continuous action. He does not shy away from the controversial, such as the leadership challenges of difficult relationships, the horrors of combat and the ethics of fighting a savage and bloody war of attrition. He portrays his story in a way that exposes the good, the bad and the ugly realities of war, in a manner that takes the reader into the heart of battle, with pace, excitement and a palpable sense of danger.

I have been enormously fortunate to get to know David and have the privilege of walking former battlefields with him, listen to his stories and have the opportunity to probe him for the details. Throughout, I was struck by his humility, humour and generosity of spirit. In the early part of 2016, I was honoured to be able to accompany David to an investiture in London, where the French Ambassador awarded him the *Légion d'honneur*. In receiving France's highest decoration, he was typically modest and talked of the real heroes being those who did not live to tell their stories.

There are few surviving veterans of David's lucidity and exceptional character, which also led him to become a national motor-racing champion in his sixties and a highly successful businessman. His story of war is an extraordinary one that deserves to be told.

Stuart Tootal

INTRODUCTION

Even today, the entry in the Sherwood Rangers' war diary regarding the fighting the regiment took part in near the Dutch town of Nijmegen makes hard reading. The report states simply that on 25 September 1944:

> A Squadron operating in the North experienced considerable enemy shelling. Lieutenant H. Heenan was killed.

Two brief sentences written in military-service style. Clipped, precise and to the point. No doubt penned by some tired staff officer in the regimental headquarters at the end of another interminably exhausting day; the loss of a young officer, just another grim minor statistic in the massed ranks of an army at war.

What the entry doesn't tell you about is how Harry Heenan died. The tragic circumstances involved, that his grieving parents never came to terms with the loss of their only child, that he lost his life saving mine or that he was my best friend. It tells you nothing of the German 88mm anti-tank gun that had us in its sights, the wild screaming crash of the incoming rounds or the dread terror as its shells struck about our immobilised tank. When I read it now, I still wince at the memory of the ear-splitting crack of the high-velocity projectiles, as they gouged lightning-quick furrows in the ground around us and sprayed the tank with dirt.

The Sherwood Rangers Yeomanry received more battle honours than any other unit in the Second World War and official documents, such as the regiment's war diary, form an important part of military history. But war is not just a matter of dry official accounts of the actions of units, or records of their manoeuvres captured by red Chinagraph arrows marked on maps by staff officers and senior commanders. War is about the soldier at the sharp end of battle with all its privations and dangers. Dog-tired, filthy men, exhausted by combat, lack of sleep and the stress of constant danger. Men who must force themselves back into their tanks, to start over again what they did the day before, wondering whether they would survive another day. Each dawn requiring them to prepare to advance to the next enemy-held feature, take another village, or once again lead the squadron's advance up a lonely road with the expectant anticipation of the first shot of hostile shell. Hoping and praying that it would not hit you and, if it did, that it would not turn your tank into a blazing inferno of hell.

Official reports and dry sanitised regimental histories tell you little of that. But such accounts are the lifeblood of historians and professional writers, of which I am not. Indeed numerous authors have written credible accounts of the fighting that took place in northwest Europe from D-Day to the defeat of Germany in the last year of the Second World War. But however commendable their works, they tend to cover the entirety of the campaign or focus on the complete compass of a particular operation or unit. In doing so, the emphasis tends to be placed on the generals and their broad sweeps of strategy and operational plans. While recognising that the experience of men in combat is vital to our understanding of war, the views of the

Introduction

ordinary soldier or young officer are largely confined to individual anecdotes or random snapshots of grassroots tactical activity from a range of different units covered in just a few short lines of text.

This book is about the battles fought in northwest Europe during the last year of the war, as seen through the prism of my own personal experience of eleven bloody months of commanding a troop of Sherman tanks. It concerns the account of the individual and the small collections of men who made up 5 Troop of A Squadron in the Sherwood Rangers Yeomanry. It is not about our famous commanders, remote men like Montgomery and Eisenhower who fought battles from the maps in their rear headquarters, where the shot and shell and the fear of battle rarely penetrated. It is not about the grand design or application of their campaign plans. Where I have made reference to them, I have only done so to the extent that they had a direct bearing on our experiences in 5 Troop, or where I feel that the broader contextual background is of importance to understanding an event. What follows seeks to highlight the human dimension of war at close quarters, where the focus of minor tactical operations rarely extended beyond the view afforded from the open hatch of a tank commander's turret, the next hedge line ahead of us, thoughts about what it might conceal, whether we would be the lead troop and whether we would live to see the fading glow of another sunset.

Looking back over seven decades, you might ask me what I have got to say and why write now? I was only a lowly lieutenant in a mighty Allied army and 5 Troop was the tiniest cog in a great machine. I was just one of many hundreds of thousands who fought through northwest Europe in 21st Army Group. I can make no claim to any great acts of valour and, like the vast majority of others, I was just doing my job. My reason for writing is not about setting down some great history of the campaign, of which I was only a microscopic part; there are better works for that. But historians have often been unkind to those who struggled ashore on D-Day, fought through the tangled nightmare of the Norman bocage, suffered the agony of that terrible flooded winter in the lowlands of Holland and went on to drive into the heartland of Nazi Germany, against an enemy that far too often was unwilling to recognise when he was beaten. I want to set down a record as I saw it.

Tough and professional as our opponents were, the comparative analysis of their fighting prowess compared to the British Tommy lacks perspective. For every Wehrmacht soldier, SS trooper or German paratrooper who fought with tenacity, there were a score more who were happy to give up and surrender at the first opportunity. I have seen men of both sides break and run, just as I have seen British infantrymen stubbornly fighting through a hard-contested enemy position, or German soldiers attacking forward against our tanks at the point of a bayonet. But while they were not the heroes portrayed in the Hollywood films made after the war, nor were they victims, as many would have you believe. While infantry casualty rates often exceeded those of the First World War and the average life expectancy of a tank troop commander was less than two weeks, we were simply soldiers trying to do our job to the best of our ability.

Fear on the battlefield is the natural order of things. Ask any regular soldier who has made the army his career and served in action numerous times. But the vast majority of those who donned battledress and shouldered rifle and pack, or operated from the steel confines of a Sherman tank, even the minority among us who volunteered, were not professional soldiers. The British Army of the Second World War was an army of conscripted citizens torn from a life of peace and thrown into war by force of circumstance. Most did not want to be there but had little choice in the matter; their main preoccupations were to get the job done, survive and get home again as quickly as possible to resume their normal lives. The fact that a conscript army of infantrymen and tank crews in its fifth year of war overcame fear on a daily basis to risk life and limb is testimony to their courage in itself. Less than 5 per cent were regular, but by the end of the war the British Army had improved markedly from the dark days of 1940 to become the largest and best-equipped army this country has ever put into the field. Despite its faults it was an extraordinary fighting force and the role it played in liberating occupied Europe and defeating the Nazis was impressive.

The frictions of war – chance, bad weather, mistakes and ill fortune – are the only certainties of combat, along with death, injury and destruction. Most of our generals were far from popular with the troops, but love them or loathe them our more senior commanders were men under the severest pressure who had to make on-the-spot decisions with imperfect information. The luxury of hindsight has also often been harsh on them. But war is a random and bloody business, where the weird geometry of chance has its play and its frictions and human fallibility and fragility abound. Combat is fast moving, confusing and often bewildering. There is no perfect science, only perfect intent that is unlikely to withstand first contact with the prevailing realities on the ground once battle is joined, and where the enemy also gets a vote in the outcome. All factors were at play as we sweated in the heat and the dust of Normandy and were mired in the blood and the mud of a miserable freezing winter on the German frontier.

While I joined regimental associations and attended organised pilgrimages to former battlefields after the war, I never thought deeply about what we had experienced. Nor did I trouble myself with the debates that raged about the quality of our tanks, whether our commanders lacked the aggressive drive of the German generals or whether as an army we missed the opportunities our opponents would have seized. Instead, I submerged myself in building a business and bringing up my family. No doubt some mental-health counsellor would describe this as some form of self-therapy. It wasn't, I was just busy. However, as I advance into my early nineties and the ranks of my former comrades, just teenagers and young men in their early twenties at the time, have been depleted and wearied by age, I am conscious that I am living on the edge of living history. Thus, I want to set down my version of events before night falls.

I have no intention of providing a detailed analysis of the major operations that I took part in, or the 'what ifs' of history. Again there are others who have felt better placed to do that. What I have attempted to do is tell my story and that of those that made up 5 Troop and the wider characters that had a bearing on how we lived, fought and, some of us, died in our Sherman tanks. I have sought to tell the story of the British tank soldier, with all his vices and virtues. How we communicated, the vernacular used, what we wore, how we were equipped, how we fought together with the other combat arms and what worked and what didn't. These themes, along with what we cared about, what we hated and what we thought about, all form threads of the story, as much as the realities of war. The frictions of fatigue, weather, miscalculations, friendly fire and pure bad luck also have their place, as do the emotions of loss, fear and excitement mixed with the fortitude and forbearance of the human spirit. Additionally, as in any parable, the interaction of personal relationships, some good and some bad, as well as the place of comradeship, small-unit cohesion and leadership all have parts to play too.

I kept no diary; few of us had any time or inclination for that. Consequently, my recall is less than complete. The distance of time has no doubt taken its toll and while some recollections are retained in vivid Technicolor detail, as if they happened only yesterday, others are masked by obscurity and I have only a vague sense of the time and space in which they occurred. The minutiae of certain details have been burned irrevocably into my mind, while the compass of more significant events remains beyond my ken. I can still remember the satisfying feel of my beautifully balanced blue-black Luger pistol in my hand, with its wonderfully smooth action. But for the life of me, I can remember nothing of the German I took it from or where and when he was captured. The awful, sobbing shriek of the enemy's Nebelwerfer rockets and the shattering explosions, as they detonated round our position, will never leave me. But ask me the exact place and the date when they caught us in the open and I will be hard pressed to tell you.

One should remain wary of accounts claiming authoritative and absolute recollection. On the battlefield total recall is neither complete nor precise. In some instances my memories of events have varied from the views of others and official accounts, just as they would have done if they had been captured in the immediate aftermath of battle. But where there are patches of amnesia I have done my best to remember and through writing this book certain events have re-emerged from the mists of time; often coaxed out of me by my co-author, as we walked, talked and debated over former battlefields.

On occasion insistence on visiting a hedge line again, or investigating a particular track to see over the brow of an innocuous-looking hill, unlocked my cognitive functions, as I found myself overlooking a piece of ground that I had not seen for seven decades. And then, suddenly, I see them again; a column of Wehrmacht infantry, a field-grey mass stark against the forestry block in the shallow valley below us. Standing but 400 yards away from where the ghosts of those men marched, I can once again hear the crash of our high explosive (HE) shells, the chatter of the machine guns and see the strike of the tracer as it began to chop them down. The fog hanging thick in the trees above Briquessard, just as it did all those years ago after a spat with a fool of an infantry major, provokes a flood of reminiscence that takes me back to the morning when 5 Troop advanced through those eerie woods alone and without the support of his company.

Other memories I will never forget. The savage blinding flash of sparking light beneath my legs, followed by the sudden darkness of thick black smoke filling the inside of the tank and the caustic taste of burned explosives in my mouth, when we hit a mine. Looking inside a knocked-out tank and, on witnessing what was inside, vowing to never do it again, or the hatred and arrogance that burned through the clear blue eyes of the young fair-haired SS trooper we captured in the fighting to the south of Tilly. The shock of seeing the rockets ripple off the wing of an RAF Typhoon and watching them streak down towards us, praying that we wouldn't take a direct hit. The comradeship and laughter that I shared with my fellow troop commanders that did so much to carry us through. The sympathetic kindness of my loader/operator, who made sure that I always had something to eat when I might otherwise have gone hungry. And of course, I will never forget the ominous click on the other end of the radio net and finding out that it meant that Harry Heenan was dead.

As an officer my concerns extended beyond the more self-orientated interests of my troopers, preoccupied primarily with eating, sleeping and staying alive. Encased within the steel hull of a Sherman, their view of the world was limited to what they could see through the glass of their crew station's one-by-six-inch periscope. But my broader perspective of the bigger picture at the time should not be overstated. It remained restricted to the role of my troop of four tanks, its part in the squadron's task and only a thin sense of what the rest of the regiment was up to, let alone the divisions of infantry that we were supporting. But hindsight and deeper re-examination has provoked a better understanding of the implications of the strategic context in which we operated. It has also brought about a clearer appreciation of chronology and the sequence of events, which have been woven in from the point of retrospection. Where my recall has diverged from the recollection of a tired staff officer or varied from the recall of others, I have told it how it was, as it appeared to me at the time, balanced against an analysis of the probable. However, any errors or faults in accuracy are mine, and mine alone.

Introduction

All the events described in the following pages actually took place and all the people mentioned are real. However, I have not used the actual names of some of the characters that appear in this book out of respect to them and to spare their relatives, where I feel that details might cause them distress. My only other concern is that I have done justice to the courage and fortitude of the men that I fought with all those years ago. In the risk-averse and self-obsessed nature of modern-day society they were a remarkable fraternity born of smoke, danger and death. They did an exceptional job with the resources they had available to them and in the circumstances they faced. It is a privilege to have served with them.

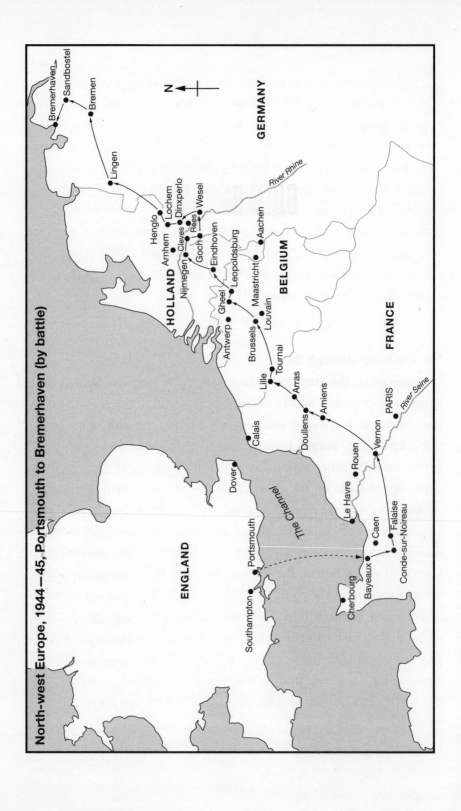

North-west Europe, 1944–45, Portsmouth to Bremerhaven (by battle)

1

GOLD BEACH

The sun broke through the clouds and projected bright beams of light that danced on the grey-green water as it rolled in waves towards the shingle. There was a steady offshore breeze, but it was nothing like the wind that had raged and battered the lines of ships and landing craft as they surged towards the beach all that time ago. I had stood with the other veterans wearing my regimental tie, suit and campaign medals on my chest, while the bands played, the dignitaries spoke and we paused in silence to remember the dead. After the pomp and ceremony finished, I slipped away from the crowds to wander alone on the beach to see if I could find the spot where I had landed. It was different; the tide was out and the grass-topped sand dunes were absent the coils of barbed wire and the smashed remains of collapsed German trenches. It was a hundred times quieter too without the crash of artillery and the crump of exploding rounds. But as I stood with the wind on my face and looked out to sea, my imagination took over and I could see them steaming towards me, the shells reaching out to greet them, just as they had done seventy years ago.

The rain had stopped by the time the cold grey light of morning began to creep over the eastern horizon. But the tail end of the storm that had swept through the Channel still blew strong enough to slap five foot high waves against the sides of the landing craft of the 15 and 43 Landing Craft Tank flotillas, soaking their decks with spray. To the men of the Sherwood Rangers Yeomanry, who sought scant shelter between the Sherman tanks chained to the open decks of the landing craft, the assault from the sea seemed relentless. Of all the ships that had sailed from England, the LCTs were the smallest and suffered for it. At just over 117 feet long, with their flat-bottomed hulls pulling a draught of less than three feet, the vessels pitched and tossed violently in the surging ocean, as the unseasonal summer squall that had delayed the sailing of the invasion fleet by twenty-four hours played itself out. The soldiers' sodden battledress, endemic seasickness and the vomit that sluiced between the tracks of their armoured vehicles were testimony to the three days of misery that they had endured on the heaving LCTs since embarking at Southampton Water.

Each LCT carried five Shermans packed close together and the sun had shone as the men loaded the tanks at the Hampshire town of Calshot on the western shore of the Solent. But once at sea the weather had changed, as an anticyclone forming up over the Azores brought in high winds, a low rain-laden cloud base and heavy seas. As the storm hit, the atmosphere of excitement and apprehensive enthusiasm that had accompanied the frenzied activity of embarkation following months of training soon dissipated in the wretchedness of ceaseless vomiting and retching, as they pitched at anchor, were soaked by the driving rain and then ploughed through the foaming ocean. The hyoscine hydrobromide seasickness tablets they had been issued had little effect and the men were not aware of General Dwight Eisenhower's decision to postpone the operation until a gap in the weather predicted by his meteorologists appeared. Had they known of the decision, the men of the Sherwood Rangers imprisoned in the heaving, sick-strewn filthy craft would have cursed the Supreme Allied Commander for it.

From the lurching deck of his LCT, Captain Leslie Skinner, the Sherwood Rangers' padre and the man responsible for the unit's spiritual welfare and for ministering to its dead, took in the scene around him as men were woken from a fitful slumber and began to prepare for battle. They folded their soaking spew-fouled bedrolls and lashed them to the back of their vehicles. A can of self-heating soup offered a meagre breakfast for those who could stomach it. The light of the odd cigarette, cupped in hands to shield its glow, illuminated the faces of the men briefly, as they huddled in small shivering groups or sought a private corner away from the wind and the spray. Somewhere in the receding darkness ahead of them the enemy coastline loomed closer. The approaching shoreline and the coming of daylight heralded the nearing of the end of their seaborne-inflicted agony, but the real trial of combat was about to begin. Skinner glanced at his watch; it was 0515 hours DST* on Tuesday 6 June 1944.

As Skinner looked out to sea, the advancing dawn revealed an almighty armada, stretching out across the ocean in every direction as far as the eye could see. The vast array of naval vessels, over 6000 craft of all shapes and sizes, constituted part of the largest combined-arms invasion force that the world had ever seen. Battleships with their huge 15-inch guns, cruisers, rocket ships and destroyers, complemented by support ships and landing craft, all ploughed through the surging swell of the stormy sea. In their midst, they carried over 130,000 troops that would form the first assault wave to land on the Normandy coastline, now only a few miles ahead of them. Overhead the air reverberated with the drone of hundreds of bombers, the black

---

* DST – Double Summer Time – was two hours ahead of GMT and constituted a wartime daylight-saving measure used by the Allies.

shapes of their wings discernible against the lightening sky, as they flew inland to unleash their payloads against the enemy's defences. Minutes later the orange flashes of their exploding bombs momentarily lit up the underside of the dark clouds on the horizon ahead of them. Skinner glanced back at his watch. It was 0520 hours and the turn of the naval task force to add their lethality to the mix.

Inside the steel confines of the battleships, naval gun crews cocooned in the red half-light of their turrets sweated in their boiler suits and anti-flash hoods, as they manhandled heavy shells from their operating hoists and rammed them home into gun breeches. The ships shuddered as they fired broadside in a blinding flash of flame and clouds of thick black smoke. The crews of the cruisers firing in front of them could feel the overpressure of each round as it passed over their superstructures. Those stationed on their bridges and decks watched as the small light traces burning in the rear of each dustbin-sized shell hurtled towards unseen targets ashore. Then their own 6-inch guns and those of the destroyers added to the cacophony of terrific noise, accompanied by the *whoosh, whoosh* of the rocket-firing ships as they unleashed their projectiles inland. Skinner watched in awe as the naval task force pulverised the shoreline defences with ten tons of high explosives a minute and the LCT flotillas ploughed on relentlessly towards the shore.

Ahead of them, the devastating weight of the naval bombardment was landing among the shoreline defences of Hitler's vaunted Atlantic Wall. Since the end of 1943, half a million Wehrmacht soldiers, slave labourers and locally conscripted workers had been employed in building bunkers, concrete gun positions and pillboxes and laying extensive minefields along a narrow strip of coast that extended from Antwerp to the Pyrenees. With the changing fortunes of war, the Germans had been anticipating that an Allied invasion of northwest Europe would come in the summer of 1944, but what they didn't know was where. The man responsible for defending the Atlantic seaboard of Nazi-occupied Europe had a hunch that the Allies might attempt a landing along the Normandy coastline. But although a favourite of Hitler, Field Marshal Erwin Rommel was at odds with the orthodox thinking of the German High Command and the Oberkommando der Wehrmacht or OKW, who believed that Pas de Calais would be the most likely area for an Allied invasion.

As Commander-in-Chief of Army Group B, Rommel's command included the Wehrmacht's 7th and 15th armies, which were responsible for defending 560 miles of coastline stretching from the Belgian frontier to the Spanish border. The German 15th Army was centred on Pas de Calais with an area extending to the River Dives in the Calvados region of eastern Normandy. Seventh Army's area of responsibility started on the other side of the river and ran west across the Norman Cotentin Peninsula and south into Brittany. It was Calais that attracted the priority of resources and the bulk of the German armoured panzer units were held back under the command of OKW and positioned to be able to cover this threatened sector. In the 7th Army area, Rommel had only three panzer formations immediately available, but the authority to release these divisions for battle was also retained by OKW and Rommel would have to seek German High Command's permission to use them in the event of an Allied landing.

Initially, Rommel had agreed with the OKW assessment that the Pas de Calais area offered the Allies obvious advantages, which made it the most likely place for the coming invasion. It provided the shortest distance across the Channel from England and the most direct route into Germany. Landing around Calais would also give the British and Americans a major port from which to sustain the logistical inflow of men and materiel necessary for a subsequent breakout from their bridgehead. But Rommel also considered a landing further south in the Bay of the Somme or along the Cotentin Peninsula as a distinct possibility. Consequently, as well as wanting to build up the defences along the whole shoreline he also wanted to be able to call on more panzer divisions.

Rommel's energetic command style and constant inspections of the Atlantic Wall had led to significant strengthening of the defences all along the coast. Millions of mines had been laid and every beach was covered by encased gun positions, pillboxes and a mass of obstacles tipped with explosives that could rip the bottom out of landing craft. But Rommel also knew there were still gaps and despite the improvements to the static defences they were only a thin crust that would delay the Allies getting ashore. Furthermore the defences were manned by under-strength and under-equipped static 'Fortress Divisions', made up of older men, convalescing wounded from the Eastern Front and Russian 'Hiwi' units composed of former Soviet prisoners of war and Poles and Czech soldiers of 'near German' extraction. Lacking motorised transport or armour and often provisioned with obsolete captured French, British and Czech weapons, these formations were of dubious quality. To defeat the invasion on the beaches, Rommel would still need armoured units positioned sufficiently close to the coast to attack the Allies as they struggled ashore and before they could establish a defendable beachhead. For that he needed more panzers and Hitler was the only man who could give them to him. Consequently, as the men of the Sherwood Rangers approached the Norman coastline in the darkness with the rest of the Allied invasion force, the commander of Army Group B was absent from his headquarters.

Erwin Rommel had left his headquarters at the chateau de La Roche-Guyon near Mantes at 0600 hours on 5 June to drive to his home in Germany near Ulm so he could spend the night with his wife Lucie. It was her birthday the next day, but Rommel's main purpose for being away from the front was to have an audience with Adolf Hitler at his mountain retreat at Berchtesgaden in Bavaria. The

Führer's staff had indicated that Hitler might be able to see the field marshal later on 6 June. Rommel was not overly concerned about being away from the front. German meteorologists had also predicted the approach of the storm from data they had received from U-boats stationed far out in the Atlantic. The forecast was one area of analysis Rommel and his superiors agreed upon. While OKW still predicted that Normandy was not the threatened sector the weather was another reason to expect a quiet night. The heavy sea states and high winds they forecasted were deemed as being unsuitable conditions for the Allies to attempt to make a landing. What they had missed was the improving gap in the weather coming behind the storm.

The Allies had no idea of Rommel's whereabouts or his appreciation that Normandy might be the likely location for the invasion. However, they had every reason to seek to underpin the misperception of OKW's prevailing conventional strategic assessment, which remained wedded to the Pas de Calais. It was an appreciation that was reinforced by German intelligence failures and a successful Allied deception known as Operation Fortitude. Since the beginning of 1944, double agents had duped the Germans' intelligence service, the Abwehr, into believing that the blow, when it came, would fall on Calais. The presence of dummy landing craft and the high volume of signals traffic relayed and rebroadcast from Kent, combined with heavy bombing raids, suggested that the British and American armies were poised to strike across the Dover Straits and supported the official orthodoxy of OKW thinking. It was an analysis that was enhanced by reconnaissance failures. Due to Allied air superiority over the Channel, Luftwaffe aircraft that might have reported the build-up of the invasion fleet in the ports further to the west of England had been unable to penetrate British airspace since the end of May. As a consequence the German High Command remained blind to the true nature of Allied intentions.

Codenamed Operation Overlord, the Allied invasion plan entailed the landing of the British 2nd Army and the 1st US Army, under the command of General Bernard Montgomery, on five separate beaches spread across twenty-six miles of Normandy's Cotentin Peninsula. In the leading assault wave two American infantry formations, the 1st US and 4th US divisions, would land in the western sector on two beaches codenamed Utah and Omaha. To their right, infantry from the British 3rd Division would land on Sword Beach on the Allies' eastern flank, with 3rd Canadian Division landing next to them on Juno Beach. The 50th Northumbrian Division would land on Gold Beach; a five-mile stretch of sand that lay between the small seaside resorts of Le Hamel and La Rivière. To secure the flanks of the invasion, capture specific objectives and assist the troops on the beaches by neutralising specifically identified enemy gun batteries, three Allied airborne divisions would be dropped in the darkness ahead of the seaborne forces in the early hours of D-Day. The 6th British Airborne division would land around the river Orne in the east and the American 82nd and 101st airborne divisions would jump into the area of Carentan in the west.

Although only eight divisions would be involved in the first assault wave, the Allies had thirty-seven divisions stationed in England for the invasion, but it would take weeks to get them all across the Channel. Success depended on breaching the Atlantic Wall, establishing an initial bridgehead by capturing key French towns, including Bayeux and Caen in the British sector, and then getting enough further divisions ashore before the Germans could bring the combined weight of their panzer divisions to bear. As the Allied officer responsible for planning D-Day and overall land forces commander, Montgomery believed that the first few hours and days would be critical. He knew that a successful breakout from Normandy could only come after the Allies had won the race to build up sufficient force ratios to beat off the German armoured formations as they moved to counter the landing.

Learning from the experience of launching the disastrous raid on Dieppe in August 1942 and subsequent invasions of Sicily and Italy, the Allies recognised the importance of using tanks to assist the assaulting troops by providing intimate fire support and traversing obstacles to allow them to get off the beach. It was an experience that bore the fruit of ingenuity in the form of specialised armoured vehicles known as 'Funnies' and Duplex Drive or 'DD' swimming tanks. The Funnies belonged to the British 79th Armoured Division, made up of a variety of converted tanks crewed by the Royal Armoured Corps and the Royal Engineers. They consisted of adapted Sherman flail tanks fitted with forward-mounted revolving drums of heavy chains to detonate mines, plus a series of heavier Churchill tanks equipped with a range of outsized Petard mortars, flamethrowers, extending bridging equipment and gap-crossing fascines made from bundles of logs. The role of the Funnies was to flail gaps through minefields, blast and burn out concrete bunkers, breach obstacles and create exit points that would allow the infantry and follow-up troops and vehicles to get off the beach.

Ingenious in their conception and design, the role of each 'Funny' was specialised and both they, and the assaulting infantry, would need the fire support of main battle tanks. The answer lay in the theory of buoyancy and the imagination of the émigré scientist Nicholas Straussler, who conceived the DD variant of the Sherman tank by fitting and surrounding its hull with a collapsible canvas screen which, when raised, displaced a sufficient volume of water to allow the tank to float. The screen was raised by means of pumping compressed air into rubber tubes sewn into the fabric, which was then held in place by flexible struts that helped keep the canvas taut. Two rear-mounted retractable propellers driven by the tank's track drive provided propulsion. The name of the tank was derived from this combination, which gave the DD a steady speed of four miles per hour through the water towards the shore once launched from a landing craft. By the passage of instructions from the commander standing on the back deck of the Sherman to the driver, the tank could be steered through the water by altering the angles of the propellers. The DD was equipped with a hand-operated bilge pump to deal with any ingress of water and on reaching land the propellers could be retracted and the flick of a lever would collapse the screen and enable it to operate as a conventional armoured fighting vehicle.

The Sherwood Rangers was one of four regiments in the 2nd British Army to have two of its three squadrons equipped with DD tanks for D-Day, with each squadron being allocated sixteen of the adapted Shermans. Two US armoured regiments were also provided with the DD tanks for use on Omaha and Utah beaches. On the British beaches, the intention was that the DDs would be launched from their LCTs three and a half miles from the shoreline, from where they would swim to their allocated beaches ahead of the first wave of the main infantry assault force. Landing on the beaches five minutes before the landing craft carrying the specialised armour arrived to deposit their cargoes at 'H' Hour, the DDs' task was to protect the Funnies as they began to prepare exit lanes across the mine-strewn sand. The DDs would then provide intimate fire support to the infantry arriving behind the specialised armour at 'H' Hour+5 minutes as they fought through and cleared the enemy's defensive positions. In the case of the Sherwood Rangers, B and C Squadrons of the regiment's three subunits were given the role of crewing the thirty-two DD tanks allocated to the unit, which was tasked with supporting 231 Brigade of the 50th Northumbrian Division while it was landing on Gold Beach.

The regiment's third subunit, A Squadron, was equipped with standard Shermans and would land on Gold Beach with the subsequent assault waves at 'H' Hour+90. The allocation of the subunit roles on D-Day reflected the fact that A Squadron had borne the brunt of the fighting the unit had experienced in the desert during the North

African campaign. In their desert battles the regiment had been equipped with a mixture of Crusader, Sherman and Grant Lee tanks. Manned by A Squadron, the Crusaders were lighter than the other tanks and their superior speed was utilised to provide a screening force to advance ahead of the rest of the regiment. A Squadron's job was to establish and maintain contact with enemy armour in order to fix them for the heavier tanks of B and C Squadrons. Although fast, the Crusaders were lightly armoured, mechanically unreliable and under-gunned. These shortcomings and the dangerous nature of their role meant that A Squadron had suffered more than the rest of the regiment in terms of tanks and men lost. Having had five tanks shot out from under him in one day during the desert campaign, as the officer commanding A Squadron, Stanley Christopherson shared the relief of his men that they would not be the ones swimming ashore in the DD tanks on D-Day.

While Straussler's application of the theory of buoyancy may have been sound, there was much that could go wrong when launching a 34-ton steel tank into the sea to lead the assault on a well-defended enemy coastline. If the screen succumbed to heavy seas and collapsed, or became shredded by shellfire while afloat, the armoured vehicle would founder and sink like a stone. As a contingency, all DD crews were issued with a modified version of the Davis Escape Apparatus issued to submarine crews. Worn about the chest and consisting of a mask attached to an oxygen cylinder by means of a rubber tube, the device would provide a submariner or sinking DD crewman with a twelve-minute emergency supply of air. Learning to operate the device necessitated practising escaping from large submarine water tanks at HMS *Dolphin* on the south coast.

If the prospect of having to swim from their tanks wasn't enough, the escape apparatus training was particularly detested. Its use provoked a small mutiny, when some of the enlisted men initially refused to take part in the training. One senior NCO was unrelenting and lost his stripes. The ire that resulted from what they were being asked to do was compounded when the cookhouse rumour that they would receive Combined Operations Pay, awarded to special operations units such as the SAS and midget submarine crews, turned out to be untrue. To men who had risked their lives in the desert and felt they deserved to be rewarded for being ordered to undertake such a hazardous mission, the false realisation added insult to injury and many of the rank and file felt that it was just not 'fooking on'.

Like it or not, the unit had become adept in the operation of their amphibious tanks by the time they moved to their pre-embarkation bell-tented transit camps outside Southampton. Across the south of England, thousands of troops who would take part in the invasion were moving to similar camps near the embarkation points and airfields. At midnight on 25 May, all the camps were locked tight. Military policemen patrolled the barbed-wire perimeters and no one was allowed in or out in order to preserve the secrecy surrounding the forthcoming opening of the Second Front. The date for D-Day had been set for 5 June and once incarcerated the invasion troops received extensive and detailed briefings on their objectives. In tune with the obsession for preserving operational security, the actual names of the locations they would attack had been replaced with codenames and would remain secret until commanders were handed their final sealed orders once at sea.

With the improving daylight, tank commanders made a last check of their maps and it was possible to see land through the mist and the smoke. As the men completed the removal of the chocks and chains that fastened their tanks to the holystoned decks of the LCTs, they felt the surge of the marine diesels as the craft began to make a hard turn to starboard to bring each of the flotilla's vessels into line astern. As the LCTs ran parallel to the coast, the tank crews began their final preparation for combat. Tank engines coughed grey-blue smoke as their engines started and burned off the oil that had collected in the bottom of the cylinders during the voyage. The crews mounted up and loaded HE shells into breeches, belts of machine-gun ammunition were slapped into feed trays and radios were switched on and netted into command frequencies. The pitch of the LCTs' engines changed again, as they turned to port to bring them into line, picked up speed and began their final run in to the shore. Skinner glanced at his watch; it was 0700 hours and the men of the Sherwood Rangers were stood to and mentally readying for battle.

Standing on the observation platforms at the rear of their Shermans, tank commanders were able to catch erratic pitching glimpses of the beach and the small shapes of beachfront buildings beyond the bow ramps ahead of them, erupting in flashes and blasting sand and smoke as the naval bombardment continued to strike among the enemy's defences. The powerful pulsing throb of the LCTs' racing diesels and the smoky rumble of the tank engines combined with the terrific ear-splitting roar of the ships' gunfire to make a constant wall of noise. Fear gnawed at stomachs, long emptied by the ceaseless vomiting and retching, as men wondered silently about what awaited them ashore. In the sea behind the LCTs, assault infantry cross-decked from troop ships by scrambling down the nets hanging on their sides to get into the smaller landing craft that would follow them onto the beach. The distance to the shoreline continued to close and the tank crews began to get ready for the moment when the LCTs would slow and the throttling back of their engines would indicate that they were about to be launched from their ramp bows. But the ramps stayed up and the LCTs ploughed on through the swell, with each man willing the interminable pitching and waiting to be over, while wondering why they hadn't launched. Ahead of them the naval bombardment lifted and shifted further inland. The padre's watch told him that it was 0710 hours and a minute later it started.

The 716th Division was a classic static Fortress Division made up of two under-strength German infantry regiments, supported by horse-drawn 105mm artillery. It lacked any significant armour and was equipped with a miscellany of foreign heavy weapons, plus a limited number of 75mm and 88mm anti-tank guns. Suspecting a quiet night due to the weather, it was at a low level of alert when the Allied bombers and naval gunfire began blasting its positions as dawn broke. For two hours it had suffered a devastating weight of bombardment, but much of the bombing had missed its targets and the heavy gunfire from the ships could not neutralise every position. As the fire lifted and the dust and smoke began to clear, stupefied Wehrmacht soldiers dug out weapons from collapsed trenches, cleared out the clogging sand from breeches and barrels and readied their machine guns and mortars against the landing craft heading towards them from the grey murk of the Channel as their artillery began to fire.

At the edge of the small village of Le Hamel on the western side of Gold Beach, the crew of a captured 77mm Polish gun remained untouched in the concrete encasement of their bunker. A thick re-inforced flanking wall spur on the seaward side of the gun emplace-ment had helped protect them from the worst of the Allied firepower. It also prevented them from firing out to sea, but their position gave them an excellent field of fire to shoot enfilade across the beach above the waterline, from the narrow firing embrasure that looked out over several hundred yards of sand to their front. Stood to around their gun, the crew at le Hamel watched and waited.

The LCTs continued to plough through the heaving ocean towards the ever-closing line of sandy beach. They had passed the planned launching point of 6000 yards, but still they pressed on as the dis-tance to the shore reduced and the sporadic fire of German ranging shells began to bracket them. Estimating that the fast-running tide and heavy sea state threatened to swamp the DDs, the skippers of the LCT flotillas had consulted with the tank squadron commanders and decided to launch the swimming tanks as close in as possible to increase their chances of making it to the beach. It was a brave decision on behalf of the naval crews, as by reducing one risk they increased another. As the distance to the shore shortened, the accuracy and concentration of the enemy's fire increased. Thick angry columns of white water shot up in the sea around them and mortar bombs sent up fountains of soaking spray when the LCTs came into range of the smaller calibre weapons, as the yards between the tight-packed vessels and the land continued to count down. Many of those that had survived the fighting in the desert thought that they were pushing their luck.

Through the waves splashing over the bow ramps, the commanders stationed on the back of the Shermans could make out the square features of seafront villas on the shoreline and the grey squat outline of pillboxes, marked by the jagged muzzle flashes of their machine guns. The pitter-patter of small-arms fire striking the metal superstructure of the landing craft was audible over the din, as the order was given to inflate the DD screens. The valves of the compressed-air bottles were opened and rubber tubes and support struts stiffened as the canvas round the tanks began to rise. From his vantage point at the rear of his Sherman, Lieutenant Stuart Hills of C Squadron could see that some of the other landing craft were lagging behind, while others forged ahead as his own vessel began to slow. The decision to bring the LCTs closer into the shore required all the skill of the coxswains to navigate through the thicket of semi-submerged mine-tipped anti-shipping obstacles that protruded from the waterline near the shore, but it also meant that the ordered line-abreast formation of landing craft began to break down. As the military maxim that no plan survives first contact with the enemy began to play out, the men of the Sherwood Rangers were about to find out how their DD equipment, training and Allied preparations would stack up.

The wallowing motion of Hills' LCT began to ease as its skipper brought it to a dead stop 700 yards out from the beach and gave the order to lower the ramp. Sailors released the forward hawser mechanism and the bow ramp slid down on its cable chain to within two feet of the water and then slapped down hard on to the surface in a shower of foaming spray. Hills could see other LCTs were also dropping their ramps, but noticed that some were pushing past them and continuing on towards the beach, including at least one landing craft that carried a mix of Funnies on its deck. Hills' concern was to get his own tank launched and he ordered the driver to begin advancing towards the ramp. The rest of the crew stood on the tank's decks and braced themselves against the canvas sides of the flotation screen to help keep it taut when it entered the water. The steering levers were released and they felt the tracks bite into the steel deck. Then the tank started to move, as a salvo of shells burst around them. One landed close ahead of them, one struck the starboard beam and the third shell hit the ramp. Its exploding shrapnel was channelled round the sides of Hills' tank and struck men standing on the backs of the Shermans lined up behind them, wounding the Squadron's second in command, Captain Bill Enderby, and a senior NCO.

The enemy gunners had their range and the open bow ramp door was not a place to hang about. Hills shouted at his driver to keep going and the DD tanks edged down the ramp and nosed into the swell. The Sherman bobbed like an ungainly inverted Chinese lantern, as the rear of the tracks dropped off the ramp and buoyancy took effect, the crew pushing hard against the canvas screen, which was bowing with the pressure of the waves. But the tank was already sinking. Its belly plates had been holed by the shellfire and the tank began to ship water. The crew operated the bilge pump frantically, until the water pouring up through the forward crew hatches indicated that it was a lost cause and Hills gave the order to abandon the tank. The decks were awash as the crew scrambled into their small inflatable aircrew dinghy and managed to pull away just in time to watch their tank slip below the surface. Hills' tank was one of eight

Sherwood Ranger DD tanks that foundered at sea, but worse was to come for some of the armour that made it to the beach.

The disintegration of the planned order of arrival, caused by the shellfire and sea conditions, meant that some of Hobart's Funnies were landing ahead of their intimate battle-tank support. As Hills' DD began to founder, a Sherman flail tank was already wading ashore through the surf in front of modified Churchill tanks belonging to the Engineers. Clearing the water to its track-line, it blew off its waterproofing and engaged the drive to the large metal rotating drum extending from the front of the vehicle. The heavy ball chains fixed to the drum started to beat the ground in front of the tank in a thrashing blur of metal, sand and exploding mines. The tank's driver selected a gear, eased the clutch and the flail started to move forward up the beach to begin clearing the first of several lanes through the minefield. As it moved beyond the waterline of the incoming tide, it broke into the left-hand arc of the concrete-encased gun situated on the edge of Le Hamel. When its first target nosed into view, the 77mm fired with a resounding high-velocity crack and seconds later the flail was a burning wreck of flames and belching thick black oily smoke. The Le Hamel gun had claimed its first victim.

In one of the DDs from B Squadron, Trooper Bert Jenkins felt the reassuring sound of the tracks grinding on the sloping shingle of the beach, as his tank made it to the shore and he prepared to jump into the lap gunner's seat at the front of the Sherman. Water poured from the running gear as the tank drove clear from the sea and stopped to disengage its propellers and drop its canvas screen at the water's edge. But Jenkins' relief was to be short-lived. As he dropped into his seat, the tank was engaged by a burst of heavy machine-gun fire from a German position among the grass-topped sand dunes at the head of the beach. The next moment there was a blinding flash, as the tank was hit by a 77mm round that set fire to the vehicle's spare fuel and the collapsing screen of canvas. Lieutenant Monty Horley ordered his men to bail out. Jenkins and two other crew members dropped into the shallow water and took shelter at the rear of the tank. In another B Company tank, Sergeant Bill Digby heard the troop commander reporting frantically on the radio that his tank was on fire until Horley's voice stopped abruptly in mid-sentence and the net went dead.

Had he lived, Digby would have discovered that the young tank officer was killed by another burst of machine-gun fire as he tried to escape from his stricken tank. His driver, Trooper Warboys, was also killed and would be the first other-ranks name listed in Padre Skinner's casualty notebook as KIA; 'killed in action'. Two of the other crewmen from Horley's knocked-out tank were also killed by machine-gun fire as they sought shelter behind it. Bert Jenkins was hit in the legs and wounded. With no time to stop and find out what had happened to his fellow B Squadron crewmates, Digby pressed on up the beach until the almighty clang of an armour-piercing (AP) shell brought his Sherman to an abrupt stop. The AP round came into the turret, slicing through three inches of armoured steel, wounded the gunner and took off Digby's legs above the knee before ricocheting off the inside of the tank and hitting another crew member in the foot. The grotesquely injured commander collapsed onto the turret floor in an agony of mangled limbs and blood. Despite being hit, there was no fire and the vehicle was drivable. With a presence of mind born from survival, the driver threw the tank into reverse and backed down the beach out of the line of fire. Other armoured vehicles that had entered the lethal killing zone of the Le Hamel bunker's weapon arcs were also being hit. An adapted Churchill tank belonging to the Engineers disintegrated in a fragmented mass of metal and body parts that were sent high into the air before raining down across the beach.

The troublesome 77mm gun, pinning the remaining armour down against the waterline of an incoming tide on the Jig Green sector, was threatening to stall the assault on the western end of Gold Beach, which was becoming increasingly congested at the water's edge.

Any tank moving even a few yards up the shingle was being hit and there was no supporting infantry to outflank the casemate and take it from the rear. The two infantry units of 231 Brigade had landed in the wrong place, three quarters of a mile to the east and were also suffering. The failure of the 1st battalions of the Hampshire and Dorset regiments to land immediately behind the armour remains a moot point for historians. Whether due to navigational error, tidal conditions or the result of a local decision made by the lead pilot of their landing craft, to avoid the murderous fire engulfing the tanks, the failure of the armour and infantry to marry up and co-ordinate their efforts was costing both combat arms dearly.

Each forty-foot Landing Craft Assault, know as an LCA, carried an infantry platoon of thirty-plus men. The landing craft were under fire before they hit the shore, but the real devastation came as the ramps were lowered and the ranks of tightly bunched infantrymen were disgorged into the water to make their way up the slope of the beach. The German mortars and machine guns found their mark as men plunged off shifting ramps carrying sixty pounds of equipment, waded through chest-high water and struggled up the sandy shingle. In those first few minutes, the men of the 1st Hampshires and 1st Dorsets were horribly exposed. Lacking intimate armoured support, soaking wet soldiers began to fall amid the hail of bullets and shrapnel that greeted them. The assaulting troops were met by murderous automatic and mortar fire from positions dug into the sand dunes at the top of the beach and from fortified houses along the seafront. Streams of bullets from German machine guns raked the sand and the water. Some of the LCAs were hit on the run into the beach and as the ramp of one came down a mortar burst immediately to its front, killing or wounding the best part of a platoon. Some of the infantry managed to push on to the dunes and the sea wall, while others remained pinned down on the beach among the dead and the wounded.

Without armoured support and exposed on the flat, open sand, the infantry casualties mounted. The commanding officers of both the Hampshires and the Dorsets were killed in the leading assault wave. Radios damaged by seawater, or jammed with the traffic on over-crowded frequencies, prevented communication and co-ordination with the armour less than a mile to their right. Combined with the loss of key leaders, command and control began to break down. Surviving company commanders and platoon leaders began to exercise their initiative as small ad hoc groups of men fought their way into the dunes, began to clear trenches and then used the cover of taken German positions to begin to link up with any of the armoured vehicles that they could reach. But initiative and courage were not only the preserve of the infantry fighting on Jig Green Sector.

To their right, the area of beach below the Le Hamel gun's deadly arc of fire was becoming dangerously crowded, as more landing craft discharged their cargoes on to the narrow strip of the tideline, few daring to move forward into the 77mm's zone of fire. But some of the armoured vehicles had made it across the beach to the other side of the sand dunes. As the forward observation officer of the battery of Sexton self-propelled artillery supporting the Sherwood Rangers, Captain Arthur Warburton of the 147th Field Artillery Regiment knew it was imperative to get his Sherman inland to call down the fire of his guns. He had survived the hazardous trip across the fire-swept beach unscathed, until his luck ran out as he reached the road running along the top of Gold Beach and turned west towards Le Hamel. He noticed German infantry running in panic among the dunes to his left as his tank approached, then he saw the gun in the bunker 150 yards away on his right flank pointing directly at him. An instant later a 77mm round smashed through the engine and his Sherman came to a dead stop. He managed to raise one of the Sextons already ashore on the radio, gave a brief target indication and told the commander to 'Blow the damn thing up'.

Sergeant Robert Palmer knew that his 25-pounder gun would have little effect unless he could score a direct hit through the bunker's embrasure, a narrow slit-shaped aperture measuring no more than three feet by six feet. Palmer could see the 77mm gun protruding from the firing port and he also knew that he would have to manoeuvre quickly to avoid becoming the next target. With the gun loaded and with its safety catch off, to give him the few seconds of advantage that he would need, Palmer told his driver to advance at top speed. Sand spewed from the track links as the Sexton accelerated across the beach towards the concrete encasement. Fifty yards short of the bunker Palmer yelled at the driver to turn by forty-five degrees and then stop. The self-propelled gun slewed and then came to an abrupt halt directly facing the embrasure, as the driver pulled hard on his right steering lever and then hauled both sticks back to brake the vehicle's running gear. The Sexton rocked momentarily with the sudden loss of forward motion. At the moment it settled, the loader sighted his artillery piece and Palmer slapped him on the shoulder. The breech of the gun shot back against its buffer mechanism as the loader yanked the firing lever. The first round glanced off the top-right corner of the bunker in a shower of steel and concrete fragments. Another round was already in the breech as Palmer shouted adjustments and the firing mechanism jerked back once more. The second round went straight through the embrasure and detonated inside the bunker. Minutes later, what remained of the gun crew staggered out of the back of the bunker with their hands up.

It had taken nearly two hours to knock out the bunker at Le Hamel and while it would take until late afternoon to overcome the resistance of all the German positions around the village, the destruction of the 77mm gun emplacement unlocked the key to the defence of the western side of Gold Beach. The planned all-arms co-operation began to take effect as infantry started work with the armour that had been pinned to the shore. The Engineer Churchill tanks fitted with 290mm Petard mortars lobbed 40lb charges that demolished strong points before infantry rushed in to mop up the survivors. Flail tanks began beating paths through the minefields to clear lanes to the top of the beach, popping green signal smoke to declare that a lane was open to the troops behind them. Engineer demolition parties started to destroy the beach obstacles, while other sappers used their Funnies to create exit points off the beach as more men and materiel were landed on Gold Beach. The sloping sands became choked with the arrival of more and more landing craft, but they were no longer under direct fire and the routes inland were beginning to open up.

The resistance on the eastern side of Gold Beach had been much lighter than the fighting round Le Hamel and the 69th Brigade was already pushing inland with the support of DD tanks from the 4th/7th Dragoon Guards. With the destruction of the Le Hamel bunker, the infantry of 231 Brigade and B and C Squadrons of the Sherwood Rangers also began pushing out from the beach as the German 716th Division's cohesion as a fighting formation rapidly disintegrated once its coastline defences had been penetrated. Operating as conventional tanks in support of the infantry, the DD squadrons began to advance through rubble-strewn coastal villages damaged by the bombardment. B Squadron cleared Le Hamel, with the Hampshires losing another tank to a 50mm anti-tank gun. One determined German took on a Sherman at twenty yards with his rifle and was blown to pieces by an HE round from the tank's 75mm gun. Lone infantry marksmen and snipers remained a danger, as the CO of the regiment found out to his cost when he ignored advice not to dismount from his tank near Le Hamel. Having taken command of the Sherwood Rangers on their return from North Africa, Lieutenant Colonel John Anderson was hit in the arm when he went forward on foot to investigate the delay in moving up the beach. He lay in a ditch for an hour until it was safe to evacuate him.

The CO had landed directly on the beach with A Squadron of the

Sherwood Rangers at H+90. Leslie Skinner should have landed with them and he should have been travelling in one of the two half-tracks of the unit's medical section commanded by the regiment's medical officer, Captain Charles 'Hilda' Young. But before embarkation the two men had argued over their distinct roles. Young's concern was to be able to keep up with the regiment when it advanced inland in order to look after its wounded and he did not want to be distracted by the presence of Skinner and his primary concern for the dead.

'When they are dead, they are dead and you will only hold me up,' Young had snapped at the padre.

The difference remained unresolved before they sailed. As a result Skinner had landed ashore in one of the LCTs in the first assault wave and his landing craft had hit a mine as it beached, wounding the men on either side of him. After assisting the wounded he had volunteered to help roll heavy vehicle matting from the ramp of his damaged craft and then waded ashore through six feet of water. Unarmed due to his ordained status as a priest, Skinner could not take part in the fighting but instead spent an hour wielding a pickaxe to help demolish a pillbox to create one of the exits from the beach.

Despite the spat with the doctor, Skinner spent the rest of his time on the beach helping the wounded infantrymen, persuading landing-craft skippers to evacuate some of the injured and doing the best he could for them until a proper medical post was established ashore. Later that afternoon he was able to find the CO, who had been recovered from the ditch near Le Hamel, and waved him off the beach in an amphibious DUKW vehicle. Inland B and C Squadrons rendezvoused at the small low-lying hamlet of Le Buhot just over a mile from le Hamel, where they stripped their Shermans of their DD modifications and prepared to lie up for the night in a leaguer. A Squadron caught up with them after assisting a battalion of the 69th Brigade take the village of Ryes lying a mile further inland, before redeploying to help the infantry of the 2nd Essex, in one of 50th

Division's follow-up brigades, to take high ground around Bayeux several miles to the south. Stanley Christopherson believed that the ancient Norman city could have been taken that night, but the infantry battalion's CO was content to dig in and wait until morning. As the last light of day began to disappear over the western horizon, the Sherwood Rangers replenished their tanks with fuel and ammunition, began listening stags on their radios and bedded down beside their Shermans. Skinner caught up with the rest of the regiment later that night, where he rejoined the medical section that had set up camp in an orchard. He was indescribably filthy and utterly exhausted. Before falling into a dead sleep beside one of the half-tracks, he made an entry in his casualty notebook; '40 casualties to date, including the missing'.

The actuality of the Sherwood Rangers' losses turned out to be lower than Skinner's estimation. Eighteen men had been posted missing at sea and were later picked up, including Lieutenant Hills and his crew. Twenty men had been wounded and Monty Horley was the only officer killed in action, along with seven other ranks that included Sergeant Digby, who died of his wounds later that night. Eight DD tanks had foundered during the landing and another eight had been knocked out on dry land. But the relatively light casualties reflected the overall success of D-Day, where the total number of men lost had been far lower than expected. As the darkness folded around them, the men of the Sherwood Rangers had every right to feel proud of what they had achieved and the role that they had played in the first day of the invasion. The German defenders had been caught completely by surprise by the arrival of the DD tanks in the first assault wave, expecting that it would take several hours after the infantry had landed before the Allies could put armour ashore. Once married up with the infantry, the DD tanks and Funnies made a critical difference; marked by the fact that the highest Allied losses on D-Day were on Omaha Beach, where twenty-seven of the thirty-two American DD tanks foundered on their way into the shore and where specialised armour was not used.

With the success of the landings behind them, the Allies had won the first round in the battle of the beaches. They had penetrated at least six miles inland and over 156,000 men and 20,000 vehicles had been put ashore across all five beaches. The German reaction had been slow due to a hesitancy to commit their armoured reserves, brought about by a paralysis in command and the mistaken belief that the focus of the main Allied invasion would still fall on Calais. But the Allied lodgement ashore was precarious and the German response was consolidating. Rommel recognised that the battle for the beaches may have been lost, but he knew that he had to contain the bridgehead and fix it for a decisive counterattack by, as yet, uncommitted panzer divisions. Montgomery knew that he now faced a race to build up his forces and establish them firmly ashore, before the Germans could bring the full weight of their strength to bear and drive them back into the sea. The German response would not be long in coming and the battle for Normandy was about to begin.

2

HOME FRONT

The description of D-Day is of course conjecture, because I wasn't there. As the Sherwood Rangers landed in Normandy in their DD tanks, fought their way across Gold Beach and pushed inland, I was safe at home 350 miles away. Nestled in the North Yorkshire Dales, the small village of Reeth is a bleak place at the best of times. It is bleaker still for a newly commissioned nineteen-year-old subaltern in the Royal Armoured Corps. The RAC was the arm of the army that had been formed just before the war, when the cavalry regiments traded in their horses for tanks and were formed into a single corps with the units of the Royal Tank Regiment. I had volunteered for the army a year and half before, as soon as I was eighteen, and I had elected to join the RAC as I thought riding into battle would beat marching on my feet with the infantry. However, as the Sherwood Rangers loaded their armoured vehicles on to the LCTs in Southampton Water and prepared to sail for France, I was setting out to walk across the hundred-plus miles of moorland that lay between the Cumbrian villages of Drigg and Reeth and, by the end of it, my feet were killing me.

We were dropped off one by one along the lonely east coast road near the Esk estuary the Friday before D-Day. I was issued a single compass bearing and told to follow it until I got back to the army camp at Reeth, where I had been sent to complete officer continuation training with a group of other young second lieutenants who had recently passed out from Sandhurst. Billed as an individual effort exercise, we were given no food, had no map and were expected to live off the land as we navigated our way back to camp by first parade on Monday morning. The purpose, as I can remember it, had something to do with practising escape and evasion in the event of being captured by the enemy. After eighteen months of training, first as a tank crewman and then as an RAC officer, it all seemed a bit pointless to me, as it was a far cry from being in a tank and we were a very long way away from any Germans. I had something of a rebellious streak in me and I might have been tempted to question the value of the exercise, especially at a weekend. But one thing I had learned during my army training was the importance of keeping my mouth shut.

It was a tempered disposition that had failed me at school and I had suffered for it. My father had served as a captain in the Royal Engineers during the First World War, where he had been responsible for building narrow-gauge rail lines to take supplies forward to the front line, a task often conducted under intense shellfire. He put his construction experience to good use at the end of the war. Following on from the imaginative investment of a housing grant made to returning veterans after 1918, he established a construction company that was to go on to build several hundred homes in north London during the interwar period. His success meant that he was able to provide me with a public school education and at the age of thirteen I was packed off to Highgate School as a weekly boarder.

My start at Highgate was inauspicious. On the first night of prep, I whispered to the boy next to me to ask if I could borrow his rubber. Pounced on by a prowling prefect, I was put in front of the school's head boy to answer for my heinous crime of talking during prep, which was strictly forbidden. My protestation of innocence, in which I said that I was simply asking for a rubber to correct my homework and was not talking, fell on deaf ears and he used a cane to beat the backs of my legs bloody. It was a salutary lesson in misplaced authority and injustice, especially when returning home for the first weekend exeat, where my mother insisted that I must have done something wrong to be punished so savagely. Loving as my mother was, her attitude reflected my Victorian upbringing, where the authority of the establishment was accepted with little question of whether it was right or wrong. The episode bred a rebellious streak in me in the form of an ingrained determination to stand up to the unquestioning righteousness of those above me. It also got me into a lot of trouble, as my protest took the form of a refusal to work or apply myself at school.

Unbeknown to me the rise of another far greater form of tyranny was to be the saviour of my downfall. Adolf Hitler's invasion of Poland in September 1939, and the start of the Blitz the following year, resulted in my being evacuated from Highgate and sent to Westward Ho! in Devon. Safe from the bombs falling on London and released from my oppressors at school, at fifteen years old I was free to immerse myself in the practicalities of working on the land and keeping chickens. I only played a tiny part in supporting the war effort, as the U-boat menace in the Atlantic threatened to starve Britain, but I loved every minute of it until reaching the age of sixteen, when it was time to return to the family home at Totteridge on the northern outskirts of the capital.

By September 1940, the British Expeditionary Force had been evacuated from Dunkirk, the Battle of Britain was at its height and the country was in the grip of fear from the prospect of an imminent German invasion. London was bearing the brunt of the Luftwaffe's attempts to bomb the country into submission and from the high ground of Totteridge common one could look south and see the horizon beyond Westminster and the Docklands dotted with silver barrage balloons. Everywhere people seemed to be digging air-raid shelters in their gardens and screening their windows with tape and blackout curtains. Sandbags were filled and stacked thick against the doorways of municipal buildings and gas masks were carried at the ready. During the day the vapour trails of RAF Spitfires and Hurricanes battling with German aircraft crisscrossed the blue sky, and occasionally a small dot of a fighter would begin to fall with its engine trailing smoke, too far away to know whether it was one of ours or one of theirs. By night the firmament over the city glowed an ominous angry red, as the fires caused by the bombing raged through shattered buildings and dockyards.

The crisis that threatened to engulf the country assisted my view that there were more important things than resuming my education at Highgate School. It was agreed that I would start a building course at the Northern Polytechnic, which was a decision that better suited my academic disposition. It also allowed me to join the platoon of my local Home Guard unit. Numbering just fifteen and made up of other boys of my age and a few middle-aged men, we drilled at the local village hall and mounted fire watches. We made Molotov cocktails and practised fitting bent rail lines into slots that had been prepared in the road surface of Totteridge Lane to form an obstacle against any advance of German armour from the Mill Hill area. Given that our armoury consisted of one old First World War Lee Enfield rifle with five rounds of ammunition and a few petrol bombs, I doubt that we would have had much impact on the panzers that had driven our regular army out of France. However, it was an exciting time. I enjoyed being at home with my mates, doing something useful in preparing to fight off the invader and drinking the odd pint with the rest of the platoon in the Orange Tree pub on the green on Sunday morning, after a night of fire-watch duty. Of course the rebellious streak in me was conscious of my disapproving parents attending a service in the local church only a stone's throw away. When not on duty with the Home Guard, I worked in my father's business at the weekends repairing superficial bomb damage to people's houses under a local government contract scheme. Although there to help them, we attracted the ire of the homeowners, who complained bitterly that enough was enough and demanded to know when Number 10 was going to put an end to the bombing. Looking back on it, the level of hostility makes me question the extent of the Blitz spirit. I suspect if Winston Churchill had decided to lead the country to some form of appeasement with Hitler, there would have been many people who would have backed him gladly.

By 1942, Britain no longer stood alone against the Nazis, the threat of invasion had passed, America had entered the war and the tide had begun to turn in the Allies' favour. But while the beginning of the end had begun, the end was still a long way out of sight and as my eighteenth birthday approached I had already made up my mind to volunteer to join the army. That September I went to the army recruiting office on Seven Sisters Road in Highbury with nine of my mates and put my name down for the RAC. While it is likely that I would have eventually been conscripted, volunteering seemed the natural thing to do. My father had served in the Great War and my brother, whom I had not seen for three years, was already serving as a captain in the army. I had also been in the Officer Training Corps at school and the Home Guard, so the concept of military service was not alien to me. And of course, we were engaged in a total war and the enemy was still far from beaten. My friends all had similar motivations; four of them would not live to see the end of the war.

The RAC training centre at Bovington in Dorset looked a dreary place when I reported there in November to start basic training at the 16th Primary Training Wing. The mild weather of autumn had long since passed and the trees in the woods around the camp were stripped of their leaves. The long lines of wooden barrack huts added to the sombre gloom of the place. But any feelings of melancholy on entering into the army's training regime fast evaporated in six weeks of square bashing, rudimentary military instruction and bullshit. Conditions were Spartan and we slept in army blankets on mattresses stuffed with straw. The average day started at 0500 hours and we washed and shaved in cold water. When we weren't drilling, conducting PT, marching or being taught how to shoot, we were preparing for room inspections or cleaning our kit. If an item was stationary or could be worn we frantically painted or polished it, if it moved we stood to attention or saluted it. However, officers were rare and we were at the mercy of brutal NCOs who had the power to do anything they liked with us and seemed to delight in doing everything they could to make our lives a misery.

Their attitude rankled with me, not least because I had volunteered, but with the demigod-like authority the instructors had over us and their expectation of an instant reaction to orders, I knew anything but blind obedience would be counter-productive and I valued my scant thirty-six-hour leave passes too much. Those who had been conscripted and had not been to boarding school appeared to suffer most. The tyrant prefects of Highgate had prepared me well for the life of a recruit, but those plucked from their normal civilian lives struggled with having their individual identity and rights as civilians stripped away from them, as the army began honing us into small indistinct parts that would fit neatly and unquestioningly into a gigantic military machine. However, I would be lying if I said that I didn't miss the everyday creature comforts one normally took for granted, such as warm water, sleeping between sheets, proper mattresses and having a pillow instead of a kit bag to rest my head on at night. A fag break, or a cup of tea and five minutes to yourself without the petty attentions of a screaming instructor or having to clean or paint something became an unimaginable luxury.

Graduating from basic recruit training to learning how to become a tank crewman at the RAC's 58th Young Soldiers' Training Regiment was no better; in fact the bullshit was worse. Each night we polished the metal buckets in our barrack blocks until they shone like silver and spent hours on our hands and knees scrubbing the wooden floors white. Our parade belts had to be blancoed and uniforms kept spotlessly clean and pressed and an imaginary speck of dirt or a misplaced crease would result in being placed on report. Invariably this would lead to some charge or field punishment, collectively know as a 'fizzer'; in essence summary justice resulting in a loss of pay, liberty or extra PT with rifle and pack. Being one minute late back from a thirty-six-hour weekend leave pass was a guaranteed way to get a 'fizzer' from the aptly named guard sergeant, Hayter. The return journey from the small side-line village station at Wool, located a few miles from Bovington Camp, to Totteridge required meticulous planning on my part in order to avoid falling foul of Hayter's mesmerised focus on the guard clock as it ticked round to the allotted time to be back inside the camp gates.

Following a rather pointless two months of repeating much of the general military training we had already undergone at the Primary Training Wing, the syllabus at the 58th Training Regiment progressed to teaching us about tanks. All recruits received basic driver and vehicle maintenance training on obsolete Valentine tanks, as well as elementary gunnery. Initially, gunnery training consisted of practising on an indoor pellet range, where a mocked-up turret firing station was fitted with a modified air rifle. We spent hours firing pellets at models of German tanks pulled by an instructor across a sand pit by a piece of string. The simulation was no doubt to save money and prepare us for live firing on the Lulworth ranges on the Dorset coast, where we engaged wooden tank targets with live ammunition. The purpose of the training was to enable us to fill any role in a tank crew, before embarking on a six-week course of more specialist training, either as drivers, gunners or wireless operators.

The 58th Regiment was a unit designed to develop potential armoured corps officers and senior NCOs. I witnessed little evidence of this, but saw becoming an officer as a means of escaping being at the mercy of oafish NCO instructors, unnecessary bullshit and the monotony of verbatim 'naming of parts' type instruction, where the slightest deviation from sacrosanct training pamphlet drills earned a smart rebuke and often a 'fizzer' into the bargain. We were also constantly hungry and meals of powdered egg, stale bread and a dollop of porridge, all in the same mess tin, did little to satisfy the hunger of growing young men being worked round the clock. All our spare cash was spent on buying egg and chips in the NAAFI and I couldn't help feeling that the food in an officers' mess would be better and more plentiful.

After six months of purgatory as a recruit trooper at Bovington, I found myself attending the War Officer Selection Board at Warminster. The food in the large red-brick mess there was definitely better and how we ate it seemed to be part of the assessment of our suitability to be officers. At least two of my fellow potential officer candidates appeared to fall short of the required standards of dining etiquette and were 'RTU'd'. How you held your knife and fork and asked someone to pass the salt, without using an expletive, was deemed to be important. The rest of the selection process was made up of basic intelligence tests, interviews, assessments of our physical fitness and high-wire confidence courses. Hesitating to climb up to a precariously tall platform, run across narrow planks and leap across gaps, where a fall would invite serious injury, all resulted in instant RTU. To me, most of what we were asked to do was a lot of fun and I was pleased to be informed that I had passed and would proceed to officer training at Sandhurst, subject to further assessment at a Pre-Officer Cadet Training Unit.

Having spent a few weeks at the Pre-Officer Training Unit at Alma Barracks near Aldershot, confirming my suitability as a potential officer, the cycle of basic repetitive training started all over again on my arrival at Sandhurst. The petty despotism of the senior NCO fraternity was also much in evidence at the Royal Military Academy, although this time it emanated from members of the Household Division, who seemed to run the place. They believed that parade drill was the very essence of life itself. The only appreciable difference from Bovington was that they called you 'Sir', but it was quite clear that they didn't mean it. However, once the repeat of general military training consisting of square bashing and more bullshit was over, the emphasis of instruction began to be placed on leadership and, for those officer cadets destined for the RAC, on commanding tanks in battle. Our practical training took place in large Churchill infantry support tanks, backed up by classroom lectures on radio voice procedure and manoeuvring armoured formations in accordance with the doctrine laid down in regulation army field manuals.

The dogma of tank warfare theory, espoused by the interwar theories of Basil Liddell-Hart and J.F.C. Fuller, was very much in the ascendancy. In the eyes of our instructors, the decisive defeat of the Anglo-French armies by Hitler's panzer forces during the blitzkrieg campaign of 1940 vindicated their thinking. As a consequence, we were taught that the role of the tank was to deliver shock action on the battlefield, by breaking through the blood and the mud of defensive positions or by outflanking them in wide-manoeuvre sweeps, to penetrate deep into an enemy's rear and bring about havoc, chaos and defeat through the use of fast-moving massed armoured forces. To our teachers at the academy, it was an unquestionable and proven mantra. Given that the Germans had done it to us at the start of the war, the theory seemed sound enough to naïve young officers eager to prove themselves in battle. But, as we were to find out in Normandy, the thinking was already out of date.

Regardless of the focus placed on the application of the theory of armoured warfare, the culmination of our training as officer cadets, which took place at Capel Curig in North Wales, had a distinctly infantry flavour to it. We were immersed in a week of arduous field exercises from the moment we arrived in the small army camp overlooked by the craggy ridged peaks of Snowdonia. We tumbled sleepily from the back of the trucks that had made the long drive from Sandhurst, to the frenzied yelling of our NCO instructors, shouting at us to form up in full marching order of rifle, pack and webbing equipment. Any thoughts of a meal in the cookhouse were quickly dashed, as we were promptly doubled out of the camp gates. It was getting dark by the time we arrived, ten sweaty miles later, at the ruin of an old stone barn that was to be our accommodation for the night. The roof had long since collapsed and it started to rain as we bedded down under our single army-issue blankets. Our misery was compounded by the fact that they had still not fed us.

The nature of our arrival in Wales set the tone for the next five days, which were spent sleeping out in the mountains under sodden blankets and being woken at 0400 hours each morning to start physically demanding field firing exercises using live ammunition. We were run up Snowdon in full kit and made to crawl along icy cold brooks where we practised close-quarter battle tactics against pop-up targets, before proceeding to live firing attacks, as sections and then platoons. Throughout, the emphasis was on battle inoculation and we slid on our bellies in the mud under low barbed-wire entanglements and fired and manoeuvred up gullies, as chattering Vickers machine guns sent streams of bullets a few feet over our heads. The instructors hurled sticks of gelignite about to simulate grenades going off and explosive charges were detonated to simulate artillery fire, as we practised an assault river crossing on one of Snowdonia's lakes.

In the pursuit of realism, the margins for error were narrow, and deaths and injury were not uncommon. During the week of our battle inoculation training, four officer cadets were killed in live firing accidents. Losses during battle camps were not uncommon and in the grand scheme of attempting to prepare men for total war, casualties attracted little attention; and there were certainly no public outcries or demands for an investigation. What their next of kin made of it I can only guess, but in the fourth year of war homes all over the country were being shattered by the arrival of telegrams bearing dreadful news of loved ones who had fallen in far-flung places such as Burma and North Africa.

Shortly after completing the training in Wales, I passed out of Sandhurst with the rest of my intake. There was little fanfare, although the NCOs from the Guards got the parade that we had spent hours on the drill square practising for. The better connected on my course went straight to regiments where they had links through family members or friends. But with no such affiliations, I was one of a group of young officers that was sent to the RAC holding camp at Reeth, where we embarked on more arduous infantry-type continuation training. I suspect it was a measure to keep us busy while maintaining a reserve of replacement officers for the opening of the Second Front. However, D-Day was top secret and no one was about to breach classified protocol to explain the rationale of being sent to Yorkshire to the likes of us.

I certainly didn't have the faintest idea about second fronts or the invasion of Europe, as I nursed sore feet and sought replacements for boots that had been worn down to my socks during the long march over the moors. Speculation about the re-entry into the Continent may have been on the lips of those training to cross the Channel, but Reeth was as much isolated from the outside world as it was bleak. We lived in a cocooned bubble of the army's training regime, we didn't have access to radios, hardly ever saw newspapers and I have absolutely no recollection of any announcement that the momentous events of D-Day had even taken place. After eighteen months of training as an RAC trooper and then as an officer at Sandhurst, I was beginning to wonder if I would ever see service as an armoured corps troop leader. Unbeknown to me, as I contemplated my fate, my youthful impatience was about be ended by a summons to the camp's orderly room and the issuing of a rail warrant.

The orders were simple; take a train to Portsmouth, where I would be met at the station and given further instructions. I can remember little of the journey, but as the locomotive pulled further south towards the coast, the fields of the passing countryside became increasingly dotted with ammunition dumps, huge piles of stores and lines of parked vehicles. As the train drew into the station it was clear that the area around the old naval port city had become one vast armed camp. It was 7 June 1944, or in accordance with the Allies' campaign timetable D+1, although I still had no idea that the invasion of Europe had started. The captain who met me in a jeep at the entrance to the station didn't bother to enlighten me or introduce himself. Simply confirming that I was 'Render', he told me to get in before letting out the clutch and roaring down a road crowded with troops drinking tea at the side of their vehicles, as they waited to head towards the docks. We drove in the opposite direction, towards the countryside that fringed the outskirts of 'Pompey'.

The trip in the jeep was short and the captain beside me didn't bother to engage in conversation. He then pulled off the road with a screeching of brakes and bumped into a field full of sixteen brand new Cromwell tanks. A low-silhouetted, square-fronted armoured vehicle, fitted with a 75mm gun and weighing 28 tons, the Cromwell had only recently entered service with the British Army and we had not trained on them at Sandhurst. A gaggle of young RAC troopers lolled on the grass beside them and ignored us, as the reticent captain told me to grab my kit from the back of the jeep and get 'That lot', referring to the Cromwells, 'waterproofed'. Answering that I had no idea how to go about waterproofing a tank, he pointed out one that had already been completed and informed me that I had two days to do the other fifteen. Before swerving out of the field in his jeep, he shouted over his shoulder, 'Oh and make a good job of it.' With that and a crashing of gears, he was gone.

There were no NCOs among the thirty-two nonchalant troopers, so I told them to form up into two ranks and ordered those qualified as drivers to take one pace forward. I rolled my eyes as both ranks stepped towards me. I pointed to the piles of Denso Tape and tins of grease and putty and told them to pair off as drivers and commanders, take a tank each and start applying the material in the same manner as the completed example. I had twigged by then that the purpose of our task was to prepare the vehicles to be able to wade ashore from a landing craft, although I had still not worked out their likely destination. But orders were orders, so I told my indifferent first command to get cracking. As they set about sealing every likely water ingress point on the hulls of their allocated vehicles, I ordered the spare pair to forage for some food, as the administrative arrangements for our little group appeared to be decidedly wanting. Having worked into the evening, we slept on the ground beside the tanks, before starting over the next day.

At midday, our mysterious captain returned and told me to get the tanks started up and to follow him. I felt compelled to protest and inquire about what had happened to the two days he had given us to complete the task, but thought better of it, so I shouted to the crews to mount up and clambered into the jeep. Forming up as a column, we headed back into Portsmouth, leaving a trail of flapping tape and balls of half-moulded putty in our wake as we drove to the docks and a waiting tank-landing ship, know as an LST. The cargo doors in the high bows of the 5000-ton vessel were already open and the captain told me to get the Cromwells reversed up the ship's double-hinged ramp and secured to the internal tank deck. Typically, his instructions were light on the detail of how and once all sixteen tanks were squeezed inside the bowels of the ship, we set about fixing them down with davits and chains as best we could.

With a great sense of responsibility for checking the tension of every fixing point, I became preoccupied with the task of lashing the Cromwells securely to the steel decking and lost any sense of time. The darkness in the hold appeared to have crept up on me by the time we had finished. Once I was satisfied that the tanks wouldn't crash about the deck with the movement of the ship once it was at sea, I went out to seek the captain, presuming that there would be more tanks to collect, waterproof and load. I was somewhat surprised to find that the giant bow doors had been sealed shut. I was even more surprised by the response of the passing naval rating when I enquired about getting off the ship. 'Get off? What do you mean get off? Look out the bloody porthole, we are at sea.' Sure enough, I could see the harbour buildings slipping past us to port, as we headed out into the Solent. My surprise turned to mild shock when I asked the incredulous sailor where we were heading and he replied, 'Where do you think we are bloody heading, mate? We are heading to bloody France.'

3

PASSAGE

Today it takes about eight hours to cross the Channel to Normandy by ferry from Portsmouth. It took much longer on D+2. The modern-day traveller is not troubled by naval shipping timetables, the need to marshal into convoys with escort ships, restricted by the use of safe lanes swept for mines, or the requirement to employ evasive measures to reduce the threat of prowling U-boats that might be lurking menacingly somewhere beneath the surface. Of course, I knew nothing of such matters, although we appeared to spend an interminably long time in Southampton Water after heading out into the mouth of the Solent. We were at sea when night fell, but it seemed to take most of the next day before we were finally in open water among a host of other smoke-stacked grey ships steaming line abreast towards France.

As we started our journey, I noted how the Napoleonic fortifications of Portsmouth's waterfront that slipped past on the port beam had been added to by the defensive needs of meeting the threat from another more current quarter. When we navigated round the Isle of Wight, I saw the sun dipping behind the green-edged hills of Hampshire as the ship manoeuvred into our allotted convoy position to begin our torturous passage. I can't remember having any particularly deep thoughts about whether I would see my family or England again, as my situation was somewhat bemusing and I had no great sense that I was journeying to war. By accident, rather than design, I had become inextricably caught up in the wheels of the massive nautical logistics chain that was feeding the invasion. My overwhelming thought, if I had one, was whether I might be in some kind of trouble, as I had no orders and I wasn't sure that anyone even knew that I was heading to Normandy. However, I became resigned to my fate and set about looking to the needs of my men.

Eventually, I found someone in the LST crew to take somewhat reluctant responsibility for getting them fed and finding them accommodation in the cramped cabins squeezed between the tank deck and the sides of the ship. With little else to do, I headed for the wardroom. The few officers of the ship's company present, including their skipper, seemed equally unforthcoming and I began to wonder if there was some form of endemic malaise of indifference that had also afflicted the army captain who had got me into the predicament that I now found myself in. The assembled naval officers gave me the impression that my tanks and my men, as they now seemed very much to be my responsibility, were some form of great burden to them. I couldn't tell whether it was their first run to Normandy, which had perhaps bred a nervousness that manifested itself in a silent resentment of me, or whether perhaps they had been there on D-Day, knew what to expect and were equally hostile as a result. Regardless, I decided to spend as little time as possible in their company and consigned myself to one of the small cramped cabins by the tank deck. I spent most of the rest of the journey there, lying on a bunk listening to the throbbing engines and the creaking and groaning of the superstructure of the ship, as the heavily laden LST rolled in the heaving swell of the Channel and the tanks strained at the chains fastening them to its deck. I wondered if the hull of the ship would hold up to the strain as it bent and twisted like some great metal snake on the surging water. Perhaps the crew shared the same concerns, and it was an explanation of why they were so reluctant to be at sea.

The breaking of dawn on D+4 brought us within sight of the coast of Normandy. The small square shapes of buildings dotted among the fields rolling down to the sea were visible on the horizon from the ship's rail. Around us was a mass of different types of shipping; tankers and troop carriers riding at anchor, with smaller vessels and landing craft plying back and forth between the ship and the shore. In their midst a rolling barrage of a broadside from the 15-inch guns of a battleship belched fire and smoke. The noise was terrific and the towering superstructure rocked backwards in the water. I could see the overpressure from the giant shells, visible for an instant in the rolling balls of flame, strip the surface of the water as they accelerated towards targets inland. Two German fighters roared towards us from the west, the leading edges of their wings flashing with cannon fire as they came in on a strafing run. The air around them popped with anti-aircraft fire, although none of the crew on the LST took any notice of them. They were focused intently on the task in hand; responding to navigation signals from the beach and following markers that had been placed to indicate the lanes that had been cleared through the water obstacles. As we came in closer to the shore, we passed through a mass of debris and oil. I noticed bodies floating facedown among the flotsam. They were British servicemen, their lifebelts still fastened about their waists. Rushing over to the other side of the deck I saw even more of them drifting in the current. I had never seen a dead person before and it provoked a profound longing for home, family and safety as the macabre jetsam drifted past in the wake of the ship.

Ahead of us a number of wrecked landing craft lay abandoned along the beach, the sand above them marked by the hulks of burned-out tanks. The skipper of the LST stood grim-faced on his bridge as we picked up speed and prepared to beach. Two ratings went aft to deploy the vessel's Kedge sea anchor. Attached to a long length of steel hawser, it would steady our approach against a rising tide and provide the purchase to get the ship off again once it had beached and blown the ballast in its tanks. I could feel a keen sense of tension among the crew as we came in closer. I was ordered to get the tanks started up and went down into the hold of the ship. The inside of the tank deck was a discord of noise and choking blue smoke as engines started, metal shackles were hammered open and men shouted to be heard above the din. Making my way back up to the rail I steadied myself against a bulkhead, as the grinding crash of metal against shingle announced that we had beached. The clam-shaped bow doors were opened and light flooded the cargo deck, casting the thick fumes from the Cromwells' exhausts in a smoky haze. The hinged ramp was released with a squeal of chains and splashed down into the water several yards out from the dry land of the beach. We were about to find out how our attempts at waterproofing the tanks would hold up as the Cromwells prepared to wade to the shore.

A strong easterly tide pushed hard against the hull and I could hear the creaking of metal as the ship strained against the force of the waves, which sought to twist us against the anchored hawser cable at the stern. The irate skipper yelled at me in no uncertain terms to get 'my fucking tanks' off his ship. He seemed keen to be rid of us and back out to sea as fast as possible. I nipped back down into the tank hold and gave the order to the young trooper stationed in the commander's hatch of the tank at the front of the ship. The engine of the first Cromwell revved and coughed more smoke as its tracks bit into the steel decking and started forward out of the open doors of the ship. Its front nosed into the water, sending a small bow wave back up the ramp. I expected it to level out as the tracks made purchase with the shingle, but it kept on going into the water at an alarmingly steep angle. As the rear of its tracks left the ramp, it seemed to float for an instant and was then caught by the strong drag of the current.

It listed heavily on one side and then flipped over, turning turtle. I glimpsed the underside of its belly plate, shiny with water, before twenty-eight tons of tank sank beneath the waves like a stone, taking the two young crewmen with it.

I stood aghast at having just watched two men die. Then pandemonium broke out around me. The skipper was down on the tank deck and came charging towards me. A stream of invectives flowed from his mouth, as he set about berating me. Shocked by what I had just witnessed and the torrent of abuse that clearly fixed the blame on me for what had just happened, I was too frightened to ask what I had done wrong. The skipper didn't bother to explain. The engines of the ship screamed in protest as they were thrown back into reverse and the whole ship racked with shuddering vibrations as it laboured to get itself back off the beach. I grabbed tightly on to a handrail as I followed the skipper back up to the bridge, where he continued to shout expletive-edged orders and curses at everyone around him. The noise of the howling engine and the jarring of straining metal added to the surrounding din from the retort of naval gunfire and anti-aircraft guns. Then the Kedge anchor cable snapped with a sickening crack and the parted end of the thick steel cable sliced through the metal superstructure down the starboard side of the ship as if it had been made of paper. Another stream of oaths followed from the frantic naval commander, who was beside himself with rage. But the ship lifted and the engines pulled us away from the beach into deeper water.

I was racked with guilt by the feeling that I was in some way responsible for the loss of the two troopers in the foundered Cromwell. But regardless of the responsibility and shock that I felt, the tragedy appeared to be of little concern to the captain and his crew in their frantic preoccupation with repositioning the ship. Any significance attached to the men's passing was lost in the storm of foul language and frenzied activity as the LST made another attempt to beach at a slightly different point along the shore. Grounding to a halt in shallow water, I was once again ordered to remove myself and my tanks post haste. I held my breath as the first of the fifteen remaining Cromwells nosed off the ramp into the waves. This time, its tracks bit into the seabed and levelled out in about four feet of water. The waterproofing held and it was able to wade the several yards to shore without mishap. The other tanks followed and by the time the last of them reached the firm sand of the beach the bow doors of the LST were already shut and the vessel was making ready to lift off and pull back out to sea.

Gold Beach was a hive of activity. Engineers worked to improve the routes across the sand and the exit points, while obstacle clearing parties were still busy demolishing the submerged landing obstructions to make way for the building of Churchill's brainwave idea: the Mulberry floating harbour that would facilitate the rapid offloading of troops directly onto the beach. Groups of dishevelled German prisoners were marched in ragged columns to the water's edge, where they would be picked up and ferried to POW cages in England. Other craft were landing their cargoes of vehicles and beach masters were busy marshalling them up the beach into assembly areas where they would wait to be called forward to the front. My tanks became part of the process and our Cromwells were directed to a field beyond the sand dunes that was laid out like a huge disorderly taxi park of trucks, tracked personnel carriers and limbered artillery pieces.

Lacking any detailed direction, my tactical training kicked in and I pushed the tanks against the surrounding hedgerows to give them a semblance of cover. I expected to receive some orders, but none came and once again I tasked a forage party to seek out some food. Later that day, a truck drove up and a party of tank crewmen dismounted, took over our Cromwells and drove them away. A short time afterwards, another truck pulled up and picked up the troopers that I had landed with. But there were still no orders for me and by last light

I was beginning to feel decidedly forgotten. I lay in my bedroll and listened to the distant rumble of artillery, its muzzle flashes flaring briefly in the distance on the horizon. German bombers droned overhead, using the cover of darkness to drop pressure mines into the sea. As I drifted off to sleep the night sky was lurid with flares and the bright arc of tracer looping up into the sky to meet them.

D+5 dawned bright and clear and a light breeze blew in from the sea. I was still without orders and thought a stroll along the beach might do me some good. As I walked along the tops of the vacant German positions dug into the dunes, the evidence of the fighting that had taken place five days previously was still all around. Blackened shell craters and discarded equipment were strewn across the sand. Small neat lines of dead, with their hobnail boots protruding from the filthy grey army blankets they had been sewn into, were arranged by the side of medical tents; a macabre indication that fighting was going on inland. I was lost in my loneliness when there was a sudden angry buzzing about my feet. For a moment I thought I must have disturbed a nest of swarming bees, as the fine-grain sand of the dunes stirred and whipped up around me. Then the dark shadow of a Messerschmitt 109 flashed over my head, immediately followed by a Spitfire, hard on its tail with its guns blazing. The angry bees were the overspill of the Spitfire's machine-gun bullets, added to by the fire of another Messerschmitt that swept in, almost low enough to touch, and sped after the RAF fighter that was on the tail of his comrade. In turn a further Spitfire followed the second German aircraft and flashed past as a fourth great speeding shadow. It happened so quickly that I didn't have time to react, but as I sought the comparative safety of the vehicle park, I was somewhat shaken by my near miss.

In less than two days I had accidentally become part of the invasion, had seen two of the men in my temporary command die before I even had chance to get to know them, the rest had been taken away from me and I had narrowly escaped being killed by fighter aircraft intent on killing each other rather than me. It seemed a particularly peculiar way to go to war. On my own and at a loss what to do next, I was beginning to contemplate that my only option was to find a ship to take me home, so that I could report back to the holding unit at Reeth; although quite what I would say when I got back to the orderly room was beyond me. I wondered if I might end up on a charge for being AWOL. Sitting on my kit in the middle of the vehicle park as the second day of doing nothing in Normandy began to draw to a close, I was feeling decidedly sorry for myself when a dispatch rider pulled up on his motorbike. I can't even remember his rank. He certainly didn't tell me his name or where he was taking me when he told me to grab my kit and get on the pillion seat behind him.

The sun was dropping below the western horizon as we motored out of the vehicle park and rode inland through twisting country lanes and villages built of distinctive yellow-grey Norman stone. The bridgehead beyond the beach seemed extremely crowded as the Allies built up their forces. The roads were busy with military transport, supply trucks moving forward, ambulances and jeeps fixed with stretchers carrying casualties heading back towards the beaches. Wooden posts at every major junction were festooned with tactical markers displaying unit locations and giving directions to logistical facilities; a clear sign of an army establishing itself ashore. We passed large dumps of ammunition and packed fuel set up in the patchwork of small-hedged fields at the sides of the road. Larger fields were reserved for batteries of medium and heavy artillery. Under the cover of camouflage netting, their crews worked stripped to the waist as they laboured to service their guns as they responded to calls for fire from the front just a few miles away, adding to the growing ensemble of noise as we approached the forward area.

The terrain began to undulate as we gained the higher ground away from the coast towards Bayeux. The twin spires and green-domed capped tower of the ancient Norman cathedral were just visible in the increasingly fading light, as we skirted to the east of the city along a rough bypass route that had been created by the engineers to support the flow of traffic to the front. Heading southeast the ground became clustered with orchards and high hedgerows that had been grown to shelter the apple crop from the ravages of the wind. The stands of apple trees made good leaguer sites for military vehicles, as they afforded a degree of partial cover from view while providing sufficient room to park up trucks and tanks and allow their crews to carry out administration and maintenance when out of the immediate battle area. The last vestiges of light were being blotted out by the approaching darkness, when we turned off a fork in the road and bumped down a narrow track that led into the orchard where the Sherwood Rangers Yeomanry were preparing to leaguer for the night.

Sherman tanks were parked beneath the apple trees and their crews worked around them in the gathering gloom. The last of the cooking fires were being extinguished as tarpaulin sheets were pulled down from the sides of the vehicles to form lean-to shelters and men were laying out their bedrolls beneath them. The motorbike came to a stop by a Sherman with a small tent set up behind its rear engine decks. Dismounting, I followed the dispatch rider, who pulled back the tent flap and ushered me inside. An officer wearing battledress looked up from a map that he had been studying in the inadequate light of a hurricane lamp. John Semken was twenty-three years old and, although only a captain, was the officer commanding A Squadron. Elegant and tall, with a head of thick dark hair, he looked much older and possessed a calm aura of authority that had been born from considerable front-line experience. After my treatment over the past four days, the warmth of his reception surprised me. Semken welcomed me to A Squadron and told me that I was to be given command of 5 Troop after receiving a day's instruction the next day from one of the squadron's officers. What John Semken didn't tell me was that I was taking over the troop because an enemy sniper had killed the previous troop leader. He also neglected to tell me that I was joining the Sherwood Rangers after several days of particularly difficult fighting that had followed their landing on D-Day and that D+5 had just been their worst day.

A Squadron had supported 2nd Essex's capture of Bayeux the day after the Allies landed. On the day of the invasion the inhabitants had cowered in their cellars as the massive bombardment had swept in from the air and the sea to pound the coast only a few miles away. As the British infantry dug in on the high ground to the north of the city, when last light began to fall, the majority of the German garrison took advantage of the cover of darkness and slipped away during the night. An eerie quiet descended on the streets of Bayeux, as the city's population waited subdued and frightened in their basements. Emerging from their places of shelter in the early morning of 7 June, their disbelief at seeing British troops and the tanks of A Squadron patrolling cautiously through the centre of the town turned to ecstatic jubilation as they realised that their liberation was at hand. With the bulk of their forces having fled, enemy resistance was limited. One isolated German machine-gun post in the south of the town held out briefly, but was dealt with quickly by a few rounds of HE from a Sherman. The ancient bells of the cathedral were still tolling in celebration when A Squadron received orders to return to rejoin the rest of the Sherwood Rangers that were assembling with 8th Armoured Brigade to the northwest of the city. Bayeux was the first major town to be captured by the Allies and the people of Bayeux had been blessed by the fact that their city had been taken undamaged and without any serious fighting; other towns and villages in Normandy would not be so fortunate.

The Sherwood Rangers formed part of the 8th Armoured Brigade, a tank formation that included two other Sherman-equipped cavalry regiments from the 4th/7th Dragoon Guards and the 24th Lancers. The Sexton self-propelled guns of the Essex Yeomanry, which had made such a crucial difference on Gold Beach against the Le Hamel bunker, provided the brigade's dedicated close artillery support. Officially designated as the 147th Field Regiment Royal Artillery, the unit fielded three batteries of eight Sextons mounting converted 25-pounder guns that could hurl a 3.45 inch HE shell just over seven and a half miles. Integral infantry support came from the 12th Battalion of the King's Royal Rifle Corps. With an approximate strength of 800 men, the battalion could field four rifle companies mounted in Bren carriers, giving them an ability to keep up with the advancing tank regiments of the brigade. Eighth Armoured Brigade was one of six similarly equipped formations that would eventually be fielded by the 2nd British Army in Normandy. The principal role of the armoured brigades was to provide direct tank support to the infantry divisions, by detaching armoured regiments and squadrons to the infantry formations' individual brigades and battalions when needed. Possession of its own integral infantry and artillery also gave the 8th Armoured Brigade the ability to conduct its own independent combined arms operations.

With much of his infantry digging in after landing in Normandy, Montgomery was impatient to exploit the initial collapse of the Germans' coastal defences and continue to push inland. Twelve miles to the west of Bayeux, the primary D-Day objective of Caen had not been taken and German forces were consolidating their positions around the city. Monty believed there was an opportunity to outflank the city from the eastern end of the British sector. As part of his plan, 8th Armoured Brigade was ordered to form a mobile column and advance ten miles south of Bayeux along the line of the Seulles river to capture the important hub of road junctions that runs to and from the town of Villers-Bocage. To protect the left flank of the advance, the Sherwood Rangers were detached to support infantry battalions of 50th Division and seize and hold the high ground to the north of the cluster of villages located around the larger village of

Passage

Tilly-sur-Seulles, which sat astride the Seulles river and marked the halfway point of 8th Armoured Brigade's intended route of advance towards Villers-Bocage.

Lying just six miles away, the highest point overlooking the shallow Seulles valley is a sloping piece of ground marked on the map as Point 103. The Sherwood Rangers met little significant opposition as they advanced towards the hill feature, although Lieutenant Victor Vernor was seriously wounded when he was hit in the chest by a sniper as he commanded his Sherman from its open turret hatch. He was to die of his wounds a few days later. Having fought through the desert, he was an experienced troop leader and a significant loss to A Squadron and the men he commanded in 5 Troop. The regiment's route took them through the village of Audrieu. They took little notice of the imposing chateau situated on the southern side of the village as they pressed on to Point 103. Follow-up units of the brigade would later make the grisly discovery that it was the place of execution for forty-five Canadian prisoners of war. It was later established that they had been shot out of hand by soldiers of the 12th SS Panzer Division *Hitlerjugend*, prior to withdrawing from the chateau at the approach of British armour. A callous and wanton act, it was also a harbinger of the savage nature of the fighting that lay ahead.

The regiment was in position on the Point 103 feature by 1600 hours. The high ground provided a commanding view over the rooftops of the hamlet of St Pierre, nestling a mile and a half distant down its forward slopes on the outskirts of Tilly. Two miles to the west of Tilly, the edge of the larger village of Fontenay was also visible. A forward edge of a ridge sloping towards the enemy is a dangerous place for tanks, as it would expose them to the fire of any Germans located in the villages below them. A reconnaissance on foot of St Pierre was conducted by two officers, as the tanks held back from the ridge in the cover of trees and hedgerows on the reverse of its crest. One of the officers was the second in command of A Squadron, Keith Douglas, who was to become a celebrated war poet. Later considered to rank among the best of the twentieth-century soldier-writers, Douglas had been wounded serving with the regiment in North Africa and had written about his experiences in a memoir entitled *Alamein to Zem Zem*, although he would not live to see it published.

Speaking French, Douglas was able to coax a frightened civilian out of his cellar, who reported that there were Germans in the vicinity. This was confirmed when the two officers bumped into a small group of enemy and beat a hasty retreat back to the ridge. The Wehrmacht patrol was part of the leading elements of Panzer Lehr and evidence that the Germans had recovered from the initial surprise of the Allied landings. Equipped with 229 tanks, Panzer Lehr was a formidable German armoured division. Positioned at Chartres when the Allies landed, it had taken it two days to motor the hundred miles to Normandy and it was beginning to move into positions around Tilly as the Sherwood Rangers were arriving in their own positions on Point 103, which were also being reinforced by infantry 17-pounder anti-tank guns and a company of Vickers machine guns. To Panzer Lehr's right in the village of Fontenay, the 20,000 *Hitlerjugend* soldiers of the 12th SS Division had already formed into line and could field 185 tanks, including 81 of the new highly capable German Panthers.

Point 103 became an increasingly dangerous place as the German reaction began to take form. Enemy tanks probed the slope from the lower ground and artillery and mortar fire began to fall on the exposed British positions. In an ideal tactical situation, a tank seeks to engage the enemy from a 'hull-down' position behind a solid piece of ground, high enough to shield its hull, but low enough to fire over. The forward incline provided the Sherwood Rangers with little opportunity for concealment or protection and they suffered for it, losing three Shermans on their second day of occupation. Frustrated by not being able to get into a fire position without the risk of being knocked out, Keith Douglas made the decision to go forward on foot.

He did so without the permission of his squadron commander and it was a decision that cost him his life when he was killed by the blast from a German mortar shell.

Relieved that night by the tanks of the 4th/7th Dragoon Guards, the regiment was operating on the top of the feature again the next day and helped beat off a German infantry attack with the prolific support of artillery and naval gun fire. The dangerous nature of the ridge diminished later that morning, when the 24th Lancers attacked and captured St Pierre in support of the Durham Light Infantry. The capture of the village also allowed Leslie Skinner to get forward and look for the regiment's dead. He found Keith Douglas in a ditch and buried him under a hedge near where he had fallen. Alarmed that his body lay unattended, Skinner had pushed Major Mike Laycock for permission to go forward and recover Douglas's body the day before, but as acting commanding officer of the unit since the CO had been evacuated on D-Day, Laycock had refused. The padre later recorded that Douglas had shared the premonition of his death with him after the last church service he had held before the regiment had embarked from England. It reflected a fatalism held by many who had survived the fighting in North Africa and considered that a fresh campaign in Europe put them on borrowed time.

The taking of St Pierre had not been without cost to the 24th Lancers, who lost twelve tanks during the fighting for the village. The light from their burning hulks cast eerie shadows over the battlefield as night fell and the Sherwood Rangers moved in to relieve them. Standing to throughout the night, in anticipation of a German counterattack on St Pierre, the men of A and C Squadrons were short of sleep when they began operations the next day in support of the British 7th Armoured Division in the area of Tilly and along the higher ground to the north of Fontenay. B Squadron remained in reserve with regimental headquarters. RHQ consisted of four Sherman command tanks that were fitted with dummy 75mm gun barrels.

The removal of the breech inside the turret created extra space for additional radio equipment and the staff officers that supported the CO's command of the regiment. Deriving from their Nottingham heritage, the four tanks were known as 'Robin Hood', 'Maid Marian', 'Friar Tuck' and 'Little John'. While the configuration of the RHQ tanks facilitated command on the move, when static it was common for the CO and his staff to set up their HQ in a suitable building.

On the morning of 11 June they were parked up in a small enclosed farmyard on the northern side of the village and the adjacent farmhouse was being used to hold an orders group with infantry officers from the Durham Light Infantry (DLI). The group had broken up and the assembled officers were walking in the cobbled courtyard when the first shell struck. The courtyard was no bigger than the size of an enlarged tennis court, so the impact of the 105mm projectile in the confined space was devastating. With splintering cobbles adding to its lethal effect, jagged-edge shrapnel and sharp broken flint scythed into the group of officers, killing the CO, his adjutant and the intelligence officer and wounding three more. In an instant the heart of the Sherwood Rangers' headquarters had been cut down and Mike Laycock's dream of commanding the regiment that his father had once led ended in a storm of steel and stone.

Later that morning Skinner buried the bodies, laying Laycock next to his adjutant Captain George Jones. Jones had been the son of the head woodsman on the Laycock family estate at Wiseton in Nottinghamshire and had worked for Mike Laycock's father. After joining the regiment as a trooper, Jones had risen through the ranks to become a trusted and efficient officer. From similar origins, but very different backgrounds, the near feudal relationship between the two men continued into death, as they lay consigned side by side in the rich Norman soil.

An urgent radio message calling him to return to RHQ informed Major Stanley Christopherson of what had happened. He wasn't the most senior squadron commander, but he was the obvious choice to take charge of the regiment. His official status as the new CO was confirmed the next day. He was the Sherwood Rangers' sixth commanding officer in a little over a year; two had been killed in action towards the end of the desert campaign and Lieutenant Colonel Anderson had of course been wounded on D-Day. It was an attrition rate that underlined the perilous nature of commanding a front-line unit. Along with the deaths of Keith Douglas, Laycock and those that had died with him in the farmyard, it also reflected the danger of being caught in the open by enemy indirect fire when out of a tank.

The loss of Keith Douglas, combined with Christopherson's elevation to acting command of the regiment, also meant that A Squadron was without a leader and had no second in command to step up and replace him. The vacant position was filled by John Semken, who had already served as a troop leader in the desert. On returning to England after the campaign in North Africa, Semken had been promoted to the rank of captain and had become the Sherwood Rangers' technical adjutant, where he was responsible for overseeing the maintenance and supply of the unit's vehicles and weapons. It was an important job in a unit where the availability and reliability of its equipment was critical, but with the loss of so many commanders and the demands of the tactical situation, there were more pressing needs for Semken's talents and experience.

Christopherson had little time to mourn the passing of his second in command or the deaths of Laycock and Jones, who had been his friends. A heavy German counterattack was brewing and he had to look to the defence of St Pierre. The main body of Panzer Lehr had arrived in the area and was ordered to mount an offensive to break the British line. The brunt of the German attack fell to the west of St Pierre and managed to penetrate as far as the location of 8th Armoured Brigade HQ on the outskirts of Tilly. Fiftieth Division was also under pressure and was forced back on to Point 103. It meant that St Pierre had to be given up, forcing the Sherwood Rangers to withdraw to the higher ground, leaving their dead and several knocked-out tanks behind them in the village. But the Germans suffered for their gains and lost several tanks to the regiment's Shermans. Additionally, while Panzer Lehr's attack was supported by heavy artillery fire, the British response was heavier. The combined fire of several Royal Artillery field regiments and the large-calibre guns of the naval battleships stationed off the coast raked the advancing Germans and decimated their ranks. As the shadows of the early evening began to lengthen across the battlefield, Panzer Lehr's attack began to run out of steam and both sides prepared to lick their wounds and reorganise their forces with the onset of the coming darkness.

I knew little of the detail of what had taken place on the day of my arrival at the regiment and knew even less of the fighting that had preceded it since the unit's arrival in Normandy. Looking back on it, John Semken must have given me some form of introductory briefing on the tactical situation, but what I can remember is that the CO had been killed, the regiment now had a new CO and the subunit that I was joining had a new boss. What I didn't know at the time was that Semken's appointment as A Squadron's commander would have a profound impact on my own service in the Sherwood Rangers; that, of course, was in the future.

I made my way to the Sherman parked up among the apple trees that Semken had pointed out to me from the flap of the tent. A fleeting moon shone through the scudding clouds, its radiance illuminating the tank's outline against the inky darkness that had descended over the leaguer. The sound of shallow snoring coming from beneath the black shape of the stretched tarpaulin slanting down from its side confirmed the presence of the crew as I approached. I laid out my bedroll and crawled in beside the sleeping bodies. The crump of artillery and mortar fire sounded off in the distance and bright flashes briefly lit up the night, as I settled down to try and get some sleep.

Passage

No doubt somewhere not far away from me in a different part of the leaguer, Stanley Christopherson was also thinking of the approaching morrow and his new command. The difference was that he was a decorated tank officer with a considerable amount of combat experience and was a known quantity in the regiment. I was something entirely different.

4

BAPTISM

I am not sure that as the new commanding officer Stanley Christopherson would have managed to get much sleep during his first night in command. In the fighting around Point 103 and St Pierre the regiment had lost thirty-seven men injured and dead. Twelve of the casualties had been officers, six of whom had been killed. Having collated the casualty return reports at his headquarters that evening, Christopherson set about the grim task of writing to their next of kin. It was the dread responsibility of any CO, and now it fell to him to set pen to paper and hope that the words he struggled to find in the early hours of the morning would bring some solace to shattered parents and grieving wives. Troop leaders were not weighted down with such burdens of command. My responsibilities would rest with the immediate leadership of the unknown men that I had bedded down next to and with the crews of the other two Shermans that made up the ranks of 5 Troop.

The spaces next to me in the tank shelter had been vacated by the time I woke. Beyond the canvas, the first light of an uncertain dawn was creeping from the shadows and the leaguer was shaking itself from a few hours of exhausted sleep. I glanced at my watch as I emerged from under the tarpaulin; it was a little before 0400 hours. Around me tank engines were being started and cooking fires flared in the receding gloom, as men prepared for another day of battle. Three of my sleeping companions were busy about their ablutions and making breakfast, intent on the frying pan that sizzled and spat on an old biscuit tin filled with flaming petrol. Their new troop leader went completely ignored. I noticed the desert ribbon of the North Africa Star on the left breast of the battledress jackets. Introducing myself provoked little reaction, other than a cursory glance in my direction before their attention returned to preparing their first meal of the day.

I didn't wait to be invited to join them. Training on Churchill and Valentine tanks, I had only seen a Sherman once in the eighteen months I spent at Bovington and Sandhurst. But most tanks were similar in concept and design and my training had taught me the importance of checking the bore alignment of the main armament to the sighting system, prior to commencing operations in any tank. Misalignment would mean that the gun could not be fired accurately and was likely to prove fatal in an engagement with a German panzer. I asked the nonchalant trio squatting round the fire which one of them was the gunner. A surly-looking individual stood up. My inquiry as to whether the gun had been properly tested and adjusted produced an indifferent shrug of the shoulders from the man who was responsible for ensuring that the gun was properly sighted. When I told him to get in the tank and check it, he told me to 'piss off' and 'check it myself'.

I was taken aback by his insubordination. But as a brand new subaltern who had worn his lieutenant's pips for only a few weeks, I was less than entirely comfortable with my new status as an officer and I said nothing. Instead I set about checking the alignment of the gun myself. Climbing into the turret through the commander's hatch, I contorted myself round the rear of the gun's breech, which filled the middle of the fighting compartment. Applying all my strength, I forced the breechblock lever open and then twisted my way back out of the turret. Climbing down to the front of the gun, I followed my training and used blobs of grease to affix two long grass stalks into slits cut into the muzzle edges to form a crosshair across the end of the barrel. Dropping back into the turret I squeezed into the gunner's seat. Squinting up the open breech, I was able to look up the shiny steel bore of the barrel to see a circle of daylight at the other end. Using the gun's traversing and elevating mechanism, I brought the centre of the crosshairs at the end of the barrel on to the high branch of a prominent tree two hundred yards distant. Screwing my eye into the rubber eyepiece of the gun sight, I expected to see the fine lines of its optical crosshairs aligning precisely with the aiming point I had laid the barrel on to.

I was alarmed to discover that, instead, the gun sight was pointing straight down at the ground a few yards directly in front of the tank. Had the gun been fired, the round would have been a long way off from its intended target and likely as not would have posed more risk to us than any enemy tank. Engrossed as I was in making the necessary adjustments to align the sight to the gun, I was aware of someone dropping into the turret behind me. The lance corporal who had eased into the loader's seat on the other side of the breech glanced across at me. For the briefest of moments, I detected a hint of warmth and a trace of sympathy in his face, before he became absorbed in working on the radio behind him. My task complete, I climbed out of the turret to the squawk of radio static, as he worked intently on the dials of the set to tune it into the regimental frequency.

With their breakfast complete, the other three members of the crew had rolled up the tank shelter and stowed their personal gear on the back of the tank. My own kit sat forlornly on the ground where I had left it. After lashing my bedroll and pack down tightly on the back deck, I sought out the troop sergeant to confirm that the sights of the other two tanks in the troop had been properly tested and adjusted. Sergeant Arthur Harrison was a large, dark, square-faced Yorkshireman in his mid-forties. He was roughly the same age as my father and seemed like an old man to me. I suspect that as far as he was concerned I was just a snot-nosed kid. Forbidding in his appearance and age, he had the mark of a veteran about him. Joining the Sherwood Rangers as a mounted yeoman trooper before the war, Harrison had been called up as a reservist in 1939 and had fought through the desert campaign, as the ribbon of the Africa Star on his soiled battledress jacket bore witness. The impression that he didn't like young officers was confirmed when he dismissed my query about the sighting of the other troop tanks by telling me that it was none of my 'fooking business'.

Remonstrating with the most senior NCO of the troop was likely to be pointless. There was no time and technically I was not yet officially in command, as I still had to spend the day under the instruction of a more senior officer in the squadron. The engines around the leaguer were already bursting into life and some crews were beginning to move out when Neville Fearn appeared at the side of my tank. He was the squadron's battle captain, but he didn't bother with lengthy introductions and simply got to the point of briefing me on the key points of my induction. Firstly, I was to follow him, stop when he stopped and fire when he fired. He instructed me not to close down, but to have my head out of the turret at all times and to keep looking through my binoculars. He then told me to wear my black tank beret and not bother with my tin helmet, as it wouldn't fit over my headset. Instead, he said, I should fix it to the machine gun bracket at the rear of the commander's hatch with the goggles strapped to it, pointing out that it was a useful draw for German snipers to aim at, instead of my head. Fearn also told me to watch my voice procedure over the net and never to raise it excitedly. Finally, he warned me not to dare to go to sleep. With that he headed back to his tank. The crew of my own Sherman were still milling around the tank, when a major started shouting at us for standing about in the open and to get mounted up. I was later to find out that it was Stanley Christopherson, who was still to put up the rank of a lieutenant colonel, and I can distinctly remember him berating us and yelling that 'We didn't bring all these bloody tanks over here to have no one left to crew them.' No doubt Christopherson was making reference to the loss of Keith Douglas and the event in the farmyard the day before. The majority of casualties the regiment had taken since landing in Normandy had been as a result of being caught out in the open by shell and mortar fire. We didn't wait to be told twice.

Mounted up with the engine running, I watched the eighteen Sherman tanks of A Squadron begin to move off in column, their tracks spilling great clouds of chalky grey dust into the air as they left the leaguer. I spotted Neville Fearn's tank at the rear of the line of armoured vehicles. Putting the black Bakelite hand microphone to my mouth, I ordered my driver to advance. With a crashing of gears and a roar of the engine, our own tank swung in behind him at the head of 5 Troop. Although Fearn had not briefed me on the nature of our task, the regiment had been ordered to protect the left flank of 7th Armoured Division as it attacked in the Tilly area to our east. Following the attack by Panzer Lehr, 8 Armoured Brigade was still in possession of the ridge that ran for two miles from Point 103 above St Pierre to another piece of higher ground in the west known as Point 102, centred on a chateau at Boislonde. A Squadron was tasked with clearing the area of some German tanks that had penetrated into the woods that ran down the forward slope of the ridge towards the village of Fontenay.

The squadron operated as four troops, each consisting of three Sherman tanks equipped with a standard 75mm gun. Additional firepower was provided by two 0.3-inch machine guns, one mounted coaxially to the main armament and the other located in the forward hull of the tank. John Semken commanded the squadron from his own tank, which was one of two Shermans that made up his squadron headquarters. In addition to the standard troops, A Squadron also had a separate troop of four Sherman Firefly tanks that operated under the command of the squadron headquarters. The Firefly was a modified Sherman that mounted a heavier 17-pounder anti-tank gun designed to provide additional firepower to the standard troops. The Firefly had only one coaxially mounted machine gun, as the hull-mounted 0.3-inch weapon and its gunner had been removed to accommodate the stowage of the larger-sized rounds fired by its 17-pounder gun. From my training I was of course aware of the configuration of a battle tank squadron, but what I did notice that was not standard RAC practice was how all the tanks had been given names that started with an A painted in white letters on their sides. My Sherman was called 'Aim' and the other two tanks in the troop were 'Archer' and 'Arrow'. I also noted that another A Squadron Sherman was called 'Akilla'.

The journey to our area of operations was not an overly long one, but I felt the wind in my hair that comes with the thrill of being in command of an armoured fighting vehicle, as we travelled at twenty-five miles per hour along a series of farm tracks. Capable of reaching a maximum speed of thirty miles per hour, the Sherman tank was fast for its day. But while speed was an important part of its design characteristics, crew comfort was not. The white painted interior of the tank was incredibly cramped. The driver sat in the forward front-left compartment of the hull with the tank's steering levers in front of him, which would also act as brakes when he pulled back on them. The accelerator pedal and clutch were located at his feet. On his left, a simple small green control box of dials and switches allowed him to start the engine and monitor its speed, revs and temperature. The gear lever was on his right attached to the large gearbox transmission that converted the power from the engine in the rear of the tank to the forward drive sprockets that drove the tracks.

The hull gunner who crewed the forward-mounted 0.3-inch machine gun sat on the other side of the gearbox from the driver. Both had their own hatches although these were normally closed down, restricting their view of the outside world to the one-by-six-inch viewing slit of the periscopes fitted into the hatches above their heads. Shells for the main armament, boxes of ammunition for the machine guns, rations, cooking equipment, water and a few crew incidentals were crammed into every space behind, between and around them. The space in the turret for the other three crew members was little better. The loader sat on the left of the gun and was afforded barely enough room for hoisting shells into the gun breech, ramming them home and slamming the breechblock shut before reporting the gun 'ready' to the gunner who sat on the right-hand side of the main armament. He was also in charge of keeping the machine gun, mounted coaxially to the left of the main gun, fed with belted 0.3 inch ammunition, as well as being responsible for maintaining and operating the radio mounted behind him in the back of the turret.

The gunner had even less space than the loader. With his left shoulder almost touching the recoil mechanism of the gun and his right brushing against the rough steel of the inside of the turret, he was able to swivel the gun left or right by a twist of his right hand on the metal grip of the power-traverse handle. A periscope set at eye level gave him a similar external view to that of the driver and hull gunner, while the separate telescopic sight fitted to the side of the gun provided him with a larger magnified image of an intended target area once properly aligned to the main armament. The gunner had just enough space for his feet to fire the 75mm gun and coaxial machine gun by means of two separate firing buttons fitted to the floor of the turret, which were connected to electronic solenoids. As the commander, I either sat on a small collapsible button seat just above and behind the gunner, or balanced on any suitable foothold inside the turret that gave me sufficient purchase to see out of the two open semi-circular split hatches of the commander's cupola.

The best stance to get my head and shoulders above the ring of the turret hatch was a semi-hunched position. It also allowed my knees to absorb some of the impact of the bucking and heaving vehicle. Lurching over uneven ground made the inside of the tank akin to being inside a rocking iron maiden, where every fixing seemed designed with bruising or shin-skinning purpose. The inside of the tank also reeked from the stench of fuel, grease and body odour. The crew wore a mixture of cotton tank suits and battle dress, but I doubted that they had been able to wash their clothes since the landing on D-Day. Apart from those who had pistols fixed in a holster, none of us wore any webbing equipment, due to the lack of room and the need to avoid the risk of snagging in the event of having to escape from the vehicle if we were hit.

The roar of the twin General Motors Detroit six-cylinder diesel bus engines was deafening. Mated together at the back of the tank, the power train ran under the turret and only a thin metal firewall provided any separation from the crew compartment. The noise they produced precluded normal conversation between the crew, other than by means of the intercom. Connected to the headset and microphones we wore, the '19 set' radio had three settings on a control panel in the turret. If I switched to 'B' setting, I could communicate with my other two tanks on the troop net. Selecting 'A' would allow me to talk on the regimental or squadron frequency, while the 'I' setting for intercom would allow the crew to talk to one another and was the means by which I could issue orders and direction to them. However, there was little conversation as we drove out of the leaguer that morning and, despite the noise, I could detect an appreciably sullen atmosphere in the tank.

In training, we had been taught to operate with commander's hatch closed down. While minimising exposure to shell splinters and small-arms fire, to do so would deny the commander the visibility and situational awareness he needed to fight the tank effectively. But having one's 'head up' was not without its risks. However, operating with the commander's hatches open was just one of the many instances where army training doctrine was discarded. I also noted how the breech guard for the main armament, designed to protect the turret crew when the breech leapt backwards into the compartment on firing, had been stripped out to provide just a little more room for the loader and gunner to operate in. It meant that we would have to be doubly cautious when engaging with the main 75mm gun, as the force of being hit by its recoil could crush bones and fatally injure a man. Smoking inside a tank was also strictly forbidden, but judging from the smoky-blue fug that had already built up inside the Sherman, as every member of the crew smoked incessantly from the moment that we left the leaguer, it was clearly another aspect of regulation that was being totally ignored. I was already a smoker, but joining 5 Troop was the start of a consumption rate that would soon become a hundred-a-day habit. Open commanders' hatches, discarded safety rails and smoking were minor affairs compared to the need to meet the tactical realities of fighting the Germans in Normandy, which would require us to completely tear up the rule book and throw it away.

Although we had travelled only a short distance from the leaguer, everything was covered in a layer of talcum-powder-fine dust by the time the squadron column stopped in the dead ground of a track by the side of a large orchard. The sun was climbing into a clear blue sky and beginning to gild the still unripe corn in the fields around us. In the fields put to pasture I noticed the dead cattle killed by artillery fire. They were strewn across the countryside, legs set rigid by rigor mortis pointed macabrely into the sky, as their distended bellies split in the warm sunshine to attract swarms of flies. The stench was indescribable and was to become a gut-churning feature of the

Normandy campaign. Up ahead, the lead troops of the squadron were preparing to advance. They moved off at a much slower pace towards a distant wood line and I noticed how little dust they threw up. Neville Fearn's tank then peeled off the track into a small hedge-bound field. I followed him with my troop in tow. He paralleled the line of its hedgerow and then manoeuvred his tank into a gap where he could bring his gun to bear. No sooner had he stopped than he opened fire with his main armament and machine guns at another hedge line lying 200 yards away across the next field. I had no idea what he was firing at, but positioning my own tank in a similar fashion off to his flank I directed my gunner on to the line of bushes and trees where Fearn's rounds were landing and ordered him to open fire.

Trooper Sid Martin had already proved that he was not one to respond to my orders with alacrity and he showed a marked reluctance to fire. I repeated my order to fire at unseen targets in the distant hedge line and slapped him hard on the shoulder to reinforce the imperative. The first HE shell crashed from the gun's barrel as the breech block shot backwards into the turret. The coaxial machine gun started to chatter before the brass case of the first 75mm shell had clanged to the floor. Lance Corporal Mayo had the second round in the breech in a flash, slammed it shut again and screamed 'Ready!' I was impressed by the speed of his loading and ducking down below the hatch ring I shot him an appreciative look through the acrid smoke that filled the interior. Through the dissipating haze it was met by the trace of a smile, but then he was already turning to cradle another of the 18-pound HE rounds onto his lap. I was also impressed by the efficiency of the air filtration system in the Sherman. Designed to keep the armour-cased engine in the back of the vehicle cool, it also sucked out the fumes of the gun from the crew compartment, clearing it almost completely from smoke in a few seconds during the pauses in firing.

I still didn't have the faintest idea of what we were firing at, as we pumped round after round into the bushes and trees in front of us. I kept straining my eyes through my binoculars, then I saw the flash and caught what was to become the distinctive buzz-saw sound of a German MG42 machine gun firing in reply. Even through the wall of noise that surrounded me, I heard the *brrrp, brrrp, brrrp* of the Spandau, followed by the hammer rattle of its bullets striking against the sides of our tank. This time Martin didn't have to be told twice and the other tanks also had the location of the offending Jerry gun in their sights. Rounds were already in the air as we fired and the muzzle flashes and distinctive sound stopped after a storm of 75mm shells smothered the hedge line with high explosive.

Fifteen minutes later, Fearn's tank stopped firing almost as abruptly as it had started. I gave the order to cease fire. Mayo took the opportunity to change the belts on the .30 calibre and to start disposing of the brass shell cases from the main armament through a small ejection port in the side of the turret above his left shoulder, exercising care to avoid the most recently fired ones, which were still hot enough to burn his hands. He kept one back to use as an impro- vised disposable urinal that then began the rounds between the crew. Fearn's tank began advancing towards the hedge line in the next field. My troop corporal's tank conformed on mine as we manoeu- vred forward, although I noticed that Harrison's tank appeared to be hanging back. The hedge was shot up again briefly with machine-gun fire, before we adopted a similar firing position and began opening up on the next line of hedges facing us across another field. After a pause the rest of my troop followed suit. Again I could detect no presence of the enemy in the hedges in front of us, however hard I looked through my binoculars. I began to suspect that Fearn had some super-normal visual powers or an uncanny sixth sense that told him just where the enemy were. We repeated the process of brassing up one hedge line after another and jockeying in and out of different fire positions for the rest of the morning. We had fired a prolific amount of ammunition, but in all I doubt that we advanced more than a few hundred yards. It was a far cry from the grand flanking manoeuvre sweeps and deep penetrations of the enemy's defensive lines by massed armour that we had been taught about at Sandhurst. It was also very different to the long-range shoots against tank targets that we had practised at the Lulworth gunnery school. I also noted how my crew displayed a notable reluctance to fire such a prolific quantity of ammunition.

The other troops of the squadron were ahead of us, operating somewhere off in the woods to our flank, but I couldn't see them and I had little idea of what they were up to. Snatches of radio traffic on the squadron net suggested they were playing some sort of cat-and-mouse game with the German tanks that were reported to be in the woods. I could hear reports of engagements with enemy armour and, occasionally, I could make out the retort of anti-tank fire through the mush of static in my headphones. They were probably less than a mile away, but in the close country of dense hedges, woods and high-banked fields they could have been in another world, as we con-centrated on our own little battle against the thick lines of vegetation to our immediate front. Apart from when we changed fire positions, or moved to the next hedge line, we were stationary for much of the time. While the gunner, loader and myself were kept busy directing, firing and loading, I noticed how the driver and the hull gunner seemed to be cocooned in their own little world and played cards when we were static.

By midday the sun was high in the sky and beating down hard. Combined with the heat of the engine, the tank was becoming un-bearably hot. By the middle of the afternoon I unbuttoned my collar and rolled up the sleeves of my battledress jacket. The next thing I knew was that Neville Fearn's tank had drawn up close to mine. He then shouted and motioned at me to dismount and meet him at the rear of my tank, where he proceeded to deliver an almighty bollock-ing for adjusting my dress. Berating me, he pointed out that if my tank was hit and brewed up, we would have six seconds to escape the flames before it became a raging inferno. Even if I managed to get out, if my arms and neck were exposed I was likely to receive 70 per cent burns to my body and my chances of survival would be low. It was a sobering rebuke and underlined the alarming proclivity of the Sherman tank to catch fire when hit by an enemy anti-tank round. All tank crews have a horror of being burned alive in their vehicles and in the case of the Sherman 80 per cent of hits resulted in a brew up. As the campaign in Normandy progressed the Germans would nickname the tank the 'Tommy Cooker'. To Allied troops it became known as the 'Ronson' after the famous American lighter that lit every time. But its propensity to catch fire was just one of the Sherman's design flaws.

Coming into service in 1942, the US manufactured M4 Sherman had proved itself in North Africa. Designed to provide the right com-bination of mobility, speed, protection, firepower and ease of mass production, the Sherman met the Allied doctrine of emulating the stunning success of the Germans' use of massed armour in France and Russia in 1940 and 1941. The emphasis was placed on the concen-tration of tank forces to breach and penetrate gaps in the enemy line and then exploit deep into the rear areas to bring about shock action, dislocation and defeat. In the desert the Sherman had demonstrated its effectiveness against the Panzer Mark IV, the mainstay of Hitler's tank forces. But Allied theory of armoured warfare was already out of date. Germany's own tank doctrine had not remained stagnant. The Russian deployment of the heavily armoured T-34 tank on the Eastern Front in late 1941 had come as a rude shock. The need to defeat it led to the improvement of the main armament of the Panzer Mark IV and the development of new and heavier tanks in the form of the 54-ton Tiger tank equipped with an 88mm gun and the 45-ton

Panther tank, fitted with a long 75mm gun and excellent sloping armour.

The Allies first faced the Tiger in Tunisia in 1943 and were alarmed to discover that even with a muzzle velocity of just over 2000 feet per second the Sherman's 75mm gun was incapable of penetrating either its four-inch-thick frontal armour or the two-inch-thick armour on its sides. As we were to discover in Normandy, the Panther's three-inch thick sloping homogeneous frontal armour was equally impervious to our armour-piercing rounds. The 88mm gun on a Tiger and the 75mm gun fitted to both the Panther and the Mark IVs had muzzle velocities in excess of 3000 feet per second and could slice through the three-inch average thickness of the Sherman's frontal armour like butter at 2000 yards. In contrast, if we were to have any chance of killing a Panther we would have to get within 500 yards and achieve a flank shoot against the thinner two-inch armour on its sides. We had virtually no chance against a Tiger unless we were at point-blank range and could get a lucky shot in against its flank or rear. Equipping the Sherman with a 17-pounder gun in the form of the Firefly was the technical antidote to the Tiger and Panther's advantages of firepower and protection. However, the Firefly only became available in limited numbers just before the invasion and was not without its limitations.

The superiority of German tank design was not the only issue facing Allied tank crews in Normandy. The terrain in which we would have to fight our under-gunned and poorly protected Shermans also caused profound concern. The nature of the Norman bocage country stood in marked contrast to the flat open desert and came as a particular shock to the North Africa veterans. The undulating ground of rolling hills and shallow valleys, overlaid with a patchwork of woods and close-knit fields, bounded by thick high-banked hedgerows and connected by deep sunken lanes, made for poor tank country. Fashioned by centuries of farming, the topography of impenetrable hedge lines and recessed tracks formed natural anti-tank barriers that hindered and channelled movement. It was also seen to favour the defender. In the desert the old Africa hands were used to seeing their enemy; in the bocage, any hedgerow or concealed lane could hide a lurking Tiger or Panther waiting to blow you to pieces.

The terrain proved ideal for infantry equipped with anti-tank weapons. The most feared was the ground-mounted version of the German 88mm gun, which had exactly the same penetrating power as the variant mounted in the Tiger. While the 88mm was limited in numbers, the hand-held bazookas used by the infantry were abundant and every hedge, ditch or small stand of trees might contain a German soldier armed with a Panzerfaust. A few pounds lighter than one of our tank shells, the disposable three-foot-long hand-held anti-tank weapon had an effective range of approximately a hundred yards and at that distance it could punch a molten slug of metal through our armour. The bocage was also a natural habitat for snipers and operating with your head out of the turret was an invitation to have it blown off.

The significance of the limitations of the Sherman, the capabilities of the Germans and the impact of the terrain were only just beginning to dawn on me as my first day of action drew to a close. The process of plastering every piece of thick vegetation and then moving short distances to repeat the process again had continued during the baking heat of the afternoon. As the shadows began to lengthen, I heard the order over the squadron net that we were to return to a new leaguer position near Bayeux. We were positioned against another hedge that extended to a line of woods. I was about to give the driver orders to start moving, when I saw movement several hundred yards to my right down the edge of a wooded track. Screwing my eyes hard into the sockets of my binoculars I thought I caught the back of a tank disappearing behind the trees. Then another vehicle followed it, briefly visible as a dark lumbering shape silhouetted in the daylight at the end of the ride. It was a German tank not 400 yards off, side on and within range. I made to speak into my microphone, but the radio net was busy and when I looked again it was gone.

It was routine for tanks to withdraw out of the line and move back to a leaguer as darkness approached. Unlike modern tanks that are equipped with night-viewing devices, we rarely operated after last light, because at night we were blind and highly vulnerable to enemy equipped with anti-tank weapons. The regimental leaguer near Bayeux took longer to get to, as it was further back from the front line, and the sun was setting behind us as a bright ball of orange by the time we pulled into the orchard and began positioning the tanks under trees and against hedges in accordance with the squadron sergeant major's instructions. There was no chatting between the crew on the intercom and their sullen disposition seemed to have been unbroken by a day in action. But our work wasn't yet done.

The vehicles of the regiment's logistic echelon were waiting to greet us as we parked up. Wooden- and cardboard-cased boxes of 75mm shells, .30-calibre ammunition, rations, water and cans of fuel were being offloaded from trucks. As we switched off our engines and dismounted, I had expected the troop sergeant to burst into energy, directing the crews to start stripping down the cases to bomb up with ammo and top up the fuel in our vehicles. Instead, Harrison was conspicuous by his absence. Searching him out, he informed me that he had plenty of fuel, hadn't fired that much and didn't see the need to bomb up. The rest of the troop were pulling down their shelters and lighting their cooking fires before it became too dark to cook. I stopped them, called them together and gave them direct orders to get the tanks replenished and the essential maintenance completed first.

A Sherman was designed to carry seventy-five shells for its main armament, but an imaginative crew could stow almost a hundred with creative packing. But with each shell weighing 18 pounds, a full load of ammunition exceeded a ton in weight. Consequently, it was backbreaking, shin-skinning work, requiring the skills of a contortionist, to load up the 75mm ammunition and everything else we required into the cramped confines of a Sherman.

Replenishing its 160-gallon fuel tank was the equivalent of filling up twelve cars by hand. I began to understand why there had been reluctance to fire when we were in action. The troops were also knackered. In midsummer the days were long and the nights of darkness were short; knowing that the next reveille might only be three or four hours away, the crew wanted to eat and get their heads down as quickly as possible. But I also knew that if we didn't do it then and there, we risked going into action without the fuel and ammunition we needed to fight with. The crews got on with it after my intervention, although Martin rolled his eyes and moved slower than most. Again, perhaps, it was another moment when I should have called both Harrison and Martin out for their behaviour, but the task was now getting done and I was required at the squadron O group.

An O group was the orders conference that the squadron commander held at the end of each day, where John Semken might discuss the events of the action we had just been through and would then issue his orders and allocate tasks to each of the troops for the next day or operation. Joining the other three troop commanders, squadron second in command and sergeant major, I sat on the floor of Semken's tent with my knees drawn up and my map case and notebook to hand. Semken gave us the good news first and informed us that the regiment had been pulled out of the line for two days to rest and reorganise. It was welcome news, as it was the unit's first break from combat since landing on D-Day. The bad news was that an anti-tank gun had knocked out a Sherman Firefly commanded by the squadron sergeant major when supporting the forward troops in the woods near Boislonde. Thankfully, the crew had managed to bail out unscathed. Sergeant Major Hutchinson made little of the incident as he sat with us. What I didn't know at the time was that Hutchinson had been the squadron's senior NCO in Africa and had been awarded the Military Medal for being wounded when rescuing crews from knocked-out tanks under fire.

Semken went through some administrative details and then asked us if we had any questions. As the junior officer present, my turn came last and I mentioned the two German tanks that I thought I had seen just as we pulled back to the leaguer. Semken asked me why I didn't engage them; I made some inadequate reference to not being sure about their identification and wanting to report them, but hadn't as the net was busy. Semken might have torn a strip off me, but he didn't. Instead he emphasised the importance of firing first without hesitation and to keep firing, then move to a new fire position and fire again. He had been in command of the squadron for less than a day himself and it was a point that he was making to all the commanders present. As I was to discover, it was typical of John Semken. Arriving in France, he recognised that the focus of the Allies' training for Normandy had been on getting ashore. For Semken it had occupied everyone's sleeping and waking thoughts and very little attention had been paid to what happened after the landings. Drawing on his experience of commanding Shermans in the desert, Semken recognised that in the bocage the rules of the game had changed.

Smothering hedges with HE before we advanced was Semken's way of bringing our advantage of numbers to bear and utilising collective firepower to neutralise snipers and anti-tank gunners, as well as flushing out concealed tanks. It also reflected his recognition that the bocage was double-edged and that how we approached it was likely to make a crucial difference to whether we stayed alive. The nature of the terrain reduced the average engagement range to a few hundred yards and in doing so significantly reduced the Germans' advantage of the longer range of their 88mm and 75mm guns. It also meant that we would have to learn to operate in the bocage in a manner that played to our strengths, rather than exposed our weaknesses. As a leader, John Semken exuded confidence and strength. I was glad to be under his command. I had considered bringing up the subject of Harrison, but thought better of it; as a strong leader, I suspected Semken wanted strong troop leaders who could get on and sort their own troops out.

The O group provided the opportunity to meet my fellow troop commanders. Harry Heenan commanded 2 Troop, Mike Howden 3 Troop and Dickie Holman 4 Troop. Harry and Dickie came from familiar backgrounds and were just slightly older than me, having joined the regiment on its return to England before D-Day. Due to their similar ages, both men were to become firm friends and engendered a sense of kinship and fun, which was to make a crucial difference in the tough days ahead. Mike Howden was a desert veteran and was considerably older at twenty-eight and his age and experience bred a slight distance. All three of them were immediately welcoming and ready to pass on useful tips, such as not wearing my officer rank slides, as it would mark me out as a target for snipers. Under the firm leadership and tutelage of John Semken we would become a close-knit group, always ready to learn from each other and to help each other out. But they couldn't help me out with the shortcomings of Harrison and my truculent troop. After one day of instruction in the field, 5 Troop were mine to command. The next time we went out there would be no senior squadron officer to follow or to guide me. How the troop behaved was now my problem and mine alone.

People have often asked me if I was scared the first time I went into combat. I can honestly say that I wasn't. There was a degree of first day on the job apprehension, but not fear. That would come later, to some extent, as my experience grew and I became more fatigued; in turn I would also learn to become numb to it. When I joined the Sherwood Rangers there was just too much to do and to learn as a troop leader to think much about being scared. I also knew that how well 5 Troop performed in battle would be down to me. My job would be to gain their confidence by leading from the front and showing that I wasn't scared. Whatever my own personal reservations, my biggest fear was fear of failure and making mistakes that would cost them their lives. That would require confidence in my own ability and that in turn required experience and the ability to live long enough to learn what to do and what not to do. The majority of the troop were sleeping when I got back from the O group, although I noticed that the tanks had been replenished. Ken Mayo was still awake and was manning the radio on listening watch when I poked my head inside the turret. He passed up a mess tin of food. It was the first meal I had eaten all day. There was much still to do and learn, but I felt that it was one small step on the journey to gaining the hearts and minds of my men. As I turned in for the night to snatch a few hours of sleep before reveille, my thoughts were of two battles that lay ahead of me; one against the Germans and the other to win the confidence of the troop. In facing both challenges, the real baptism of fire for me, 5 Troop and A Squadron was yet to come.

5

BOCAGE

Two days spent out of the line in the leaguer to the southeast of Bayeux provided an opportunity to observe the manner of men that I now commanded. Like most soldiers, if asked, they would have stated that their formal loyalty lay with the regiment they belonged to. It was a bond strengthened by the unit's regional identity. In the case of the Sherwood Rangers, it stemmed from an identification with Nottinghamshire and the north of England. Officially designated as the Nottinghamshire Yeomanry, the Sherwood Rangers was a Territorial Army cavalry regiment that traditionally recruited its rank and file from the Leen Valley mining communities of Mansfield and Worksop and from the country stock of Nottinghamshire villages and market towns like Retford and Newark-on-Trent. The regiment drew its officers from the landed hunting set of the county. Raised to meet the threat of Napoleonic invasion in 1794, the regiment could boast of being commanded by five dukes and a score of earls and lords.

The Sherwood Rangers went to war in 1940 as men of the shire commanded by its country gentlemen. Equipped with saddles and sabres, the purpose of its deployment, to conduct internal security duties in Palestine, differed little from that which had taken it to fight the Boers in South Africa in 1900 and to Mesopotamia during the First World War. When the requirement for policing the empire was overtaken by the more pressing need to defeat the Axis powers in the Mediterranean and North Africa, the regiment handed in its horses to train as coastal artillery. It took part in the defence of Tobruk, Benghazi and Crete, before converting again to become an armoured unit in 1941. Equipped with a mix of Grant, Crusader and Sherman tanks, the Sherwood Rangers fought its first tank engagement in North Africa as part of the 8th Armoured Brigade at the battle of Alam Halfa in 1942. It was a costly schooling in its new role and the regiment lost half its tanks to the panzers and 88mm anti-tank guns of the Afrika Korps. From the hard learning of the early desert battles, the regiment went on to make a name for itself as the only unit of Montgomery's 8th Army to breach Rommel's defensive line in the first twenty-four hours of the British offensive at El Alamein. It then played a key role in spearheading the Allied advance into Tunis that brought about the surrender of the German forces in 1943.

In war the nature and character of a unit changes through the experience of battle. The losses it takes and the churn of replacements that refills its ranks all have a bearing on the emphasis of a unit's collegiate identity that increasingly focuses downwards to its smallest constituent parts. In an armoured regiment, that focus lies with the individual tank crew and the troop that they belong to and the Sherwood Rangers was no exception. The regiment's twelve troops of three tanks were the unit's fundamental fighting components, where loyalty was fashioned by the comradeship of shared endeavour, teamwork and mutual dependence. While they often operated as part of a squadron, what mattered to the individual trooper was his crew and those of the other two tanks that made up the troop. Fifteen men who fought, lived, slept and ate together, shared obscenities and banter and got to know each other better than their own families, forming a strong sense of their own kinship and belonging.

Harrison and most of 5 Troop had been part of the regiment's collective testing in the North African campaign. They knew the dangers of an exposed position or an open flank. The men that I commanded were the product of tough won experience at places like Alam Halfa and El Alamein. I had still been in training when they had already fought through several desert engagements. As the product of shared endeavour and learning, 5 Troop had become an exclusive fraternity born of the privations and dangers of battle, which any new recruit trooper joining in the field would find difficult to break into until they had proved themselves in the heat of combat. In the case of a brand new young subaltern, it was much harder. As far as my troop was concerned I had not been with them in Africa, or trained with them in England or landed at D-Day. To them I was just a nineteen-year-old kid straight out of the factory of officer training, green and untested. But I was also their new commander and I would be making the decisions when we were in action. Consequently, my inexperience was likely to be a dangerous thing and they knew it.

Like many 8th Army veterans, most of 5 Troop felt that they had done their bit in the desert campaign and were pushing their luck to be asked to do it again in northwest Europe. The men would no doubt take their lead from Harrison, a man more than twice my age with a wife and family, who had already risked his life in North Africa and now just wanted to survive and get back home to them. He clearly had no desire to get to know me or guide me. I suspect that he thought it would be a nugatory exercise given my anticipated chances of living beyond the first two weeks in action, which was the estimated life expectancy of a new troop commander in Normandy. Harrison's primary concern was that I didn't get him and the rest of the troop killed before I either gained the necessary battlefield experience to lead them with competence, or got myself killed in the process.

The link between my future performance and the crew's own mortality was an undercurrent of unspoken tension during the time we spent out of the line resting and reorganising with the rest of the squadron and getting our Shermans ready to go back into action again. The .30-calibre machine guns and the breech block of the tank's main 75mm were stripped, cleaned and oiled by the hull gunner and main armament gunner. Trooper Sid Martin had already demonstrated his truculence when refusing to test and adjust the gun's sighting alignment and he retained a barely hidden hostility towards me. Martin was a former miner in his late twenties; wiry and dark, he had a sly nature about him. In a peacetime army he might have been described as the barrack-room lawyer of the crew. While slow to respond to orders, he seemed to have a habit of being quick to find a reason or an excuse not to do something. Sam Gartside, the hull gunner, was a squat, broad-chested individual of similar age and was Martin's 'mucker'. Both hailing from the Worksop area of Nottinghamshire, the two were close. As they worked on the tank's guns, I could detect from muted mutterings that they were in league in their resentment at my arrival.

The busiest member of the crew when not operating the tank was the driver. For its day, the Sherman was an extremely reliable machine, but any armoured vehicle needs constant minor servicing after a prolonged period of use. The metal-pinned links of the track need to be tightened, running-gear sprockets and wheel bogeys greased, and oil levels checked and topped up. Tall and lanky, Joe Dixon was the closest in age to me at twenty and had joined the Sherwood Rangers as a casualty replacement in Libya in time to take part in the last desert battles in Tunisia. He went about his driver maintenance tasks diligently and seemed to be the quietest of the four crewmen. As troopers, Dixon, Gartside and Martin were all private soldiers. The loader and radio operator was a lance corporal and was the only NCO in the tank. Perhaps it was due to a sense of responsibility that came with holding rank, but I detected that Ken Mayo was of a different cut to the other three.

Fair-haired and slight, Mayo was aged in his late twenties. Originally serving in B Squadron, he had been slightly wounded on D-Day and had been posted into A Squadron after recovering from his wounds.

Mayo was able and had served for long enough in the regiment to be promoted to troop corporal and commander of an individual tank in his own right. But as I was to discover, few crewmen wanted to step up to take on the individual responsibility of commanding a Sherman. It meant operating opened up with your head out of the commander's hatch, which was an invitation to have it shot off by a sniper or be hit by shrapnel. The reluctance of so many to accept the elevation to increased responsibility and the exposure that came with it was hardly surprising, given that the regiment was to lose fifty tank commanders in the first month of fighting in Normandy. This grim figure included their previous troop leader. Shot through the chest as he commanded from the turret hatch during the initial advance to Point 103, he had subsequently died of his wounds. He didn't mention it at the time, but Ken Mayo later admitted that he felt a certain amount of sympathy for me due to the risks and responsibilities that I would face as the troop's new leader. It was an empathy undoubtedly brought about by his disinclination to take on the hazardous duties that came with commanding a tank. It was also the beginning of an alliance that would play its part in my battle to win over the troop.

As 5 Troop's troop corporal, Jonny Lanes was one of the few who had been willing to assume the mantle of responsibility the others were reluctant to take. Commanding the third Sherman in the troop, Lanes was from genuine Nottinghamshire country stock and had joined the Sherwood Rangers in 1936 aged seventeen. A lover of horses, he had been tasked with looking after the regiment's mounts

on the ship that took them to Palestine and had spent the majority
of the voyage in the hold caring for his charges. Jonny Lanes had
also fought as a coastal gunner at Tobruk and had served in the
Crusader tanks of A Squadron in every action that had taken the
regiment from Egypt to Libya. At twenty-five, he was a good deal
younger than Harrison, but did not appear to be played out by his
experiences in North Africa. Initially reserved, he was no doubt also
sizing me up to see how I would perform in combat. However, unlike
Harrison, I had already noticed from the preceding day's action
that he didn't have the same tendency to hang back during an engagement and had made sure that his tank kept up and held station
with mine.

While diverse in their individual personalities and backgrounds,
my troop shared timeless commonalities with all soldiers. Firstly,
they spoke in their own form of the vernacular, part shaped by their
regional Nottinghamshire dialect that was not dissimilar to a softer
form of a Yorkshire accent, which was pleasantly blunt and direct.
The letter 'h' was generally dropped, while 'thou' replaced the second
person singular and the standard greeting among the men was 'Alrate
youth?' Someone who was lucky was a 'jammy git' and 'chuffed' was
to be pleased with something. It was a language that was mixed heavily with the use of words born of traditional army service in India, as
well as Egyptian expressions drawn from more recent exposure to the
culture of North Africa. The Hindustani word 'dhobi' was to wash
and 'jildi' was to do something quickly, while 'dekko' was to take a
look. Additionally, in the eyes of my soldiers, a woman was a 'bint'.
If they couldn't care less about something, the Arabic 'malessh' was
used and something they thought to be really superb was described
as 'quois quetter'. Their language was also liberally sprinkled with
Anglo-Saxon profanities and the F word in particular, pronounced
'fooking', replaced the normal vocables with a proclivity that would
have offended the sensibilities of a young middle-class man brought

up in a Victorian family, had it not been for the six months that I had spent training as a trooper. Like most soldiers, they also shared a perverse delight in moaning, commonly expressed in the term that something was 'not fooking on'. The British soldier is famous for his disposition to complain, but while indiscernible to an outsider who has never served in the military, the propensity to gripe did not necessarily mean that they weren't in good spirits. As I was to learn, it was when they were subdued or silent that I should be most concerned about their morale.

Food played a major part in their general sense of wellbeing and they placed great store in the rations we received. Not only because of the physical demands placed upon us, but also because it was a simple pleasure that provided a welcome distraction from battle. Each crew cooked its own meals, the ingredients for which came in ten-man compo ration boxes that would last each tank for two days. Revelling in their culinary imagination, the crew sought to transform the staple diet of army hard-tack biscuits, bully beef, beans and the frightful tins of Maconochie, an unappetising mush of poor-quality diced meat and over-stewed vegetables, into something more palatable. When we had the time, biscuits were smashed and soaked overnight, to be boiled with condensed milk and sugar to make a form of porridge. We also learned to live off the land and Gartside became an expert in bartering our fags and issued chocolate for local produce from the French civilians to supplement our rations. Runny French Camembert became something of an acquired taste to men from the mining valleys of Nottinghamshire, but a cup of tea had psychological impact that cannot be overestimated. 'Cha' was of such central importance that each crew hoarded and jealously guarded fresh tea leaves as the most precious of commodities, for they provided a highly prized alternative to the issued tins of tea with powdered milk and sugar all mixed together. A premium was also placed on tinned rice pudding and when discovered in a newly supplied ration pack, it met with the exclamation of 'quois quetter'.

The demands of my duties as the troop commander prevented me from getting involved in the gastronomic creativity of preparing meals. I was usually too busy overseeing the preparation of the troop for the next day's action, which included attending the orders group held each evening by John Semken when we returned to the leaguer. The fact that I ate at all was down to Ken Mayo. He always made sure that some food was kept back for me when I returned to the troop, although it was usually cold, as it was often well after midnight by the time I had finished passing on my own orders to the troop sergeant and corporal. But at least I was able to snatch a hasty meal from a mess tin he had reserved for me. In essence Mayo became my batman, although it was a much less formal relationship than existed in some of the smarter infantry units, where private soldiers were officially allocated to look after officers as their designated servants. I didn't ask him to do it and it was a voluntary and spontaneous gesture on his part. It meant that I could concentrate on doing my job as the troop leader. Without Mayo, I doubt that I would have survived for very long and my longevity was a subliminal issue for the whole crew.

On that first evening in the leaguer, the squadron O group had finished early and there was time to eat together. Important as it was to the life of a tank crew, food could only ever provide but a momentary diversion from the stresses and strains of battle. As I settled down to my first meal with the crew after a day spent working on Aim, I could hear the laughter drifting across the leaguer from other crews enjoying the temporary respite from action. In contrast my men were withdrawn and silent. In war no one wants to go into combat with a stranger, but I was still an uninvited outsider in their midst and I was conscious that I was being weighed up. They were wondering how I would measure up and what impact my performance would have on them when they went back into action again. The confidence the crew had in me would play a large part in their motivation and performance in battle. No doubt they were thinking that only time would tell and I sensed that I was on a form of unofficial probation in respect of whether I would have the right to earn their trust. But statistically time was not on my side and my men didn't expect to see me live it out.

If I lived for long enough, I would have a chance to gain the necessary experience and learn what to do, what not to do. Growing battlefield knowledge would not only reduce the risk to me, but also to the troop as a whole, as it would inform the decisions I made and their impact on the lives of my men. It was a vicious circle and in a veteran unit newcomers tended to suffer the highest casualties, as knowledge of what risks can and cannot be taken only comes with experience. The question was whether I would last for long enough, and learn fast enough, to avoid making mistakes, as their troop leader, that might get them killed. What they were certain of was that my arrival had just shortened the odds of their own chances of survival.

The men of 5 Troop knew a lot more about war than I did. But experience of battle can be a double-edged phenomenon. They had seen what a German 88mm could do to an under-armoured British tank and they had watched comrades die in the mangled mess of a burning armoured vehicle. That knowledge bred a degree of fear and trepidation that was compounded by the nature of the new type of battlefield that they found themselves in. In the flat open expanses of the desert the enemy was visible, or in their own words, 'thou could see tha fooking boogers'. But in the close-knit countryside of Normandy, death could be lurking in every sunken lane or waiting behind every hedge line. Terrain features that could conceal an anti-tank gun, an enemy tank or a German infantryman equipped with a Panzerfaust, ready to rip the thinly protected crew compartment of a Sherman asunder with an explosive shaped-charge warhead or an armour-piercing projectile. These were the new rules of the game and they had taken the old North Africa hands by surprise.

It was a shock that was intensified by fear of the superiority of the German panzers and especially the heavily armed Tiger tank. Although we didn't know it at the time, it was a phobia that was to be exacerbated by the actions of one German in particular that had been unfolding twelve miles to our southeast. It was also the reason why the whole regiment had been put on one hour's notice to move. Finishing our solemn first meal together that first evening in the leaguer, our kit was already packed and we knew that if we got any sleep at all that night it would be with our boots on so that we would be ready to respond with little warning to events that had been occurring at a place called Villers-Bocage.

During the six days of inconclusive fighting that had followed the Allies' initial push inland from the D-Day beachheads, 50th Division and 8th Armoured Brigade had made little headway in breaking through the German positions. With the arrival of the 12th SS Panzer Division and Panzer Lehr in Normandy, the Germans had been able to begin consolidating a defensive position to the south of Bayeux between Tilly in the west and Caen in the east. While the Sherwood Rangers had been pulled out of action to rest and reorganise, Montgomery was desperate to restore the momentum of the British 2nd Army's advance before the Germans could feed in more reinforcements to further strengthen their forces concentrating around Caen. In an attempt to outflank Panzer Lehr's positions around Tilly, 7th Armoured Division had been ordered to advance south to the town of Caumont and then swing east to exploit a gap behind the enemy's defences by driving through the small market town of Villers-Bocage. The intention was to bring about a collapse of the Germans' positions by penetrating deep into their rear. In concept it was a classic armoured warfare theory manoeuvre that would have made our

RAC instructors proud. It was also an extremely risky undertaking. But what might have worked in the desert failed to take account of the nature of the Norman bocage and the unfortunate presence of a young SS tank officer called Michael Wittman.

Just as we were pulling out of action on 12 June, Obersturmführer Michael Wittman, the commander of the 2nd Company of the 101st SS Heavy Panzer Battalion, was moving into his own leaguer position on an overgrown track on the western outskirts of Villers-Bocage. Only four of Wittman's eight Tiger tanks had survived the long journey from Beauvais to Normandy that had begun on 7 June. As fearsome as the Tiger appeared, it was extremely unreliable and prone to mechanical breakdowns. Wittman's tanks had been forced to make extensive detours to the south of Paris in order to find a bridge over the Seine that was strong enough to take their 54 tons and had not been destroyed by Allied bombers, but five days of motoring on their own tracks had taken a heavy toll on their serviceability. As dawn broke the next day, Wittman had expected to start the much-needed maintenance on his remaining Tigers. Instead he awoke to see a long column of British armoured vehicles strung out nose to tail in front of him for several hundred yards along the main Villers-Bocage to Caen road, which lay only a small field's distance away from where his own tanks remained hidden.

The 4th City of London Yeomanry might have discovered the presence of 2nd Company's remaining Tigers, had they deployed a reconnaissance screen in front of their advance. But the leading unit of 7th Armoured Division was under pressure to move quickly. Keen to push on, its drive through Villers-Bocage had been delayed only slightly by the jubilation of the population who believed that their liberation was at hand. Pausing on the sloping ground outside the town, the column stopped while its commanding officer considered the next stage of his advance. Wittman didn't hesitate, even when his own tank broke down after a few yards; he immediately cross-decked into a second Tiger and began engaging the Yeomanry. The armour-piercing rounds from his 88mm gun tore through the front and rear vehicles, fixing the British column in the road. Wittman then motored alongside the trapped line of vehicles leaving a score of burning Cromwell tanks, Bren gun carriers and armoured half-tracks in his wake. Proceeding into Villers-Bocage he knocked out another troop of Cromwells. Wittman's own tank was subsequently disabled by a British infantry 6-pounder anti-tank gun, but not before his other two Tigers and units of Panzer Lehr had been called in to join the fray.

Already the holder of the Knight's Cross, Wittman was able to add an impressive tally to the 130-odd tanks he had already destroyed on the Eastern Front. A darling of the German public for his exploits against the Russians, the Nazi propaganda machine had a field day and made much of the vaunted tank ace's 'single-handed' defeat of the advance of the 7th Armoured Division, which helped generate near-mythical perceptions of the event that have been fuelled subsequently by numerous historians. In reality, the blunting of the British drive at Villers-Bocage was never the result of one man and Wittman took no part in the subsequent fighting around the town that lasted long into the afternoon and continued the next day.

Villers-Bocage was not our battle and although we stayed at an hour's notice to move through that night and into the next day, we were never deployed to aid 7th Armoured Division. But the loss of over fifty British armoured vehicles at Villers-Bocage was a bloody setback. It exposed the complacency of Desert Rat veterans and tactics born of experience in North Africa. It also helped reinforce the myth of the Tiger's invincibility and the perception that it was everywhere. In truth, fewer than 200 Tigers out of a total of some 2500 German tanks and armoured self-propelled guns were deployed in Normandy. The majority of the enemy's tank divisions were equipped with the older Panzer Mark IVs, although roughly a quarter of their overall tank numbers consisted of the more capable and better armoured Panther tanks. In reality, the Panthers were a much greater threat and not just because there were more of them. They were also more reliable and, as we were to find out, they could traverse their gun much faster than a Tiger.

German tank numbers provided in hindsight offer useful context regarding the enemy we faced, but it was data that we were not aware of at the time. Had it been available, it would hardly have mattered. All German tanks and self-propelled guns were dangerous. If one had you in its sights it was largely academic whether it was equipped with an 88mm or 75mm gun. The nature of the terrain also compounded the risks that we faced, but the tactical implications of the bocage remained two-sided. The close country that confounded armoured manoeuvre warfare tactics that might have worked in Egypt and Libya concealed a host of threats that could spell our doom, but it also put the enemy at a disadvantage. Historians have often been quick to make much of the fact that Normandy was not good tank country and favoured the defender. But most tank-on-tank engagements took place at a distance of less than 600 yards, which significantly reduced the Germans' ability to maximise the superiority of the long range of their tanks' guns and optical sighting systems.

Villers-Bocage brought the difficulties of fighting in the bocage, and the need to adapt, into sharp relief. Seventh Armoured Division was a former 8th Army formation that had fought in North Africa since 1940 and had also participated in the early stages of the fighting in Italy in 1943. The bloody nose it received at the hands of the 101st SS Heavy Panzer Battalion and Panzer Lehr also raised questions about the battle weariness and performance of veteran units in Normandy. Combined with the Sherwood Rangers' own veteran status and experience of fighting in the Tilly area, it was a realisation that was not lost on John Semken. He recognised that there was much that we needed to learn and that we needed to learn fast if we were to avoid a fatal reckoning on the battlefield. Semken was a deep thinker and applied a first-principles approach to the challenges we faced as a squadron. He also drew on his own experiences as a Sherman troop commander in North Africa. Although under-gunned and lacking in armoured protection, Semken knew that the Sherman's mobility, shorter barrel and faster rate of fire gave it advantages that he intended to exploit. A good Sherman gunner and loader could get three to four rounds into the air before the first shell struck its target, while a Tiger's crew would still be struggling to load its much heavier and longer ammunition into its breech for a second shot. Six pounds lighter and eight inches shorter, the Sherman's 75mm HE round was excellent for dealing with enemy infantry and anti-tank guns. Additionally, a heavier German tank could be disabled by smothering it with a sufficient weight of HE fire to smash its optics and damage its tracks. In John Semken's words, the key was to 'never hesitate' but to 'fire first' and 'keep firing'.

Semken also placed a key emphasis on his four troop leaders. He knew that as the squadron's principal commanders we would be central to influencing the outcome of an engagement and how we went about our business would determine whether an attack was successful or not. Equally, we could get a troop wiped out if we were overcautious, reckless or ignorant of what was required in battle. Consequently, Semken placed a premium on making sure that we knew when to lay down speculative fire, adopt a hull-down position, keep off a skyline or avoid the dangers of an open forward slope. He continuously impressed upon us the importance of using ground to our advantage to improve our survivability and maximise our lethality against the Germans. The ability to read the ground and a map was also an absolute imperative, as an error in navigation could get you killed.

John Semken was an expert when it came to appreciating the tactical relevance of terrain. As we moved ahead of him, Semken would call out topographical features to our front over the radio, spelling out their significance and how we should approach them. I can remember hearing him in my headset.

'Hello Sugar 5. Watch the wood line on your right. Stop and make sure you brass it up properly before advancing.'

Initially, I thought that he must be able to see each of his troop leaders in order to know how to direct us, but later I realised that he was reading the ground from a map sheet in the turret of his own tank and guiding us accordingly. Hearing him talking to us calmly over the net made a huge difference and did much to boost the confidence of a young officer. Although John Semken would be the first person to tell you that he was no soldier, his skill in reading ground and guiding us was a testimony to his reputation for professional competence and his abilities as a leader. As the officer commanding A Squadron, he was open, friendly and looked after his men. It meant that we came to revere and love him. However, he never hesitated to grip us, or put us right, especially over the air and I certainly received my fair share of bollockings for numerous tactical transgressions.

Although he didn't share his thoughts with us at the time, Semken also knew that some of the veterans in A Squadron were played out by their experiences in Egypt and Libya. Secretly, he was appalled that the older men with families who had been conscripted to risk life and limb in the desert were being asked to do it again in Europe. At full strength the Sherwood Rangers had a complement of thirty-seven officers and 655 other ranks. Approximately 300 served in the fighting echelon of the unit's front-line squadrons and troops. On the Sherwood Rangers' return to England many had been posted out of the regiment, or transferred to less dangerous jobs in the unit's logistics and support troops, but at least half of those that had served in North Africa remained in the forward sabre squadrons. They included men like Sergeant Arthur Harrison who, if asked, would no doubt have commented that it was 'not fooking on'.

Semken understood the tendency of some of the more seasoned NCOs, like Harrison, to hang back if they were not confident in a young troop leader's competence and it was why he invested so heavily in our development. Even though I was the most inexperienced, as I had not trained with the regiment or landed at D-Day, with the exception of Mike Howden none of the troop commanders had served in the desert. But combined with the high standards of our technical and leadership training, Semken also recognised that our lack of combat experience had some advantage. Having recently passed out of Sandhurst, we were used to obeying orders without hesitation. Additionally, because we had not fought in North Africa we held few preconceived assumptions about how we should fight in the Norman bocage, which to some extent held fewer surprises for us as we had nothing else to compare it with. Tinged with a fresh eagerness and an arrogance of youth, we were hungry to learn and prove ourselves and represented an unprejudiced raw product that Semken could work on to mould into effective troop leaders. The opportunity to begin applying the lessons John Semken was so keen to instil in us came soon enough when we went back into the line.

With the failure to break though the German defences at Villers-Bocage, the once porous front line had begun to congeal and the fighting broke down into a series of small holding actions and piece-meal engagements, where success was measured in advancing a few hundred yards to snatch possession of another hedgerow, a small wood or a Norman hamlet. As the Germans probed our positions and we fought small battles to make some impression on theirs, large-scale tank engagements were rare and our primary role became one of supporting the infantry formations that had dug in along the front. Having initially supported the 50th Northumbrian Division since D-Day, 8th Armoured Brigade was placed under the command of a new infantry division on 17 June. Like the 50th Division, the 49th West Riding Division consisted of three infantry brigades, each made up of three infantry battalions supported by their own divisional artillery of four field regiments of 25-pounder guns, a Vickers machine gun battalion and engineer squadrons. The Sherwood Rangers were tasked with supporting the division's 147th infantry brigade, made up of the 11th Royal Scots Fusiliers and the 6th and 7th battalions of the Duke of Wellington's Regiment, know in military jargon as 11 RSF, 6 DWR and 7 DWR respectively.

Recently arrived in Normandy, 49th Division had been ordered to capture the small German-held village of Cristot and consolidate the high ground of Point 102 a mile to its south, which had been penetrated by enemy probing attacks. The task fell to the division's 146th brigade supported by the 24th Lancers. As the Sherwood Rangers were supporting the 147th brigade, we were kept in reserve. A previous attempt by 50th Division to take Cristot on 11 June with the 4th/7th Dragoon Guards was a bloody failure that cost 90 per cent of the leading squadron's tanks and caused 250 casualties among the infantrymen of the Green Howards that they were supporting. This time they were taking no chances and the attack on the village was preceded by the combined fire of all of 49th Division's artillery, as well as that of the 50th Division. The collective weight of eight field regiments, each fielding twenty-four 25-pounder guns, on an area no more than half a mile square, was devastating. It proved too much for the defending elements of 12th SS Division and forced them to withdraw. Our own operations scheduled for 17 June were postponed due to the prolific expenditure of artillery rounds and the regiment remained in reserve. However, the 24th Lancers pushed on to secure the high ground around the Point 102 feature and lost eight Shermans in the process.

We went into action the next day to relieve the 24th Lancers, who were supporting the 147th brigade in the area of Le Parc de Boislonde, located on the forward slopes of Point 102. Having been fought over continuously since 8 June, the relatively small area between Cristot and Tilly, three miles to the southeast, was scarred by the marks of the last eleven days of fighting. As we headed towards Point 102 via Cristot in the early hours of the morning, I noticed how great rings of corn in the surrounding fields had been scythed flat by artillery. The odd burned-out Sherman, forlorn and broken, made grim milestones to mark our progress. Located in a shallow depression in the road leading to Point 102, Cristot was a desolate shambles of death and destruction. The fields on the outskirts of the village, where the attack by the Green Howards had been stopped short, were still full of their dead; their bodies, putrefying in the summer heat, added to the all too familiar stench of rotting cattle. In the village itself the wax-like dead of both British and Germans were mingled together in the gardens and side roads. We steered to avoid a cadaver stretched out in the small winding high street and passed a handcart full of corpses with a German soldier dead in its traces. The passing scene had a sobering effect on the crew and we drove in silence as we made our macabre progression through the village. Though they were closed down, they could see enough of the carnage through their periscopes and the smell of death pervaded my open hatch. The scenes we witnessed in those few hundred yards were testimony that there is no glory in war.

The air was fresher on the gentle heights of Point 102 and we were relieved to have put the charnel house of Cristot behind us. The squadron deployed on the higher ground looking south over the chateau woodland of Le Parc de Boislonde and C Squadron deployed on our right flank. The trees of the park obscured the large chateau and outbuildings and the infantry of 6 DWR were reported to have dug into the woods beyond them, but although they were less than 200 yards away they were out of sight. Scanning the ground to my front through my binoculars, over the tops of the trees, I could make out the slate rooftops of the village of Fontenay glistening in the sunlight, less than a mile distant. It was quiet and I decided to advance forward down the slight slope to get a better sense of the detail of the ground to my front.

The rebuke I might have expected to receive from John Semken over air didn't come from him and it wasn't direct, but the voice I heard through the mush of static in my headphones was unmistakable and caught my attention as I drove down towards the wood line.

'Able 4. Did thou see that?'

It was Harrison and the reply, 'Able 5. Aye but ee'll learn' came from Sergeant George Dring, who was the senior NCO in Dickie Holman's 4 Troop and commanded the tank called 'Akilla'.

Naturally, Harrison had not followed me and I had broken one of John Semken's cardinal rules about the use of ground by taking the risk of exposing my Sherman unnecessarily on a forward slope where I would have been an easy target for an enemy panzer or an anti-tank gun hidden in the trees ahead of me. We were on the regimental net, as we were operating with C Squadron, and I knew that everyone in the unit, including my own crew, would have heard the exchange. Rather meekly and somewhat chastened, I turned Aim around and headed back up the slope to find a position of better cover among some oak trees and the hedge line on the crest of the ridge I had just left.

The rest of the morning was uneventful, as we sat in overwatch of the wood with the other troops of A Squadron strung out along the contour line of the ridge and waited for something to happen. But nothing did and apart from the low rhythmic throb of the idling engine and the buzz of static on the radio net it was quiet. It was also another stiflingly hot day. By the early afternoon the heat inside the tank was oppressive and I relented in allowing Dixon and Gartside to open up their hatches, although I stopped short of granting their request to dismount to stretch their legs and take a leak, as we kept an empty 75mm brass cartridge case for that. I kept scanning the area ahead of us with my binoculars and made the occasional reminder to Martin to do the same through his gun sight. While strictly against regulations, Mayo got a brew on using a small primus stove set up on the floor of the turret, while Dixon and Gartside played whist, sitting either side of the tank's large gearbox and using it as a makeshift card table. We all smoked as we watched and waited and the hours drifted past against the somnolent background of the vibrating hum of the engine, the crackle of the shortwave radio in our headsets and the buzz of flies around the open hatches.

The sun was past its highest point in the sky when the woodland ahead of us burst into life in a series of short sharp cracks, as enemy mortar and artillery fire began to land in the trees. The sound of explosions and bright flashes rocked us out of our balmy trance and shattered the relative peace of a summer's afternoon. It was Gartside who saw them first, exclaiming: 'Thou fooking boogers!' Then I saw them. Infantry were breaking from the cover of the edge of the wood to our front and running towards us at full tilt. They were our infantry and were followed by several Bren gun carriers that came hurtling up the slope away from the wood. Overtaking the running figures, they ignored any pleas to stop and pick them up. The infantry were shouting as they streamed past us, but I had to dismount to try and make sense of what they were saying over the noise of our engine. I couldn't get anyone to stop and tell me what was going on and there didn't appear to be any officers with them. They just kept yelling about 'tanks' and 'Tigers' and that 'they were coming'. The troop were already alert and scanning their arcs with the .30 calibres and 75mm by the time I got through to John Semken on the radio to tell him that the infantry were bugging out. He asked me if I had seen any tanks and I said, 'No. Nothing.' He told me to stay where I was and to watch and shoot if German armour started emerging from the woods. Moving forward with his own tank, he made sure that his gunner was covering off a British 17-pounder anti-tank gun

sited to fire along a wooded ride, which had been abandoned by its
fleeing crew.

For several minutes nothing happened, as we waited tense and uncertain. The enemy artillery and mortar fire had stopped and there
was no movement from the wood to our front. Then it started from
an unexpected quarter, as our own artillery opened up and brought
down a heavy curtain of final protective fire on our position. Provoked by the unauthorised panicked retreat of 6 DWR* and fearing
that a German breakthrough was imminent, every gun available to
49th Division was brought to bear on the sector of the front that we
were holding. We didn't hear the whine of the approaching shells,
but they arrived with a shattering crash of violence that tore a pattern
of destruction across the ground, heaving up fountains of earth and
spraying out jagged pieces of shrapnel that could cleave a man in
two. I shouted at the crew to 'Close down! Close down!' as I pulled
half of my own turret hatch down, hoping that none of the splinters
of steel would seek me out through the opening above me. The risk
was greater as many of the shells were landing in the trees, where
the branches caused them to airburst and spray their lethal contents
down on top of us.

I have no idea how long the 'stonk', military vernacular for a concentration of artillery fire, on our own positions lasted. But it seemed
like an age, as we listened to the dreadful sound of exploding shells
and chunks of metal moving at high velocity smacking against the
sides of the tank. Inside Aim, we could survive anything but a direct
hit, but some men had been caught out of their tanks or in the opening of their hatches. Not surprisingly it was the tank commanders

---

* An Army Board of Inquiry was later held into the unauthorised withdrawal of
6 DWR from the position at Boislonde. A month later, Montgomery deemed that they
were no longer fit for battle. He sacked the commanding officer and had the battalion
broken up, sending its men as casualty replacements to other units.

who suffered. Two NCOs in A Squadron were wounded, as were two officers in C Squadron, one a young troop commander who had only just arrived in the regiment. An NCO in the reconnaissance troop of eleven Honey light tanks was never found. He was last reported in a dismounted observation position before the shelling started and it was speculated that he had been obliterated by a direct hit. Today such 'blue on blue' incidents would cause outrage, but in the total wars of the last century they were common. In an army of several hundred thousand men, where the fighting was often confused, communications far less developed and weapons precision technology unheard of, what is perhaps more remarkable is that occurrences of 'friendly fire' were not more common. Although it was not to be the last time that our own side engaged us.

When it was over, I lifted my hatch to see the ground around us littered with smoking fragments of metal and pockmarked by dirty black gouges in the earth. Without infantry support, the regiment held the line on its own late into the evening. Twice the enemy attempted to probe our positions with a few tanks, but each time they were repulsed and forced to withdraw. Although I didn't see him, when listening to the regimental net the CO seemed to be everywhere, talking calmly over the radio, directing A and C Squadrons and the recce troop to make sure no gaps appeared in the line. At 2200 hours, 7 DWR began sending infantry patrols back into the woods from which their sister battalion had fled eight hours previously. Stanley Christopherson brought his command influence to bear, pushing and cajoling them to ensure that their operations were co-ordinated with the regiment's. His presence did much to restore their confidence and ours and demonstrated how firm leadership can prevent panic and restore a situation. It also highlighted how all-arms co-operation was essential if we were to prevail in the challenging environment of Normandy. But the difficulty of working with the infantry was to become a persistent theme and it was not something that was going to be overcome easily.

Like us, the infantry also had to learn and adapt. The 49th Division had not been in action before and the combined all-arms training the units had gone through in England had generally been conducted in more open terrain in places like East Anglia and on Salisbury Plain. It was insufficient preparation for meeting the prevailing conditions in Normandy and reflected the initial doctrinal weakness of British armoured warfare theory, which lacked imagination. In North Africa the infantry and the tanks could afford to operate as almost separate independent arms, but the bocage demanded far greater levels of integration and co-operation. Consequently, whether a veteran formation or not, most infantry divisions lacked experience of working closely with tanks and there were no common operating procedures for doing so. Being part of an independent armoured brigade, we were also constantly switched between different infantry formations. Just as we were beginning to develop ways of working with one infantry division, we were reallocated to support another. We would then have to start over again in devising mutually agreed tactics. Often redeploying at very short notice, we rarely had time to do this before commencing operations with a new unit.

The first actions in Normandy had made for painful learning, but there would be insufficient time to absorb all the lessons required to fight in the bocage. With the failure at Villers-Bocage and the arrival of more German reinforcements the front line stabilised, ushering in a period of relative quiet, as we spent the next few days engaged in largely passive holding operations, with each squadron taking its turn to support various infantry units of the 49th Division. But it was not to last for long. Monty remained desperate to restore mobility to the battlefield. He was building up his forces for a large-scale operation to break the impasse and we were being rotated out of the line two squadrons at a time to retain a degree of freshness for the coming offensive. On 18 June, the wind picked up and threatening storm clouds darkened the sky from the west. That night the weather broke. The next day we relieved B Squadron on Point 102 where the wind drove the unabating rain into our faces and the ventilation fans sucked it into the insides of our tanks. It was an ominous portent of what was about to come.

6

SPURS

It was still raining hard a day later when Leslie Skinner emerged at the side of my tank. We were located in a good hull-down position facing across a wide-open field. The enemy were on the other side, although we had heard nothing from them since earlier that morning, when we had been briefly engaged by a troublesome machine gun, which had fallen silent after we plastered it with HE fire. Skinner was crouching down and appeared to be about to go forward when I shouted at him, gesticulating with my arm and raising my voice to be heard above the noise of the engine.

'Hey Padre! What the hell are you doing? There are bloody Jerries over there.'

He stopped and I scrambled out of Aim, dropping over the rear of the tank to make my way round to him. The padre explained that he wanted to go out and see if he could identify and bury the body that lay in the middle of the wet open field 150 yards distant. The prone figure of a British soldier had been there all morning, lying like a bundle of discarded rags.

I told Skinner that he was mad and would get himself killed, but he was insistent. There was clearly no point in arguing with him, so

I said we would cover him and wished him luck. We held our breath as Skinner started to crawl out across the saturated field towards the body. Our machine guns were made ready and the gunner had a round up the spout of the main armament, which he laid on to the opposing hedge line. I drew hard on a cigarette as Martin watched him through the telescopic gun sight and muttered 'Fooking 'ell' as Skinner moved further out into the field on the flat of his belly. He was fifty yards away from the body and nothing had happened. There was still no response from the German positions when the padre finally made it to the dead soldier. After a brief search of the man's clothes and one failed attempt to pull him backwards, Skinner appeared to complete a prostrate prayer of spiritual succour over the lifeless figure. Then he crawled back to us through the sodden grass while the Germans held their fire.

From the ID disc the padre brought back with him, it transpired that the dead soldier was one of ours. Trooper Lywood from recce troop had been killed the day before when he was working dismounted with the missing reconnaissance NCO. It was unclear whether Lywood had been killed during our own artillery bombardment called down after the rout of 6 DWR, or by enemy machine gun fire; Skinner believed that both had hit him. Regardless, it was typical of the Sherwood Rangers' padre, who was obsessed with locating the regiment's casualties and making sure they received a decent Christian burial. But with Lywood's body being exposed in full view of the Germans, he reluctantly abandoned the idea of digging a grave, climbed back into the small Dingo armoured scout car he had borrowed from RHQ and went off to see if he could find the body of the missing NCO.

Stanley Christopherson later ticked Skinner off for taking such risks and banned him from going to the forward areas to look for bodies. The CO's admonishment didn't stop the padre from going up to the front line to continue his hapless search of the forward areas, but the fighting that had occurred further back from point 102 provided him with plenty of business. On returning from one fruitless foray, he was stopped in Cristot by some infantry and asked to bury two dead troopers from the 4th/7th Dragoon Guards. Their bodies had been exposed to the elements for six days since the attack on the village and were crawling with maggots. Smoking furiously to ward off the stench, Skinner stitched the unfortunate cavalrymen into the standard shroud of grey army blankets before interring them in the Norman soil and giving a short service for the deceased. Then he was violently sick.

The 'Great Storm', three days of gale-force winds and persistent driving rain, had finally begun to blow itself out on 21 June. Severely damaging the British Mulberry Harbour at Arromanches and destroying the American facility, the atrocious weather had seriously hampered the Allies' schedule for landing more men and materiel in France and had impeded the race to build up sufficient forces to stage an attempt to begin breaking out of the Normandy bridgehead. The storm had forced Montgomery to delay his forthcoming offensive known as Operation Epsom, but within two days the British floating port was back in working order and delivering 6000 tons of stores and equipment per day. The start date for the operation was set for 25 June and the passive situation that had allowed Skinner to traverse the battlefield to minister to the dead was about to end.

The offensive would focus on launching the newly arrived VIII Corps into a set-piece battle with the purpose of breaking through the German line on a front running five miles east from Tilly. Driving south through the Odon river valley, the corps, consisting of two infantry divisions and one armoured division, would then seize the high ground on the other side of the valley known as Hill 112. The intention was to outflank the original D-Day objective of Caen from the west in order to threaten the city from the southwest. By causing significant attrition to the enemy and fixing more German panzer divisions around Caen, the offensive would also set the conditions for further offensive operations to clear the way to the more open ground of the Falaise Plain to the south of Caen; beyond which lay the route to Paris and ultimately to Germany itself. Involving 60,000 troops, 600 tanks and 700 guns, the main attacking formations would consist of the 43rd Wessex Division, the 15th Lowland Scottish Division and the armoured units of 11th Armoured Division. The operation would be supported by a diversionary attack on 25 June, made by 49th Division and 8th Armoured Brigade, codenamed Operation Martlet. The purpose of this subsidiary element of the offensive was to distract the Germans and secure Epsom's right flank by capturing the villages of Fontenay and Rauray and securing the high ground beyond the villages that dominated the Odon valley from the north.

However, 5 Troop knew little of Monty's great plan and our major preoccupation in the days leading up to the attack was to keep dry. As we sat wet and miserable in our tanks watching the front, John Semken and the other squadron leaders attended numerous planning conferences with the CO at 147th Brigade headquarters, which was the infantry brigade of 49th Division that we would be supporting in the diversionary attack. The concept of operations they thrashed out was a three-phase plan, where each squadron would be allocated to support one of the brigade's battalions. Fontenay would be captured in the first phase by C Squadron supporting 11 RSF, B Squadron would support 7 DWR on their left, while we remained in reserve with the rest of A Squadron. After the second phase of capturing the high ground south of Fontenay had been completed, we would then push through the village and attack Rauray in the third and final phase of the attack. The other regiment from 8th Armoured Brigade, 4th/7th Dragoon Guards, would be supporting the division's 146th Brigade on the right of our attack. The planning details were not shared with us as they were worked out. But at each of his O evening groups, Semken gave us the heads up on the outline of A Squadron's likely role and shared the concerns that the CO had about working with the infantry; not least as A Squadron would be supporting 6 DWR, which we had last seen cutting and running on Point 102.

While the majors, colonels, brigadiers and generals laid their plans and waited for the weather and the supply situation to improve, we continued to rotate in and out of the line and focused on more immediate practical concerns. We didn't know much about the enemy we would be fighting, but there was talk at Semken's evening conferences that we would be facing the 12th SS Panzer Division. We knew they were tough bastards, made up of fanatical former Hitler Youth members and commanded by equally fanatical diehard Nazi officers. There were also rumours that they had executed nearly one hundred Canadian soldiers they had captured in the first few days of the landing.* I had yet to see any German soldiers at close quarters, but I wanted to be ready for them and I was concerned about the quality of the personal side arms that we were issued.

Unlike the infantry, where the .303 Bren light machine gun and Lee Enfield bolt-action rifle were the standard personal weapons, tank crewmen were issued with .38 Webley Mark IV revolvers and 9mm Sten submachine guns. The Sten was cheap and simple in both design and manufacture. Costing five shillings to produce, its simplicity also meant that it was prone to discharging accidentally. You only had to drop it on the ground, or tap its butt against a hard object with a bullet in its breech, and it would fire off without the trigger being touched. Its horizontally fitted side magazine also made

---

* On 7/8 June, soldiers of the 12th SS Panzer Division *Hitlerjugend* executed twenty Canadian POWs at Ardenne Abbey in Saint-Germain-la-Blanche-Herbe, just outside Bayeux.

it awkward to handle from the hatch of a tank. As well as being dangerous, it also had a propensity to jam. The .38 revolvers were also standard issue throughout the army. Utterly reliable, they were also completely useless. Although it kicked like a mule and required you to fire it cowboy style with the aid of your left hand over the top of the weapon, the revolver lacked penetrating power. Additionally, it was highly inaccurate and you would be lucky if you could hit a man-sized target from twenty paces. The characteristics of these weapons hardly made them conducive for use in the close confines of Shermans or in situations where they would need to be brought to bear quickly and effectively. Consequently, I was resolved to replace them as soon as possible and traversing ground that had previously been held by the enemy provided an opportunity, as the quality of their automatic small arms was much better than ours.

I can't remember exactly where and when I found it, as the abandoned German positions around Cristot and Point 102 were strewn with discarded equipment and weapons, but the MP40 Schmeisser machine gun pistol I picked up was the answer to a maiden's prayer. Although slightly heavier than a Sten and despite being designed much earlier in 1938, the German Schmeisser was a superior weapon. Made of stamped steel and plastic, it had a folding stock and a vertically fitted magazine that suited the ergonomics of a turret hatch and made it handier to stow and easier to get into a firing position. It used the same 9mm rimless ammunition as the Sten and had the added advantage that it held more rounds in its magazine. Harry Heenan ribbed me about carrying a captured German weapon and was content to stick to his issued Sten. It was a friendly difference of opinion and preference that was to have dramatic consequences for us both. However, like the other troop leaders, we were both agreed that the issued revolver was rubbish and that the German automatic Luger was a much better alternative. They were highly prized items and taken quickly by any Allied soldier who found one on a captured enemy. Consequently, we would have to wait for the start of the next offensive action for the opportunity to acquire one. It would not be long in coming.

On the evening of 24 June we received our final orders for the diversionary attack on Fontenay and Rauray in support of Operation Epsom. The army follows a standard orders format that is little changed today. John Semken started by giving us an overview of the general situation, outlining the position of our own forces and the enemy. He then highlighted our mission and how it would be executed, before covering the co-ordinating administrative detail of logistics, command arrangements and communications. At the end of it, Semken took questions, then we synchronised our watches, gathered our maps and tucked away our notebooks before going off to brief our troops. I kept what I passed on to Sergeant Harrison and Corporal Lane and my own crew to the necessary minimum, concentrating on A Squadron's task and the role the troop would play within it. Although as the troop leader my horizons were broader than the men in my troop, I had little interest in what the rest of the regiment would be up to, let alone the bigger picture activities of the brigades and division above us. My focus was on the specifics of the villages and road junction features we had been ordered to take and the battles we would have to fight across individual fields and hedge lines to get there.

The leaguer was a hive of activity on the final afternoon, as we prepared for battle by completing minor maintenance, refuelling and bombing up the tanks. Given the close nature of the ground we would be advancing across, we packed in as many HE shells and extra boxes of .30-calibre ammunition for the machine guns as we could. I ignored any reluctance from Harrison and made sure that the gunners had properly bore sighted all of the 75mm guns. Then I tested my Schmeisser and made sure it could hang within handy reach inside the turret. As the evening approached Ken Mayo tuned in Aim's wireless to the issued frequencies that would net us into the squadron and regimental command channels. When he was satisfied that they had been set and tested, he locked them into place by turning a small screw on the control panel of the radio. It was dark by the time we had finished and the petrol-tin cookers that had heated our last proper meal before the off had long been extinguished by the time I crawled into the tank shelter and brooded on the morrow, wondering how what we had learned in the last few days and my own performance would stack up.

It was still dark when we were woken from a few fitful hours of sleep. I looked at my watch; it was 0200 hours and time to go. There was just enough time to grab a quick mug of hot sweet tea and a hasty breakfast before climbing stiffly into our tanks and starting the engines. The grey light of dawn was still over an hour away as we drove under radio silence to the assembly area near Point 102 and were marshalled into the start positions for the attack. At H minus one hour, the artillery opened up; it was 0330 and the enemy were about to be pulverised by sixty minutes of intensive indirect fire. The horizon behind us was lit up by the muzzle flashes of 250 guns stabbing fire from their barrels into the retreating darkness. The 5.5-inch guns of the medium corps artillery, which fired projectiles weighing one hundred pounds, supplemented the 25-pounders of the divisional gunner regiments and provided four times the destructive power of the lighter field pieces. The noise was terrific and the shells screamed through the clouds overhead as a solid wall of sound. We could hear the crash of their explosions as the rounds landed unseen in the misty darkness less than a thousand yards ahead of us.

I wondered how anyone could survive such a bombardment, but the delay in opening the offensive had allowed the Germans time to prepare their defences. The experience of facing heavy Soviet artillery fire on the Russian Front had taught them how to dig deep well-constructed bunkers that could withstand anything but a direct hit. The villages of Fontenay and Rauray had been turned into veritable strong points with dug-in tanks and anti-tank guns. A thin screen of well-concealed machine guns, snipers and infantry armed with Panzerfausts were dug in forward of the villages. Their job was to absorb and reduce the power of our attack before it reached the main defensive locations and these would be the first positions that our troops would encounter. If the plan of attack was to work, success in overcoming the German defences in depth would depend on the infantry, armour and artillery working together to maximise their relative strengths, while minimising their vulnerabilities when working apart.

The arrival of dawn an hour later had begun to grace the battlefield with a damp misty half-light that revealed a patchy fog. It was cold and there was a steady drizzle as the engines of B and C Squadron's Shermans roared and they started to move off behind the leading infantry down the slopes of Point 102 towards the village of Fontenay, which lay in the bottom of the shallow valley. The artillery was still firing, but it had been adjusted to fall as a rolling barrage that would land a few hundred yards ahead of the infantry and would be crept a hundred yards further forward every three minutes as they advanced. The guns could suppress and momentarily neutralise a dug-in enemy position, but not destroy it. Artillery is not a precision weapon and a significant number of the defenders would be expected to survive. Consequently, it was essential that the battalions kept up with the barrage, as it would give the Germans little time to recover their poise and prepare to meet the assault before the leading infantry companies were upon them. The thirty-odd Shermans of B and C Squadrons would fire in the infantry attack and could then be called forward to deal with dug-in machine-gun posts and enemy armour. Tanks don't like close country, where they are vulnerable to anti-tank weapons, so in turn they expected the leading infantry to have cleared any hedges or buildings that might conceal German infantry equipped with anti-tank guns or Panzerfausts.

Remaining in reserve on Point 102, we watched them go. With a roar of their engines and squealing tracks, B and C Squadrons moved off into the swirling mist down the forward slope towards Fontenay. The infantrymen moved in column beside them with their rifles at the port. Within minutes they were completely obscured, as they advanced together into the thickening ground fog that had condensed in the lower reaches of the valley floor. Our artillery continued to land out of view ahead of them. Then we heard the unmistakable battlefield signature of the German MG42s barking unseen through the mist. Soon it was joined by the sharp retorts of German anti-tank guns and the crump of enemy mortar fire. The success of the attack would depend on the infantry keeping up with the barrage and maintaining contact with the tanks as they advanced. But as enemy machine-gun fire and high-explosive shells tore into their ranks, the infantrymen stopped and went to ground.

With visibility reduced to zero and the exposed infantry seeking cover, the integration between the two arms disintegrated and the momentum of the assault began to break down into confusion and chaos. Listening to the regimental net, we could hear that the attack was in trouble. But while the tanks could talk to each other on their 19 Set radios, the infantry '18 Sets' operated on different frequencies and the companies and squadrons were unable to communicate. Pinned down and not daring to move, infantrymen hacked at the earth with their entrenching tools to get even a few inches below the ground. Company commanders shouted at their men to get up and move forward, but it is hard to rise from the safety of a piece of cover when death reigns around you. As the mist began to lift, the Germans concentrated their fire on scattered groups that had bunched together, causing more casualties, and the desperate cries for stretcher bearers were added to the frantic yelling of infantry officers trying to galvanise their men.

The padre had already determined that his place was forward with the medics, assisting with the wounded and providing succour to the dying. Moving up behind C Squadron on the right flank of the attack, Skinner ran fast and low looking for casualties, taking cover from machine-gun fire in folds of ground and hastily dug shell scrapes. Diving to avoid a burst from a Spandau, he toppled into a foxhole occupied by a young Scots Fusilier who made it clear that he was going nowhere, as heavy automatic fire cracked a few inches above their heads. Frightened and alone, but not wounded, Skinner took advantage of a lull in the firing to find someone who was. The clearing mist revealed plenty of infantrymen that were in need of the padre's assistance, the location of some marked by the sombre indicator of a bayonet-fixed rifle driven into the ground next to the casualty. Skinner was helping the stretcher parties move injured men back to the Regimental Aid Post when he was caught by a splinter from an exploding mortar bomb. Had he been able to look at his watch it would have told him that it was 1130 hours.

The improving visibility restored some momentum to the attack, but by the time the tanks of C Squadron had reached the outskirts of Fontenay three hours later, there were not enough infantry with them to engage in the necessary close-quarter fighting through the buildings to take the village. With a number of 12th SS panzers remaining resolutely dug in on the southern outskirts, the attack had petered out and the Sherwood Rangers and the two infantry battalions they were supporting were ordered to withdraw back to Point 102 to regroup and lick their wounds. It is easy to be critical of the infantry, especially if you have never taken part in a dismounted attack or seen infantrymen dying in one around you. Unlike us tank men, they were not impervious to shell fragments and machine-gun fire. We also had a better radio. With one allocated to every vehicle, the 19 Set provided us with greater situational awareness and an ability to co-ordinate our actions. The three sections of ten men that made up a platoon didn't have radios and those issued at company level to direct the activities of its three platoons were inadequate.

The infantryman's lot was not a happy one and we had immense sympathy for our unarmoured, dismounted counterparts, whose bleak sobriquet was the 'poor bloody infantry' or 'PBI'. Infantry fighting is a wretched business. Unlike us, they were beasts of burden carrying sixty pounds of equipment or more. Weighed down by rifles, packs, digging tools, rations, grenades, bandoliers of .303 ammunition and extra magazines for the Bren light machine gun, they had to march into battle on their feet, while we drove in our tanks. Given the advent of heavy body armour and the bomb-jamming equipment they carry today, I struggle to imagine how modern infantrymen coped in places like Afghanistan. But like the soldiers of today, the infantrymen of the Second World War also lived out in the elements with all its privations and the infantryman's home was the hole that he dug and what he carried in his pack. Unlike us they didn't pull back from the line into a leaguer at night. The infantry stayed forward. If they weren't patrolling, they would be digging or manning standing positions in the darkness. If it rained, they might be lucky enough to crawl under their gas capes with a sodden army blanket or greatcoat, if they had one, to snatch a few moments of miserable exhausted sleep in the cramped confines of a hastily dug trench. We felt sorry for them, especially when we saw them coming out of action, their faces ashen white with the shock of combat and the loss of mates and the look of utter exhaustion. The poor sods all seemed terribly young and although our casualties were high theirs were much higher.

While the infantry only had their Mark II pudding bowl steel helmets to protect them, the feeling of sympathy was mutual and they would not have traded places with us. They knew we were out-gunned by the Tigers and Panthers and were vulnerable to infantry anti-tank weapons. Unlike them, we could not go to ground at the approach of incoming shells and dive for cover into the shelter of a ditch or trench. Instead they saw us as being trapped inside a steel coffin that could be turned into a raging inferno in seconds. They knew that an armoured-piercing round could slice through our vehicles in the blink of an eye and many had seen the aftermath of a tank being hit. Seeing crews rolling about on the ground on fire trying to put themselves out and the ghoulish features of badly burned men was enough to make most infantrymen glad that they went into battle on their feet.

While neither arm would trade places with the other, the events of the day highlighted the requirement for better infantry–armoured co-operation and the need for a new plan of attack. C Squadron and the Royal Scots Fusiliers were sent back into action later that evening. Attacking under the cover of darkness, they gained a foothold in the village. It was gradually extended the next day after more difficult fighting that included taking the second objective of the higher ground to the south of the village. Throughout, we had continued to remain in reserve. With the first objective taken after thirty-six hours of bloody combat, it was our turn. A Squadron were ordered to move through Fontenay for the third phase of the assault on Rauray, which lay a mile and a half away to the south. With most of the day already gone and the operation running behind schedule, the CO stitched a hasty plan of attack together with the infantry commander and the senior gunner officer. Their impromptu conference took place in an orchard in the middle of Fontenay, which was under heavy mortar fire. After the mauling they had already received, the infantry were reluctant to advance across open ground and it was agreed that we would lead. Our own artillery would put down a concentration of shells in front of our advance and the infantry would follow us for the first mile and then dig in.

After an equally hasty conference with John Semken, I was ordered to proceed through Fontenay to the southern outskirts of the village and then go firm to wait for the rest of the squadron to catch up. The scattered houses of Fontenay had been badly knocked about by our own artillery and I noticed how the stout Norman farm buildings had been incorporated into the Germans' defences as strong points. A number of dead Germans lay wax-like and stiff around their former positions, but there was no sign of their armour that had been dug in among the houses and outbuildings. Files of our own weary infantry marched by the side of our tanks or were digging into the side of the road.

Sheltering under a raincoat draped over the turret hatches of his tank, Stanley Christopherson was talking into his microphone; no doubt he was co-ordinating the final adjustments to the plan of attack when I passed him at the side of a bend in the village's main street. I pushed on for another 500 yards, drove over a crossroads and then led my tanks into a large field on the right-hand side of the road. We shook out into extended line and halted. I told Semken that we were firm and then waited, as he sent the rest of the squadron through Fontenay to join us. Neville Fearn was the first to arrive and as he was the squadron's battle captain I dismounted from my tank and climbed up on to his vehicle to speak to him. I can't have been there for long when movement to my right caught my attention.

Travelling proud above the top of the high-banked hedge that flanked the road that I had just left were the head and shoulders of a tank commander motoring back towards the village. For a moment I thought that it must have been one of C Squadron's tanks, as they were securing the higher ground ahead of us. Then I caught sight of the distinctive headgear the man was wearing and the field-grey flash of the tank's paint. The hat was the black silver-edged side cap favoured by panzer commanders and the man wearing it was commanding a Tiger tank.

'Shit!' I said to Fearn. 'It's a bloody Jerry and he is heading straight for the crossroads and A Squadron!'

I was already yelling at the crew to turn Aim around as I took the side of the tank at a sprint and hauled myself into the turret. I screamed at the driver to get back into Fontenay as I scrambled for the headset and microphone to send a warning to Semken over the radio, but I couldn't raise him on the net. We had broken back on to the road and were heading at full tilt back into the village when I heard the first rounds of tank fire ring out and saw billowing smoke less than 200 yards ahead of me on the other side of the crossroads.

The German Tiger was already advancing down the top of the main street into Fontenay, as we started to make after him. He was closing up on the bend where Christopherson had parked his unarmed headquarters tanks, when Semken's Sherman turned the corner from the opposite direction. At only sixty yards' distance from each other, it was an unanticipated meeting for both parties. Following his own principles of tank warfare, Semken had an AP round up the spout of his 75mm. He fired first and kept on firing. Within less than a minute, Semken's gunner had pumped six rounds into the Tiger, forcing it close into the wall of a large farm building and filling the road with the smoke from the phosphorous tracer element in the back of the AP rounds. The crews of both tanks were unable to see for the obscuring smoke, but Semken had got his shot in first and with the target acquired he ordered his gunner to keep firing until they had expended ten rounds. They stopped when a report came over the radio that the crew of the Tiger had been spotted bailing out.

It was all over by the time I got there and the smoke was beginning to clear. Semken had hit the giant tank six times at close range, but not one of the rounds from his Sherman had penetrated the Tiger's main armour. It subsequently transpired that one of the

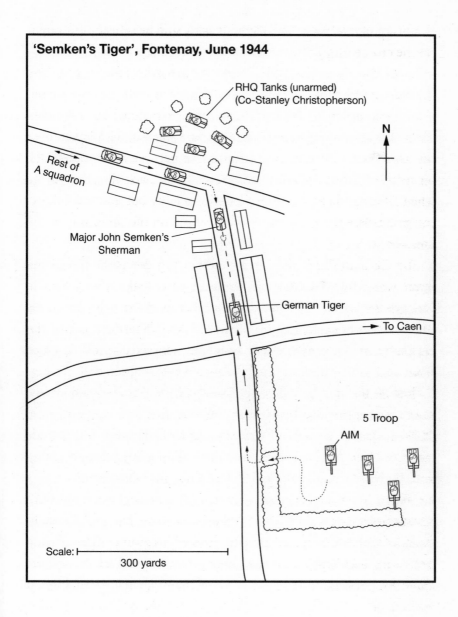

'Semken's Tiger', Fontenay, June 1944

RHQ Tanks (unarmed)
(Co-Stanley Christopherson)

N

Rest of
A squadron

Major John Semken's
Sherman

German Tiger

To Caen

5 Troop

AIM

Scale:
300 yards

AP rounds had deflected off the Tiger's gun-mounting armour to hit the much thinner armour of the driver's turret hatch, scabbing off sparking metal from the inside. As a result of the impact, it is likely that the driver claimed he was hit. With his tank potentially immobilised and under fire, the commander of the Tiger then ordered his crew to bail out. It was the first Tiger to be captured intact in Normandy and it was the result of an extremely lucky shot. But as far as we were concerned John Semken was a man who made his own luck. Practising the principles that he preached had undoubtedly saved his life and those of his crew. With half his squadron strung out on the main street behind him and the CO's unarmed RHQ tanks but a hundred yards away next to the infantry headquarters, it is highly likely that Semken had prevented another 'Wittman' or 'Villers-Bocage' taking place. Although I doubt that he felt in the mood, there was no time to celebrate as it was already getting late and he needed to get the rest of A Squadron forward for the attack on Rauray.

Rauray is a smaller village than Fontenay, made up of some forty-odd houses. The area between the two villages runs for 2500 yards and consists of large fields interspersed by hedgerows and the odd tree. The ground was much more open than anything we had previously traversed and allowed A Squadron to shake out on its start line with two troops forward and two troops back. Harry Heenan's 2 Troop was on the left and 5 Troop was the right forward troop. Semken placed himself at the centre behind Harry's troop and mine. He then grouped the squadron's four Sherman Firefly tanks with his own, which he referred to as his 'Praetorian Guard'. The infantry of the DWR formed up next to us, crouching on one knee with their spiked pig-sticker bayonets fixed to the end of their rifles. The patchy fog that had plagued C Squadron throughout the day finally began to lift and the early evening sun reflected off the ripening fields of corn ahead of us. There was no fixed time for H Hour, the appointed time for an attack to start, as our artillery support was on call as soon as we were ready to go. C Squadron had already secured the start line for us earlier that afternoon after clearing the higher ground just outside Fontenay, as phase three of the operation. But they had lost two tanks in the process and their knocked-out hulks continued to burn. One smudged the sky with an ominous thick oily smoke stack. I wondered whether the crew got out and whether they had been badly burned. My own crew was apprehensive and tense as we waited for the artillery to commence firing and for the squadron commander to give the order to advance.

I heard Semken's voice come up on the net an instant before the fire from our guns started to crash 'danger close' less than 200 yards ahead of us.

'All stations. All stations. Advance.'

Dixon didn't need to wait for my command. He let the steering levers go and Aim lurched forward as the gears transferred the engine's power to the forward drive sprockets. The infantry were with us, moving through a sea of waist-high corn, as we fanned out and crushed the crops flat with our tracks. We stopped to plaster every hedge in front of us with fifteen minutes of HE and machine-gun fire before moving forward another bound. Despite our speculative fire and the artillery barrage that had preceded it, a German Spandau opened up from the bottom of a hedge. The infantry went to ground and stayed down. NCOs and officers shouted commands and some of their soldiers made desultory attempts to return fire with their light machine guns. But a thirty-round magazine-fed Bren gun was no match for the MG42, which dwarfed it with its crushing firepower. With a distinct perforated heavy fire barrel, it could manage a cyclic rate of 2000 rounds per minute. I was always amazed that the Spandaus never seemed to run out of ammunition, but when one opened up it was our cue to get forward and deal with it.

The MG42 fire rattled off the side of the tank like a jackhammer, as I ordered Martin to fire three rounds of HE to airburst in the foliage above the machine-gun nest. The explosive force of the fragmenting rounds and a few belts of .30-calibre fire were enough to silence them. I ordered the crew to cease fire and we moved forward cautiously. Suddenly there was a blur of movement to our front, as field-grey clad figures broke from the cover of the hedge line in a desperate bid to get away from our advancing troop of tanks. Martin and Gartside didn't wait for me to order them to fire; the coaxial and hull MGs burst into life, cutting them down in a hail of bullets. The hull gunner's station had limited traverse, but Dixon instinctively slewed the tracks to the left and right to reposition the tank, allowing Gartside to bring his machine gun to bear on the fleeing figures. Mayo already had a new belt of ammo to hand ready to slap into the feed tray of the coax as soon as it needed to be reloaded. I watched in fascinated admiration as the crew worked like a well-oiled automatic machine, as practised drill and killer instinct combined to deadly effect. There was no trace of a desire to conserve ammunition in order to avoid the lengthy task of re-bombing the tank when we pulled back to the leaguer later that night. But the crew knew the dangers of having German infantry in their midst, regardless of the fact that they were running away. A fleeing enemy can easily go to ground and pick up a Panzerfaust to return to the fray with deadly intent. A retreating soldier also lives to fight another day and we were not going to give the Germans the chance to do that.

The inside of the tank was a thick haze of choking smoke when I gave the order to cease fire, a last few desultory rounds chattering on until repetition of the order put a final halt to the fire. The job was done and the riddled remains of several Germans lay sprawled face down along the line of the hedges. An instant later the smoke in the turret had cleared and our own infantry were already stabbing and firing among the dugouts the enemy had vacated, searching out any remnants of the defenders by firing Bren guns into bunker entrances, followed up by a grenade for good measure. Then they cleared them of any remaining occupants at the point of a bayonet. One shell-shocked prisoner, punch drunk from the weight of fire that had fallen on his position, emerged from the trench, his hands stretched out in supplication above him. He was extremely fortunate not to have been killed by the momentum that carried the infantry's assault through the position. An infantry assault is a frenzied and adrenaline-charged thing and the blood of the men from the attacking battalion was up, not least because several of their mates lay dead in the stands of wheat behind them.

Not all the captured Germans were so lucky. As the close-quarter fighting raged along the hedgerows, a young SS soldier was dragged out from an earth-covered bunker by a group of infantrymen who pushed him unceremoniously towards where Aim had taken up a fire position. He was wearing a camouflage smock with its distinctive SS flashes on the collar. The SS soldier was dirty and dishevelled from having spent days under bombardment dug into the bottom of a hedge. A shock of matted blond hair fell across his face, which was bloody and swollen from the rifle butts and boots that had been used to prise him out of his hole. Probably not more than eighteen years old, he was clearly angry that he had been captured and a Teutonic arrogance shone out from his clear blue eyes. He refused to put his hands up as he was searched for his pay book and looked up at me as if I was something off the bottom of his boots. Suddenly, enemy mortar fire crumped in around us. The infantry threw themselves prone into the dirt and some scuttled behind the tank, to shelter from the blasting shrapnel. But the young SS man stood his ground and didn't move a muscle. He laughed at those who had taken cover and I can still remember the startled look of momentary surprise on his face as a shell splinter struck him square on the forehead and he crumpled dead onto the ground.

Our tanks had advanced just over a thousand yards and Rauray still lay almost a mile ahead of us. Their part in the plan complete, the infantry halted and began to dig in along the hedge line that we had just cleared. The squadron pushed on. Without the infantry in support, we would have to be even more wary of snipers or Germans equipped with Panzerfausts waiting to get close enough to fire a lethal shot from a concealed position in the corn around us. Conscious that we were now on our own, Semken took his time. Calling on his experience from the desert, he was waiting for the sun to begin to dip behind us. He controlled our movement over the radio, ordering one troop to move forward a tactical bound at a time while another went firm. There was about 100 to 150 yards' spacing between each tank and 200 to 300 yards between the two troops. Semken kept the Sherman Firefly tanks further back under his personal control so that he could move them into a position where they could provide overwatch with their heavier and more capable 17-pounder guns. Before each troop moved we still brassed up every likely piece of cover with HE and machine-gun fire, as the distance between us and Rauray continued to count down and the artillery fire crept sporadically forward ahead of us.

I have absolutely no idea where the first enemy tank round came from, but we were closing in on the outskirts of the village that lay less than a thousand yards away. The Germans used a propellant that had a lower flash base to it, which made the flash of their muzzle blast difficult to spot, especially if they were dug in among trees or buildings. I scanned left to right across the houses and vegetation to my front, as another high-velocity crack, followed by another, announced that more rounds were being sent out to greet us. Harry Heenan's troop on the left was already returning fire, as incoming high-velocity projectiles ploughed themselves deep into the ground around us. Semken was calm on the net, calling out that we had enemy armour to our front and bringing the other troops up to support us. Firing into the sun made it more difficult for the German tanks to pick us up in their sights and the weight of fire from the squadron was also affecting their aim. Then I saw a glint of light on metal that drew my eye to the low hull-down shape of a panzer.

I gave a fire-control order over the intercom: 'AP. Traverse right. Eight hundred yards. Enemy hornet dug into the right side of prominent building.'

Martin clenched the spade grip and the turret swung round, but he traversed beyond the aiming point. I shouted a correction and he traversed back again, desperately seeking the target. I heard the retort of a 75mm firing to my left. Corporal Lane was already engaging the enemy tank I had spotted. Normally the gunner screams 'On!' when he has locked on to the target indicated. But Martin had still not located the enemy through the gunner's sight. I hauled him backwards, pulling him out of his seat. Squeezing into his vacant spot, I grabbed the spade grip and brought the gun to bear. Tapping the firing pedal an instant later, our first round splashed to the right of the panzer. Shoving Martin back into his seat, I thrust my head back out of the turret and shouted the adjustment to the fall of shot. This time Martin had got him. He made the correction for line and direction and I watched the trace of the next AP round accelerating towards the German tank. We were hitting him now and so was Lane and our combined weight of fire forced him to withdraw.

All the tanks of the squadron were now firing across the entire front of our advance at a host of enemy tanks that had taken us on as we closed on Rauray. Some of the older German Mark IVs were already knocked out and burning. But there were heavier and better armoured Panthers too. Now the German tanks were plastered, fixed and damaged by the 75mm fire of the four troops, Semken moved the Firefly tanks up. Sergeant George Dring dismounted and led his 17-pounder forward on foot. Although hailing from Lincoln, Dring was a pre-war yeoman and the son of a blacksmith. He was a keen huntsman and had an eye for ground that gave him an uncanny sixth sense of using it to his advantage to stalk German tanks. He had also won a Military Medal for gallantry in the desert and was not shy of going forward to engage the enemy. Using a hedge for cover, he walked Akilla into a firing position to engage a Panther firing at us from a small wood at the side of the village. One round from Akilla's powerful 17-pounder was capable of penetrating the armour of the heavier German tanks at ranges beyond 500 yards. Dring made sure that the first round counted. In a few minutes he had repositioned his tank and knocked out another panzer, before going on to claim two more victims.

Suddenly, a Panther burst from cover to our right and drove along a road that ran east to west across our front, no more than 200 yards from the forward edge of our advance. Presenting itself side on to us, where its armour was thinner, was a desperate manoeuvre and we didn't waste it. Any tank that could bring its guns to bear engaged the Panther as it traversed down the road. Martin responded to my fire-control orders and this time he was spot on. The recoil of our 75mm shot back as we began working a well-oiled rhythm of firing, loading and firing again. An empty brass case clanged to the floor of the turret and Ken Mayo instantly had another round in the breech. Martin fired and our second round added to the rounds of other tanks that were hitting the Panther as it passed down the line of our guns. Some shots were bouncing off its armour, but it began to slow, belch smoke and stop. Two of the crew from the stricken tank bailed out and we joined in with the others as they were cut down in a hail of combined coaxial machine-gun fire from our Shermans. The volume of the combined fire of the squadron had overwhelmed the German armour defending Rauray and our turret was filled with caustic gagging smoke, until the fan filtered it out.

Semken directed me to clear a line of hedges on the western side of Rauray where enemy infantry had dug a honeycomb of trenches and weapon pits. Some died in their positions and a few were shot down as they tried to scuttle back to the cover of the houses in the village. We had to depress the coaxial machine gun to the limits as we moved closer, the turret traversing left and right to spray the positions along the bottom of the hedge with bullets. Dixon was again slewing the tank from side to side to provide Gartside with the maximum arc of fire for his hull-mounted machine gun, as I gave fire-control orders and flicked the switch on the frequency box to give directions to the rest of the troop. Lane's Sherman was up with us and I was looking over the back of the tank wondering where Harrison was, when an SS soldier tried to climb up the front of Aim. With one hand clutching a stick grenade, he struggled and slipped to get purchase on the smooth sloping metal of the glacis plate. It gave me the split second I needed to reach inside the turret for the Schmeisser. The butt was already folded and it was made ready with the safety catch off. In the time it took to bring the machine-gun pistol up to my shoulder, the German had made purchase and was on the top of the driver's hatch. His grenade arm was raised backwards when I blew him off the side of the tank with a long burst of automatic fire.

Lacking our own infantry to protect us among the houses, we were unable to clear further into the village. But A Squadron had achieved the objective it had been set and thirteen enemy tanks had been knocked out. Four were accredited to Dring, but like most of the other troop leaders I didn't keep a score. As far as most of us were concerned, enemy tank kills were attributed to collective effort. The CO informed Semken that a battalion was being sent up to relieve us and to consolidate the gains that we had made. The light was fading by the time they arrived and we pulled back to a leaguer to the sound of infantry picks and shovels clanging in the darkness as they dug in on the outskirts of Rauray. We were again held in reserve when the village was cleared the next day by the infantry and B Squadron. But it cost them eleven men dead and a complete troop of tanks lost to a lone Tiger that managed to infiltrate back into position during the night. The infantry would also suffer, but when Rauray finally fell on 27 June, nine enemy tanks were discovered abandoned in its streets. Some were still in working order, including a Panther and a Tiger.

With Rauray taken, the regiment continued to operate with 49th Division for the next five days engaging in a series of holding actions to consolidate the gains made and protect the right flank of Operation Epsom to our east. The main thrust made by VIII Corps' three divisions had succeeded in reaching the Odon and intense fighting continued around Hill 112, until it was eventually given up as Monty's first set-piece offensive ran out of steam. German attempts to counterattack were beaten off and we had a grandstand view of the bombing of Villers-Bocage, as RAF Lancasters pulverised the place. The large lumbering aircraft came in low over our heads with their bomb-bay doors open and we could clearly see the bombs slung inside their fuselages. We watched in fascination as thousands of pounds of steel-cased high explosive ordnance fell away from their bellies and rained down hell on the wretched town. The bombers then altered their course to the north and left the prevailing wind to cover us in brick dust from the devastation they had wreaked, as they headed for home. But while a deep salient had been driven into it, the German line remained unbroken. On 4 July the Sherwood Rangers were pulled out of action to rest and refit. After nine days of near continuous operations we were utterly exhausted as we drove our tanks into a leaguer that had been established in a pleasant orchard near Chouain, six miles to the south of Bayeux. Although we were dead on our feet, the crews started the process of bombing up the tanks without complaint; except Martin, of course, who rolled his eyes. But for him I took it almost as consent and I handed the Player's cigarettes round, we lit up our fags and got started. Then, unshaven and dirty, we slept the sleep of the dead.

The regiment spent the next five days resting, reorganising, replenishing and replacing the tanks that it had lost. The unit's B Echelon vehicles that carried its second line of supplies were brought up from the beaches to join us at Chouain. It was the first time since landing in Normandy that all elements of the Sherwood Rangers had been together. As well as carrying the regiment's second line of ammunition and other stores, the B Echelon vehicles also carried sundry supplies that were not normally needed when the fighting element was forward in combat and also items such as pay and mail. Most importantly for me, they brought with them a Sherwood Rangers cap badge.

I had exceeded the expectation of survival. In three weeks of fighting, I was not only still alive, but I had gained vital combat experience. Under John Semken's guidance I had begun to develop an eye for ground, with an ability to read a battle and a growing awareness of how to exploit the vulnerabilities of the enemy and maximise our advantages in numbers and weight of firepower. We had demonstrated that the Tigers and Panthers could be beaten and we had been tested in combat and not found wanting. There had been no major breakout and the fighting had been a hard bloody slogging match to gain a few thousand yards of ground. But we had played a part in Monty's intention to tie down the enemy around Caen and cause attrition to his forces, inflicting losses that the Germans could not replace. Our superiority in numbers was beginning to tell and was proving that quantity has a quality all of its own. But it was brutal arithmetic and attrition cuts both ways. The bloody grinding machine was set to continue and there was also still much to learn, not least in the need to improve the co-operation between tanks and infantry. However, I would be lying if I said such thoughts weighed on my mind at the time. For me what was important was that I had proved myself on two fronts; firstly in battle against the Germans and secondly to win the confidence of my men. As I fixed the regimental cap badge in my black tank beret I felt at home, that I belonged and that I had finally won my spurs.

7

PROVIDENCE

If you drive along the one and a half mile stretch of the main Fontenay to Rauray road today and look across the open fields to your left, you will see a solitary screen of beech trees standing sentinel to the cemetery of Fontenay-le-Pesnel. Within the confines of neatly cut hedges lie the immaculately kept graves of 460 Commonwealth soldiers and 59 of their German opponents. Maintained by the British War Graves Commission, the cemetery also contains the graves of those members of B and C Squadrons of the Sherwood Rangers who lost their lives during Operation Epsom. Standing there seven decades later, as I have done numerous times before, I listened to the wind rustling through the beech trees and thought how my men and I could so easily have been among them. The headstones of Sergeant Green and nineteen-year-old Trooper Smith of B Squadron are testimony to the regiment's sacrifice in the bitter fighting that took place on the battlefield between the two villages all that time ago. The fact that no member of A Squadron lies buried there is testimony to John Semken's leadership.

Under Semken's command, in a few short weeks since landing in Normandy A Squadron had gelled as a team and the culmination of our competence and fighting prowess had been proved in the battle for Rauray. It was the Sherwood Rangers' largest clash with enemy armour since North Africa and the feat of arms in knocking out thirteen enemy tanks had been achieved without loss. Semken had always said that as his troop commanders he depended on us and it was the squadron's young officers who made the difference between whether a battle stalled or succeeded. While he may have relied on us, we took our lead from Semken and our confidence and the competence we gained flowed directly from him. The mutual trust he engendered extended to the rank and file of the squadron and demonstrated that in war stability in command is a vital element in the morale component of a unit's fighting spirit. But having just reached such a high point in its achievements, A Squadron was about to go through a crisis in its leadership.

Even in war, an army has to look to its future and the career development of its professional officer corps. Like 75 per cent of those holding commissions in 1944, John Semken was not a regular career soldier but a young acting major who was destined to leave the army once the war was over. As we reflected on our success, Semken was informed that he would revert to the rank of captain and return to his old job as the regiment's technical adjutant. The vacancy he created by relinquishing command of A Squadron would be filled by Major Geoffrey Makins. It was a bitter blow for Semken, but Makins was a pre-war professional officer from the Royal Dragoons who needed the combat experience of commanding a subunit in the field if he was to advance his career as a regular officer. When such command opportunities were not available in an individual's own regiment, much to the chagrin of others it was common practice to send them to another unit where a vacancy existed or could, in Semken's case, be created. Unenlightened as we were regarding the army's career development policy for its officers, it was also a devastating shock for the squadron. The replacement of Semken touched a nerve in the subunit, as they had faith in him to deliver success and keep them alive. It had particular poignancy as it came straight after Rauray and just before the start of another major attack.

On 10 July, four days after Geoffrey Makin's arrival, the regiment moved out from the orchard at Chouain to its assembly area for the forthcoming operation. Lying four miles to the west of Rauray, the village of Hottot-les-Bagues is a straggle of houses set either side of a long straight road that sits on a spur of high ground. Occupied by the enemy, it formed the key part of a German salient that jutted into the British front line. Elements of Panzer Lehr had been holding out there fiercely for some weeks and had beaten off all previous attempts to shift them. Monty wanted the salient nipped out as part of his continued intention to keep applying pressure across the whole of the German line. The attack would also support another attempt to capture the dominant feature of Hill 112 to the south of Caen. The infantry of 43rd Wessex Division would be used for that task, while we would be supporting the infantry of the 50th Division's 231 Brigade in the attack on Hottot.

It took all night to move into our positions on the start line for the attack, which would be a standard 'two up' infantry brigade affair. Two of the brigade's battalions, each supported by a squadron of tanks from the Sherwood Rangers, would form the initial assault force, while C Squadron would remain in reserve with the brigade's third infantry battalion. The usual preliminary artillery barrage began to creep forward as dawn broke over the eastern horizon and there was little time to marry up with the infantry before we began to move forward. The first light of morning revealed the nature of the ground over which we would have to advance. Sloping upwards to the northern side of the village, it was a typical bocage studded with orchards and clumps of trees among a patchwork of small hedge-bounded fields that were little bigger than a football pitch. Each would form a defensive position and each would have to be taken methodically in turn. Due to the noise of our engines, we couldn't hear the scream of the incoming enemy shells, but the infantry could and they sank to the ground like moles just before the first of the rounds began to land; those infantrymen that made it to cover, or avoided a direct hit, survived. Others caught out in the open became casualties, while we pushed on to deal with the first line of hedges.

The German shellfire was heavy and I kept my head down low in the cupola, as shrapnel struck the sides of the tank. Snipers were also active and I trusted to my helmet decoy as we hosed down every likely tree and piece of cover with machine-gun fire. The German snipers often tied themselves into trees to stop them falling out if wounded and sometimes we only knew if we had hit one when a German soldier toppled from the branches to have his fall smartly arrested by a piece of rope. With the first hedge line sanitised with fifteen minutes of .30-calibre and 75mm HE fire, we positioned ourselves to deal with the next hedgerow. If the distance between the hedges was greater and they were closer to the main German defensive positions, there was an increased chance of coming across a concealed enemy tank. But we had begun to develop new tactics to deal with them.

The fighting at Rauray had demonstrated that the Sherman Firefly was not a good general-purpose tank. Although the large, powerful 17-pounder gun made it effective against Tigers and Panthers, it was less agile than the standard 75mm-gun-equipped M4 Sherman. The length of the Firefly's barrel reduced its mobility in close wooded areas and the weight of its main armament also meant that when moving at speed, or covering any significant distance, the gun had to be traversed and fixed over the rear deck of the tank. This saved wear and tear on its turret mountings, but meant that the commander had to dismount and unfix the gun before it could be brought into action. Additionally, because the hull gunner's position had been removed from the Firefly to create the necessary space to accommodate its larger calibre ammunition, it had a distinct disadvantage when dealing at close quarters with enemy infantrymen equipped with Panzerfausts. Although it lacked the Firefly's penetrating punch, most of us favoured the manoeuvrability of the M4 and its quick-firing 75mm gun with its excellent HE round. John Semken saw the solution as mixing the two types of Sherman together and as a legacy of his command each troop of three standard Shermans now had one of the squadron's four Fireflies allocated to it.

Lance Corporal Redfern commanded the Firefly in my troop. Being a short bloke, he was ideally suited to command a 17-pounder, as the inside of the tank was even more cramped than the standard Sherman. With the possibility of enemy armour ahead of us, I pushed him off to a flank while the three M4s brassed up the hedges to our front with HE. If our fire provoked a concealed German tank to break cover, Redfern's job was to hit it and destroy it with his 17-pounder. Sometimes the presence of the Firefly was enough to get a panzer to unmask itself, as the enemy knew that the 17-pounder was dangerous so it often attracted their fire first. The Firefly also produced a bloody great flash that no German could fail to spot. The air was rich with expletives the first time Redfern fired his gun, as the flash from the muzzle burned off his eyebrows and was so bright that it temporarily blinded him. After that, the crew learned to close their eyes and at the moment of firing Redfern would duck his head down into the turret. Because the Firefly gave away its position as soon as it fired, every enemy tank or anti-tank gun within range would home in on it with everything they had. Consequently, it required careful siting and making the right decision as to when to reveal its existence.

If you stared long enough at an opposing hedgerow, you could sometimes discern the presence of an enemy tank from the shimmer it produced in the air above it. The Panther in particular was fitted with two large extractor fans on the top of its rear decks, which expelled the fumes and the heat from its engines. In the process it warmed the immediately surrounding air and created the faintest visual distortion. It took a practised eye to spot it, but when we did we would engage the area with HE. The top of the Panther's armour was much thinner than its front and sides, which meant that there was a chance of penetrating it with HE shrapnel. There was also a slim possibility that a round might ignite the petrol fumes that were expelled into the air.

Regardless of the circumstances, when a German tank revealed itself the whole troop would open up and pump as many rounds as possible at it. If we didn't knock it out, the combined weight of our fire was usually enough to force the enemy to withdraw if we were able to overmatch it with our quick-firing 75mm guns. High explosive was the preferred nature type of ammunition. We had little faith in the AP variant due to its lack of penetrating power. But a rapid rate of HE shells could smash an enemy tank's optics and damage its tracks. However, we never remained static for too long, as constant fire and movement was the way to stay alive. Having fired three to four rounds at a target in rapid succession, each Sherman would jockey backwards and then drive back into a new attack position to observe the effects of its fire and re-engage a target if necessary. We put these tactics into practice at Hottot and, as ever, Corporal Lanes was up with my tank but Sergeant Harrison's Sherman still displayed a tendency to hang back. Later, after the fighting, I had it out with him and he replied that he 'couldn't cum up as ma engine was oover eatin'. At the time I was frustrated with his lack of aggression. But I was still young and relatively fresh and as my own experience and exposure to battle increased I began to realise that it impacts on your resilience and willingness to take risks. Ultimately, you don't become battle hardened, you just become more cautious.

During the fighting for Hottot, the regiment accounted for seven enemy tanks; five were claimed by A Squadron and some undoubtedly resulted from the new methods that we were employing. But the squadron also began to take its first significant casualties. The Germans were well dug in, so instead of pulling back to a leaguer that first night we consolidated the gain of a few hundred yards made during daylight by staying forward with the infantry to bolster their morale and protect them from enemy counterattacks. The crews hated it, as it meant that we got hardly any sleep and it exposed us to danger as a result of being able to see very little at night. The onset of darkness brought out more snipers, who would creep forward to infiltrate our positions and there was always the risk that a German with a Panzerfaust might work his way through the infantry protecting us. Throughout the night, I strained my eyes into the blackness around me, closing one eye to protect my night vision when flares bathed the ground ahead of me in brilliant light before dying out to cast eerie flickering shadows around the position. The occasional stream of tracer cut through the darkness, which was alive with strange shapes that played tricks on my mind and stretched my imagination, as I struggled to remain awake and focused. Throughout, I willed the luminous minute hand on my watch to tick faster, as I counted down the hours to the coming of morning, although I knew that with the arrival of first light we would start over what we had done the day before.

It took another day of difficult fighting to grind our way slowly up the hill towards Hottot and break into the village. The enemy continued to shell us heavily as we eventually fought down the long narrow high street. The tanks would deal with the machine-gun positions and any elevated structures that might conceal a sniper or an artillery spotter, by pumping 75mm rounds into the church spire and the upper windows of any prominent building. Then the infantry would enter and clear the houses on either side of the street with grenades and bursts of automatic fire. We progressed through the village in this manner until we were engaged by anti-tank fire and forced off the road to seek cover. A first-round hit on one of our tanks caused it to brew up. I hoped that the crew got out, as within seconds the Sherman was a raging inferno. For once I was thankful for the constant noise of our own engine and the battle around me, as it would drown out the animal-like screams if any of the men were still trapped inside. By the time we had ejected the enemy from the village the regiment had lost four tanks and seven men killed or wounded. The majority of them were tank commanders and came from A Squadron; three of them were officers.

Captain Ronnie Gellis, acting as the second in command of the squadron, was cruelly maimed when he had his jaw shot away, most probably by a sniper. Mike Howden received superficial shrapnel wounds to his face when he was leading 3 Troop up the slopes to Hottot and Geoffrey Makin was seriously wounded by artillery when out of his tank. Tragically, he was to die a few days later from the wounds he sustained. One will never know whether the new squadron commander was hit as a result of inexperience or due to sheer bad luck. But it was his first action and Semken had taught us that in war you help make your own luck. As we pulled back out of the line, I noted that the helmet fixed on the machine-gun bracket at the back of my turret hatch had two neat bullet holes drilled through it; no doubt courtesy of a German sniper. Thankfully, there were no casualties in 5 Troop, but our closest shave during the battle had come from our own side.

Much has been made of Allied air superiority during the battle of Normandy and the crushing punishment the Typhoon and P-47 Thunderbolt fighter-bombers of the tactical air forces of the RAF and USAAF inflicted on the German army, but they were also a danger to us. On the first day of the attack, the advance had become bogged down and there were reports of tanks to our front. Unbeknown to us, the infantry had tasked the RAF forward observation officer attached to their headquarters to call up fighter-bombers to deal with them. The squadron was strung out along the edge of a ridge when I heard the high-pitched roar of an aero engine. I looked up behind me and saw the first black shape of a Typhoon diving towards us. The leading edge of its wings seemed to be on fire and I initially thought that it might have been hit by German anti-aircraft flack. Then it began to bank and climb upwards and that's when I saw the smoke trails betraying the presence of two rockets streaking towards us. I had just enough time to shout a frantic warning to the rest of the troop to batten down, and managed to get one half of my own hatch closed, when the screaming projectiles exploded on either side of Aim and showered the tank with steel splinters.

From the open half of the turret hatch, I could make out the black dots of three more aircraft circling in the blue of the sky above us, each one increasing in size as they dropped into a sixty-degree diving attack attitude. Swooping down one after another, more 60mm rockets rippled off their wings, to which they added 20mm cannon fire for good measure, which stitched lines of spurting earth in the ground around us. Some of the rounds hit, but none of the rockets did, which would have opened us up. Thankfully, it wasn't the precision ground attack of today, where one modern aircraft only needs to use one laser-guided bomb to guarantee a hit on a vehicle. Striking a target with unguided rockets was notoriously difficult. However, while it was over in a matter of seconds, being under air attack is a frightening experience. It was made worse by the fact that we were suffering at the hands of our own air force and the language in the tank was foul. Dickie Holman in 4 Troop was particularly upset as the RAF shot up all the presents he had just received for his twenty-first birthday, which were strapped under the tarpaulin on the back of his tank.

Once in the village, the Wehrmacht soldiers of Panzer Lehr made us fight hard for every yard of ground taken, but they were different to the SS and surrendered readily enough when they realised that their position was untenable. Once we were among them they were happy to throw their hands up. Usually the infantry dealt with them, but if they weren't with us and we were static some of the troop would dismount and cover me while I searched them for their pay books, which yielded a significant amount of information regarding the individual and his unit. This could be passed back to the intelligence officers at regimental headquarters. It was also an opportunity to loot them. Valuable items like watches and pens went to the men and by the end of the campaign seeing an Allied soldier wearing several watches on his wrist was not an uncommon sight. But we were all interested in getting our hands on a German pistol and the POWs we took in the village yielded Lugers. Designed in 1908, the weapon was still the standard German issue in 1944. It had a lovely smooth cocking action and could take our own 9mm ammunition. More importantly, it was far more effective than our .38 revolvers. In getting my hands on a Luger I had satisfied a small personal objective.

The attack on Hottot met Monty's much greater objective of straightening the front line and distracting German attention as he prepared to launch Operation Goodwood. Employing all the British and Canadian corps at his disposal in 21st Army Group, the operation was a major push to swing round Caen and open up the Falaise road. The city itself had finally fallen on 10 July. But the German line remained unbroken and more enemy reinforcements continued to arrive to shore up their defences. In launching Goodwood, Monty was determined to keep the bulk of Hitler's forces tied down in the Caen area. In doing so he sought to set the conditions to assist a much bigger break-out by the Americans in the west, which the US armies were preparing to make after securing the Cotentin Peninsula and then on 29 June capturing the port of Cherbourg. The harder Monty attacked around Caen, the more he drew German attention and their forces away from the US sector in the west, but it was a costly endeavour.

Mercifully, the Sherwood Rangers' part in Monty's grand plan was to be a passive one. On 17 July the regiment was ordered to relieve the American 67th Armoured Battalion of the 2nd US Armoured Division in the Caumont area, in order to allow the Americans to reorganise their forces for the forthcoming break-out in the west. Caumont was situated less than ten miles to the southwest of Hottot and was a relatively quiet sector of the line. Most of the surrounding villages and countryside had been untouched by the fighting, which made for a pleasant contrast to the battle-scarred areas around Tilly that we were used to. Tasked to take over the role of manning the 67th Battalion's static forward positions, the main hardships came in the form of the requirement to copy the American habits of wearing helmets and camouflaging our vehicles with foliage. We also had to dig slit trenches, but this latter aspect was a necessity born of the intermittent shelling of our positions, rather than a requirement to follow foreign field discipline. When pulled back to a leaguer during operations, we had rarely dug slit trenches, as there was precious little time even to sleep. At Caumont it was different and, although not heavy, the shelling did cause casualties.

If we were out of the tank, or the main engine was switched off and the vehicle was running on the auxiliary power of the small petrol engine used to charge the batteries, we could usually hear the shells coming. A high-pitched whistle produced by its supersonic properties announced the approach of an incoming projectile and provided a few seconds of warning time to find the shelter of a slit trench or climb into a Sherman and batten down the hatches. Mortars were different, as they travelled at subsonic speeds and didn't scream as they approached. At best you might hear a mortar bomb make a slight swishing sound before it landed with a shattering crack.

But the Moaning Minnie was by far the worst. Firing 21cm high-explosive rockets, the Wehrmacht's standard Nebelwerfer rocket launcher was capable of hurling six heavily packed explosive projectiles over a distance of three miles. The frightful noise it made sounded like the sobbing wail of some mythological creature and was caused by the rocket motor, as the incoming missile shrieked through the sky towards its target. It had a psychological effect on troops at the receiving end, who developed a particular loathing for the weapon, although compared to artillery and mortars, which tended to be fired in simultaneous salvos, the actual lethal effect of a single Nebelwefer round was often more limited. It could only launch its six rockets one at a time and the noise preceding the arrival of the first rocket usually provided enough warning to get under cover before the remainder of the incoming projectiles landed. But you didn't hesitate, especially when you were out of your tank. When I heard the first one coming towards our position in Caumont I ran to the nearest slit trench. Standing next to it was Captain Ronnie Hutton, the second in command of the HQ Squadron and one of the regimental stalwarts. Commissioned from North Irish Horse, Hutton was a tough Ulsterman who had won an MC in the desert. I don't know why he didn't take immediate advantage of his proximity to several feet of below-ground cover. But whether through a coolness under fire, or a lack of awareness, I didn't bother to find out. Pushing him roughly into the trench I dived in on top of him, as the heavy weight of explosive landed with an almighty bang. I felt the edge of its blast wave wash over the top of the trench as large fragments of metal scythed through the air above us. We counted the other five rockets in before climbing out of the trench. It was an interesting way for a junior second lieutenant to meet a man like Ronnie Hutton. After dusting ourselves off, Ronnie asked me why I had pushed him in. I said something about rank having its privileges, but omitted to mention that he was also in my way. Ronnie roared with laughter and it was the start of a relationship with a man who was to save my bacon in very different circumstances in the future.

During the time spent at Caumont, we didn't conduct any operations and, apart from the shelling, manning a relatively quiet sector of the line provided the opportunity to engage in less warlike soldierly pursuits. We traded our rations of bully beef with the French civilians for eggs, cheese, cider and their fiery Calvados. We also bought live chickens for a packet of cigarettes. We would keep them in the tank when on the move and they seemed quite content roosting in an ammunition box with a bit of straw in it. They would also strut happily around the confines of the Sherman and seemed to relish pecking Gartside on the back of his neck, as he sat forward manning the hull machine gun. They laid eggs, although too much firing in the tank tended to make them bomb happy and then they would refuse to lay. When that happened they went into the pot, much to the delight of Gartside.

We also had time to write letters and mail from home arrived regularly. Our letters were not allowed to contain any references to operations concerning units, locations or activities. In reality, few of us had any wish to expose our loved ones to such matters or give them any sense of the dangers we faced. Instead we preferred to keep to mundane topics, such as the weather, news of family members and whether a recent batch of fags sent from England had arrived. However, all letters were subject to censorship. While officers were allowed to sign their own envelopes to attest that the contents did not contain any reference to sensitive issues, the men had to present their letters to their troop leaders in unsealed envelopes, so they could be checked and censored by us prior to posting. When Martin first brought a letter he had written home for me to check and sign, he was embarrassed; I expect as much for the poor standard of his English as for anything that it contained. However, I had no desire to read the private correspondence of one of my soldiers and came to a common agreement with my troop. If they promised not to write about classified subjects, I would simply sign the letter for the benefit of the official censor without reading it. While we wrote a lot of letters, we were overjoyed to receive them. Those who have not seen military service overseas will never be able to understand what a letter from home means to a soldier's morale. Familiar handwriting and domestic subjects, however banal, provided an abstract link to the normality of the outside world and reminded us that there were things that were more important to us than war. All those devoted parents and wives who wrote regularly to their menfolk did more to bolster their spirits than they can imagine.

There were also opportunities to make forays away from the line. Mine came from an unexpected quarter when I was told to report to regimental headquarters. Being a young subaltern, I expected it was to receive a bollocking for some misdemeanour I had committed, and I racked my brains to work out what I might have done wrong, as I made my way to the unit's RHQ that had been established in an old Norman farmhouse. I became even more wary when I was told to accompany a dispatch rider to an unknown destination for an un-specified purpose. I was none the wiser as I sped up the main Tilly to Bayeux road on the back of an army-issue Norton motorbike. I noted how the dispatch rider dropped a gear, twisted the throttle hard and put his head down as we approached a large open crossroads near the small village of Jerusalem. He didn't slow down for the military policemen who popped up from slit trenches on either side of the road, but simply twisted the throttle even harder as we shot across the intersection and sped on towards Tilly.

The bike slowed down a mile or so beyond the crossroads and turned off the main road on to a dirt track that led to the remains of a large house, which had been seriously damaged by shellfire. Its rider stopped and motioned me towards what remained of a broken staircase that was open to the elements within the shattered building. The house had nothing about it to indicate that it was some form of military establishment and I drew my Luger as I made my way cautiously up the steps. I stopped at the top of the landing. The sky poked through large holes in the roof as I checked out several empty rooms before proceeding to a closed wooden door at the other end of a long corridor. I thought about knocking, but instead pushed it open with my pistol at the ready and entered a room that contained a large bed in its centre. The bed contained a figure hidden under the covers. I beaded the bedclothes with the Luger and shouted a challenge, when they were thrown back sharply to reveal a fully clothed grinning captain of the Royal Army Service Corps. It was my brother Geoffrey and it was the first time we had set eyes on each other in three years. I was overjoyed to see him.

Geoffrey had joined the RASC at the start of the war. He had fought in France in 1940 and had been through the evacuation, where he narrowly missed going down with the Cunard liner the *Lancastria* when it was bombed by the Luftwaffe and sunk off St-Nazaire. Geoffrey was on his way out to the ship in a small boat when the attack took place and he watched it go down with the loss of over 4000 lives. He had then served in the desert in a logistics unit supporting 7th Armoured Brigade and had gone on to see action at the landings in Sicily and Italy. Now he was supporting the division in Normandy. We slapped each other on the back, shared a brew and caught up on the years that had passed. He had heard from my parents that I was serving in the Sherwood Rangers and had sent the dispatch rider from his unit to find me. I wanted to show him my troop and he agreed to come back to the regiment with me. Driving back down the Tilly road in his jeep, Geoffrey explained the significance of the military policemen at the Jerusalem crossroads. The intersection was on a main supply route and had been bracketed by German artillery. The MPs' job was to marshal traffic across during pauses in the shellfire and the roughly dug graves at the side of the road indicated that it was a dangerous business. After being waved across, we didn't hang about as my brother put his foot down.

On reaching the regiment, I made a point of introducing Geoffrey to John Semken, who had resumed command of A Squadron after Major Makins had been wounded. He then met some of the troop and

I showed him Aim. I was struck by the fact that my brother showed a marked disinclination to climb inside the tank. He later admitted to me that he knew what happened to tankers on the battlefield and the risks we took. Geoffrey had seen the consequences of a brew-up when he commanded an ambulance detachment in North Africa. He was also aware of the casualty lists and had seen the grisly state of knocked-out tanks that had been recovered from the forward areas. Consequently, he had no desire to get in a tank, particularly one that belonged to his kid brother. Geoffrey used to bully me as a child and we had not been close as siblings, but from that moment on he treated me differently and demonstrated a new and profound respect that was to last for the rest of his life.

The spell the regiment spent at Caumont was the longest period we had enjoyed between operations and was a time of providence in more ways than one. I not only got to see my brother, but Semken had returned to command the squadron and Leslie Skinner had also rejoined the regiment. Desperate to get back to the unit and feeling that he had sufficiently recovered from his wounds, the padre had discharged himself from hospital in England and made his own way back across the Channel by bluffing that he was a Sherwood Rangers officer. While he clearly had some explaining to do to the army chaplains' department, which might have prevented his return to the unit, Skinner was revered in the regiment and there was not a man who was not glad to see him back. We were also fortunate not to have been involved in Operation Goodwood. Launched on 18 July, the offensive had petered out two days later having advanced only six miles with the loss of over 200 British tanks to well-placed screens of German anti-tank guns. While costly, Goodwood kept the bulk of German panzer divisions in Normandy tied down around Caen as the Americans prepared to begin their decisive break-out in the west. On 25 July they launched Operation Cobra. Facing only two of the enemy's armoured formations, by the end of the month the US 1st and 3rd armies had broken out of their sector, were driving on Saint-Lô and were poised to fan out into Brittany. With the gains made by Cobra the whole atmosphere changed and the Sherwood Rangers received orders to recommence operations as the British and Canadian armies prepared to exploit the success of the Americans along the entire length of their own sectors of the front line. The Sherwood Rangers' role in the general push began on 30 July and the day before it started John Semken informed me that 5 Troop would be leading it.

8

BREAKOUT

Nestling in a shallow wooded valley three miles southwest of Caumont, the hamlet of Briquessard is little more than a cluster of houses centred around a small sloping village-green road junction. Although unremarkable, capturing Briquessard formed a preliminary part of Operation Bluecoat, as it was on one of the chosen points at which a hole would be punched through the German front line. Three divisions of the British XXX Corps would then make a bold ten-mile thrust to the south to seize the Mont Pinçon massif. With a height of 1188 feet, Mont Pinçon is the highest feature in Normandy and dominates the surrounding countryside. On a clear day it is possible to make out the spires of Bayeux's cathedral from the top of its steep wooded slopes. As the entire area over which the British planned to advance would be under observation, holding the massif was a key element of the enemy's defensive posture. The success of Operation Bluecoat would depend on how quickly Mont Pinçon could be captured, so it lacked the usual lengthy planning preparation that had preceded previous British offensives. It was also conceived in haste to keep up with the Americans' advance in the west. As well as protecting the left flank of their advance, Bluecoat was also designed to exploit the swift progress of US forces, to assist in bringing about a predicted collapse of the whole German position in Normandy. As a consequence, an emphasis was placed on the speed of the advance and we were told to throw caution to the wind; but that entailed risk.

Mont Pinçon is also the gateway to a region of Calvados known as La Suisse Normande, due to the alpine-like appearance of its landscape. Consisting of steep forested ridges interspersed with undulating hedged farmland cut by meandering river valleys, it is bocage country at its worst and would require close co-operation between infantry and tanks. The Sherwood Rangers were tasked with supporting the infantry of the 43rd Wessex Division. They had landed in France on 23 June, so we had not worked with them before, but the reputation of their divisional commander preceded them. Some of the divisional commanders the regiment supported, like Douglas Graham of 50th Division, were considered to be good men and were popular with their troops and ours. But Major General Ivor Thomas stood out for all the wrong reasons. Between 10 and 13 July, in another failed attempt to capture Hill 112, Thomas's division had suffered 40 per cent casualties, which earned him the nickname of the 'Butcher'. In the Sherwood Rangers we preferred to call him 'von Thoma', after a German general who had been captured in the desert; not least because we believed that many under Thomas's command were more frightened of him than they were of the Germans.

Of wiry build and with small piercing eyes set above a clipped bristly moustache, Ivor Thomas was an undoubtedly brave soldier, having won two MCs and a DSO as an artillery officer in the First World War. Determined and committed to his profession as he was, Thomas had a fiery temperament, was intense and was completely devoid of any sense of humour. He was also a micromanager. Quick to meddle in the detail of his brigades and battalions, he had a penchant for sacking their brigadiers and colonels. If they couldn't put their hands on the detail he demanded or if he believed that they were

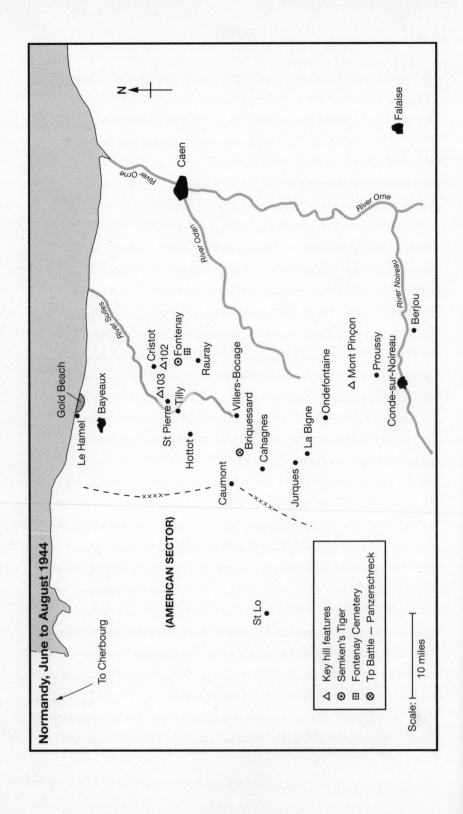

Normandy, June to August 1944

N

To Cherbourg

Gold Beach

Le Hamel
Bayeaux

River Sulles

River Orne

Caen

River Orne

River Odon

Falaise

River Noireau

Berjou

Proussy

Conde-sur-Noireau

△ Mont Pinçon

Ondefontaine

La Bigne

Jurques

Cahagnes

⊗ Briquessard

Villers-Bocage

Rauray

⊙ Fontenay
⊞
△102

Cristot
△103

St Pierre

Tilly

Hottot

(AMERICAN SECTOR)

Caumont

×××× ××××

St Lo

△ Key hill features
⊙ Semken's Tiger
⊞ Fontenay Cemetery
⊗ Tp Battle — Panzerschreck

Scale: |—————| 10 miles

not moving fast enough, or pushing hard enough, regardless of the losses their units were suffering, he had absolutely no compunction in relieving them of command. I saw 'von Thoma' on several occasions, as he traversed the battlefield in his armoured car to harass his commanders. Although I never spoke to him and, as events were to demonstrate, he looked every inch the thoroughgoing shit he was supposed to be. In any command, the senior officer does much to set the tone and style of the rest of a formation's leadership. In the 43rd Division, Thomas's brittle manner flowed downwards to many of his battalion and company commanders. A Squadron and 5 Troop had been tasked with supporting the 5th Dorsets in the attack on Briquessard and the battalion commander and the officer commanding the company that they would be working with were no exception.

The day before the attack, John Semken spent the morning at the headquarters of the 5th Dorsets tying up the details for taking the village and securing the surrounding area to facilitate the subsequent advance of the regiment and the 43rd Division's 130th Infantry Brigade. He returned later that day in high dudgeon and told me I had to get myself up to 5th Dorset's battalion headquarters to discuss the arrangements for attacking Briquessard with the company that my troop would be supporting. He didn't elaborate on the cause of his irritation, although he indicated that I would find out why when I met up with the infantry. That afternoon I returned to the leaguer equally frustrated. The infantry company commander of the Dorsets was a major called Braithwaite, who clearly had little idea of how to use tanks. There was no hard and fast rule regarding whether infantry or tanks should lead in an advance, as it would usually depend on the circumstances. The ground we would be advancing into consisted of narrow winding tracks flanked by hedgerows and thick woods. In essence it was good ambush country, which dictated that the company's lead platoons should advance on our flanks and slightly ahead of us, where they could flush out snipers and grenadiers armed with Panzerfausts. We would then be on hand to move forward and deal with MG42 positions and any armour that might make an appearance. It was a format born of experience that we had developed with the 49th and 50th infantry divisions and it depended on close co-operation. But Braithwaite was arrogant and naïve and was having none of it. No doubt he could tell I was relatively junior to him and so he was not interested in listening to me. He insisted that the tanks should lead and he might have pulled rank on me if I had been wearing any insignia. However, I didn't give him the opportunity to discern that I was only a second lieutenant and flatly refused.

My spat up with Major Braithwaite didn't augur well. When we went to marry up with his company on the start line for the attack on the village in the early hours of the next morning, we discovered that they weren't there. The creeping barrage had been dispensed with, as it had been decided that we would advance with support from the gunners on call if we needed it. Without the usual sound of artillery, and in the absence of the infantry, it seemed eerily quiet as we waited in a wood situated on the higher ground a few hundred yards to the north of Briquessard. The light was improving and a heavy dank mist hung in the trees; I was wondering what to do when I heard a sharp explosion and the crackle of small-arms fire coming from the direction of the village. Visibility was down to about a hundred yards as I led the troop in the direction of the firing along a sloping track down towards Briquessard. As we got closer, the mist began to clear and the wood, which had previously seemed so devoid of life, was suddenly full of small groups of khaki figures sheltering among the trees. The infantry weren't going forward and the rifle and machine-gun fire had died down to a few desultory Bren gun bursts and the odd snap of a Lee Enfield. It didn't appear to be aimed at anything in particular. Then a jeep appeared out of the parting mist. It bounced along the track towards us and Dixon slewed the tank to one side to let it go by. As it passed, I looked down and saw that Braithwaite was lying on a stretcher that was strapped lengthways on to a metal frame fixed to the back of the vehicle. One of the major's feet was a mangled mess of blood and hastily applied bandages, which suggested that he had trodden on a German Schu-mine. The look that passed between us, as the jeep bounced up the wooded track and took him back to the rear, said it all.

The Germans made prolific use of different types of mines. The Teller mine was an anti-tank weapon. About the same size as a large dinner plate, it was three inches thick and contained about twelve pounds of TNT; sufficient explosive to blast the track off a tank, penetrate its armoured belly plate or blow a soft-skinned vehicle to pieces. Activated by 200 pounds or more of pressure, it was unlikely to be set off by a man stepping on it. To combat enemy infantry, the most common anti-personnel device used by the Germans was the Schu-mine. Consisting of a small wooden box with minimum metal content, to avoid detection by a metal detector, the Schu-mine had a seven-ounce explosive charge that was capable of taking an individual's foot off and the unfortunate Braithwaite had stepped on one. Ill-fated as the major was, he was lucky not to have stepped on the far more deadly German anti-personnel device known as the 'S' mine. Also known as the 'Bouncing Betty', when triggered the 'S' mine threw up a metal canister full of hundreds of ball-bearings that would detonate at waist-height and spray its lethal contents in all directions, within a radius of a hundred yards. Designed to seriously maim rather than kill, a soldier's genitalia were particularly vulnerable to the 'S' mine, which was a feature that made it a weapon that was particularly feared by Allied troops.

Mounted in tanks, we were safe from anti-personnel mines. But bereft of their commander and undoubtedly concerned at the presence of mines in the leafy floor of the wood, the infantry melted out of sight into what was left of the receding mist. Briquessard lay a couple of hundred yards distant beyond the trees and no company officer stepped forward to take over from the hapless Braithwaite. I briefed the troop over the radio that we would be advancing forward without the infantry and needed to keep our eyes peeled for German anti-tank teams. Corporal Lane's Sherman was a tactical bound behind mine and he replied in the affirmative, confirming that he understood my orders. Martin's own acknowledgement was equally precise and to the point, as he rechecked the main gun to make sure that we had a round up the spout and that the safety was off; he simply said, 'Tha fooking boogers. We sh'll ay do it ussens then.' And with that I spoke into the microphone and ordered Dixon to begin moving forward cautiously.

Driving through a wooded area in a tank and entering a village without infantry is a dodgy business. But there was little choice. The rest of the regiment with the 130 Brigade of the 43rd Division was behind us and they were waiting for 5 Troop to clear Briquessard so that the general advance could begin. Additionally, working without infantry was also something that we had become accustomed to. Accounting for only 17 per cent of the total British forces in Normandy, due to the heavy casualties they had suffered, there was always a shortage of infantry throughout the Normandy campaign. Not having them with us had not stopped us before and it was not something that I was about to raise with Semken, especially as the operational imperative had been placed on speed and the need to take risks. So we cracked on down the track, keeping a distance of about a hundred yards between each of the tanks. If Aim was hit, the other two Shermans behind me would then have time and space to do something about it. The mist was clearing, but it was still patchy and pockets of fog clung to the ground between the trunks of the trees. Glancing over the rear deck, I had lost sight of Corporal Lane when the wall of a large house suddenly loomed out of the grey murk on the side of the track beside me. It heralded that we had hit the edge of Briquessard, as beyond it the track opened on to a road running through the village. We slowed the tank and crawled forward to where the end of the track intersected with the road and stopped. Forty yards to our front was a small sloping triangular village-green junction flanked by cottages on either side. I scanned the windows and gardens of each of the houses, but couldn't see anything that gave away the presence of the enemy. Apart from the idling throb of our diesel and the mush of radio static in my ears, the village was quiet and the mist continued to lift.

I waited to catch sight of Lane's tank coming along the track behind us and then told the driver to advance to the cottages on the right-hand side of the green. Dixon crashed through the gears to build up some power in the engine and we lurched forward, shot across the elevated side of the grassed road junction and stopped outside a neat white-fronted cottage. I reported that I was firm on the radio and was about to call Lane's Sherman forward when a bloody great explosion ripped into the grass bank a few feet to the left of where Aim had stopped.

The enemy bazooka team located less than thirty yards away in the garden of one of the cottages on the other side of the green must have panicked. Their second round was also a miss and went high over my head, shattering the roof of the cottage next to us and showering the tank in shards of slate. I was already shouting fire-control orders into the mike before the Germans managed to get their third shot in. Martin traversed the turret fast to the left, firing the coaxial .30 calibre as he went. Stamping on the main armament fire button as soon as the turret slewed to a stop, he was spot on with the first HE shell. He then swivelled the turret a few inches from left to right as he continued to hose the front of the houses down with machine-gun fire. Mayo had already slammed another 75mm round into the breech by the time I slapped Martin hard on the shoulder again. I watched the second round impact among a score of scurrying figures. They were trying desperately to get out of the gardens and escape the heavy weight of fire that we were pouring back at them by running between the houses. But at that range we couldn't miss and machine-gun bullets and shell fragments cut them down to a man.

It was over almost as soon as it had started. The drills in the turret and Martin and Mayo's speed of reaction had been excellent, proving that in such engagements there are only the quick and the dead. I grabbed my Schmeisser and dismounted, as Lane's tank broke into the village and covered us. The once well-ordered cottage gardens were strewn with enemy dead. When I saw them, I was surprised that they had missed with their bazooka. The bodies of the men sprawled across the well-cut lawns and flowerbeds were Fallschirmjäger. Wearing their distinctive cut-down helmets and baggy jump smocks, the German paratroopers were part of the Luftwaffe and were considered to be elite troops. They might have been expecting to encounter our infantry first, having heard the explosions of mines in the wood and the sudden arrival of tanks may have caught them off guard. We had not come across German paras in Normandy before and the weapon that they engaged us with was another first. Instead of the ubiquitous Panzerfausts, they had used a Panzerschreck. Unlike the Panzerfaust, which was a disposable one-shot weapon, the Panzerschreck was a five and a half foot long bazooka that fired an 88mm fin-stabilised anti-tank rocket and, as we had found out, could be reloaded. We had been well within its slightly longer range of 150 yards and had its rocket hit us it would have had no difficulty in penetrating the armour of our Sherman. Intrigued, I picked it up and slung it on the back decks of the tank. Later it was sent back up the line and the top brass were delighted, as it was the first German bazooka to be captured in Normandy.

With the destruction of the German bazooka team and their supporting infantry, I reported back to the squadron that Briquessard had been cleared of the enemy and climbed back into Aim to await their arrival. Minutes later I heard the heavy rumble of a large body of tanks on the wooded track behind us. The sun had burned off the last traces of mist and promised a glorious day of blue skies. Sitting in the turret waiting for the regiment to arrive, I was feeling somewhat pleased with myself. Then I first noticed the lines of Teller mines spread across the road exiting the village, which the entire unit was minutes away from driving down. Any sense of elation evaporated quickly as I scrambled down from the turret and dashed across the green to start removing them. I picked the mines up by the carrying handles attached to their sides and tossed them into the verge one after the other. The first Sherman was already turning at the junction on the green as I got the last mine off the road. I stood back as the commander waved at me from his turret hatch and the tank roared past me heading out of Briquessard. What I didn't know at the time was that the Teller mine has an anti-handling device. Had the German paratroopers armed them, I would have been blown to pieces as soon as I picked one of them up.

As the regiment advanced south, 5 Troop and the rest of A Squadron remained in the village. Semken ordered me to push my tanks up to its western outskirts and adopt a picket position until all of the columns of the regiment and the units that we were supporting had transited through. As we broke through the cover of the back of the houses we caught a platoon of Germans in the open in the middle of a field and immediately engaged them with machine-gun fire. We hit about half of them and took the survivors prisoner. But without our own infantry in support we didn't have the means to deal with POWs. After disarming them, searching them and taking their pay books, pistols and watches, we sent them to the rear where they would be picked up by our own troops. That there was less than a company of enemy infantry in the village indicated how thin the German line had become as they spread themselves out to meet the Allied threat that was now developing across the whole of their front. But Briquessard was also an indication of our potential vulnerability to relatively small groups of the enemy. The nature of the terrain restricted the advance to the use of single narrow lanes, often little more than sunken farm tracks. Twisting and winding through folds in the ground and open stretches flanked by steep wooded hillsides, the terrain we would have to push through meant that there would be more ambush country ahead of us.

More hole-punching operations for Operation Bluecoat commenced the next day in support of 43rd Division. The main effort was to capture the small town of Cahagnes three miles to the south of Briquessard. A Squadron was tasked to guard the right flank of the advance, while B and C Squadrons were ordered to work with the infantry in taking the town. Given the distances involved and the fragmenting opposition we were facing, a creeping barrage was again dispensed with, but heavy bombing by the RAF preceded the attack. We watched them come in low over our heads in the early light of morning as dawn was breaking on 31 July. The sky was suddenly full of the throbbing foreboding roar of engines as hundreds of Lancasters and Halifaxes streamed black against the grey sky. The doors of their bomb bays were already open and they lumbered on in the direction of Cahagnes. We watched as the bombs began to fall and the ground beneath our feet shook as they began saturating the German positions with thousands of tons of high explosive. Great gouts of flame and clouds of dust and debris plumed ahead of us and we were glad that we were not on the receiving end of the devastating weight of firepower they were delivering on top of the enemy. But any sympathy we felt for the Germans was short-lived as the tracer of anti-aircraft fire rose up to meet the bombers. We watched in horrified fascination as the wing of a Lancaster folded up and it began to spiral to the ground. We saw the white billowing canopy of a parachute, and then a second one, pop below the doomed aircraft. We knew the Lancaster had a crew of seven and we willed more to follow, but none did, as the crumpled, spinning black shape plummeted out of sight behind a ridgeline where a thick ball of flame plumed momentarily against the horizon. Suddenly, the bombing stopped and an uncanny silence settled across the landscape until it was broken by the sound of tank engines starting up.

In two days the Sherwood Rangers had advanced five miles. B and C Squadrons overcame small pockets of enemy and, while facing numerous delays due to mined tracks, took Cahagnes with little resistance. The town itself had suffered badly from the bombing and was little more than a shattered ruin when the regiment passed through it. A Squadron advanced steadily on the right flank and accounted for a Tiger tank and a German Jagdpanther self-propelled gun. The Jagdpanther lacked a turret but had the powerful 88mm gun of a Tiger tank and the well-protected sloped armour of a Panther chassis. The one A Squadron knocked out was disabled by the combined weight of 75mm HE fire that took off one of its tracks, forcing the crew to bail out. Sergeant Dring claimed the Tiger after walking Akilla into a fire position and then using the 17-pounder to brew it up from the flank. He spotted a second Tiger, which bogged itself down, forcing its crew to abandon it. Although there were numerous other tank engagements, the distance the regiment covered in less than forty-eight hours had been greater than any previous operational advance and was an indication that the German line was beginning to fold in on itself.

On the evening of 1 August, the CO received confirmatory orders for Operation Bluecoat, which heralded the beginning of the general advance across the whole front. The regiment's axis swung to the southeast towards Mont Pinçon. The Sherwood Rangers would continue to support 130 Brigade and ahead of us lay the villages of Jurques, La Bigne and Ondefontaine, which would be our objectives. Beyond them lay the dominating feature of the massif and 43rd Division's ultimate objective. The total distance was less than five miles, but advancing on a frontage of a single road it would take a week of relentless bloody fighting to get there. The further we advanced towards Mont Pinçon, the more difficult the terrain became, as we entered deeper into Suisse Normande and the Germans sought to make the most of the advantage that the ground gave them.

The trouble started soon after driving through Jurques in a deep sunken fold of ground outside the village of La Bigne, when a pair of 88mm anti-tank guns firing from an elevated position engaged and knocked out two Shermans from one of C Squadron's troops as they crested the steep road running out of the defile. Lieutenant Jock Campbell was the leading troop commander and he and a number of his men were killed. When a second troop from C Squadron was sent forward up the road, two German self-propelled guns engaged them. The advancing Shermans managed to return fire, damaging one of the enemy armoured vehicles, but the second German self-propelled gun hit and brewed up the lead tank commanded by Lieutenant Alan Birket.

A Sherman has a dry weight of 32 tons, but fully laden with over a ton of ammunition, a full tank of fuel, the crew and all their kit, it weighs considerably more. Struck on the brow of the sharp incline and burning fiercely, with only dead or injured crewmen inside it, Birket's tank started to roll backwards down the hill, gathering speed as gravity took effect. A nose-to-tail column of Bren gun carriers and other British vehicles had built up at the bottom of the road in the defile behind where the tank had been hit and the burning Sherman was heading straight for them. With its ammunition cooking off and exploding inside the hull, one of the squadron's NCO tank commanders managed to jump aboard the blazing tank as it gathered momentum. Reaching into the driver's compartment, he succeeded in seizing one of the steering levers and slewed the tank off the road into a ditch. The NCO's presence of mind and courage averted further carnage, but there was nothing he could do for the men still inside the blazing Sherman.

Breakout

The tanks of B and C Squadrons were still burning when 5 Troop passed them later that day. Flames roared through the open hatches, which generated an updraught of air to fan the raging inferno inside them. Fed by the vehicles' ammunition propellant, fuel and oil, each tank belched thick oil-laden smoke into the sky and their steel sides glowed a dull red with the intensity of the heat. Once set ablaze, a Sherman might take twenty-four hours to burn itself out and only then, if the situation on the battlefield made it safe to do so, could the grim task of recovering the bodies of the men trapped inside begin. In the Sherwood Rangers that burden fell to the padre. Initially refused permission to attempt a recovery the day after the incident, Leslie Skinner finally got forward to the knocked-out tanks two days later. The pelvic bones he found when searching through the ashes in Birket's Sherman were the only reminders that the tank had once been crewed by human beings. In the other burned-out tank the intensity of the fire had not been as great, although the heat of the flames had fused the bodies of the three men in the turret together. I don't know how he did it, as the fibre identity discs we wore would often not survive a brew up, but Skinner was able to identify Campbell. However, after a long, vomit-inducing struggle he was unable to separate the turret crew and had to give up his attempt to remove them for burial.

Undaunted by his grisly responsibilities, Skinner returned to the site three days later and managed to extract Campbell and his crew. He buried them near a railway crossing, conducted a short funeral service over their hastily dug graves and was then violently sick again. It was only after the war that we discovered exactly what Leslie Skinner had put himself through. Throughout the campaign in northwest Europe, he was adamant that the men of the regiment who manned its fighting vehicles should not be involved in the recovery of the dead from a knocked-out tank. On one occasion, when a squadron leader offered to lend him some men to help, he refused, stating that the 'less men who live and fight in tanks have to do with this side of things the better. They know it happens, but to force it on their attention is not good.' In his own words, he considered it his 'job'. As well as ascertaining the identity of men in a burned-out Sherman and then extracting their remains for burial, Skinner also had to collect what was left of men hit by shells or blown up by mines. Picking up pieces of men, reassembling them for identification and then stitching them into blankets for burial was a fearful job, especially if they had been exposed to the ravages of the heat and flies for several days before he got to them.

While we were thankfully spared the detail, the brewed-up Shermans in the defile on the way to La Bigne were a macabre marker of the dangers we faced in advancing on a narrow front consisting of a single road. The burning hulks must have made a dreadful sight for the brand new troop commander under instruction in the tank behind me. David Alderson had joined the regiment at Caumont just before Operation Bluecoat and had been posted to A Squadron to fill the gap in the ranks of our troop leaders left by Mike Howden after he had been wounded at Hottot. Before Alderson was given command of 3 Troop, John Semken tasked me to take him under my wing and his tank was following mine as we crested the hill where the last of C Squadron's Shermans had been hit. After passing them, we swung left off the road and followed a track that ran along a ridgeline that would put us in a position to cover the rest of the squadron as they pushed on towards La Bigne. It was a sensible deployment, as Semken wanted to make sure that he had a troop of tanks in overwatch on the high ground behind him in the event that we encountered more German armour.

The position 5 Troop adopted on the ridge looked across a small wooded dale, with the rooftops of La Bigne just visible beyond it. In providing a good vantage point, it was also an exposed forward slope position, which would make us vulnerable to any 88mm guns concealed on the other side of the valley. To minimise the risk, I spread the troop out below the skyline and told all the commanders to scan the ground to our front as hard as they could with their binoculars. The sun was behind us and I was looking for anything that might betray the presence of an enemy tank or a self-propelled gun, such as the silver glint of steel from a track burnished by road use or the reflection of an optical sight. Instead, I saw a company of enemy infantry moving in column of route along the front of a pine forestry block about a quarter of a mile to our front. There must have been about 150 of them and they were marching four abreast as if on their way to a military parade, clearly unaware of our presence. I ordered the troop to engage and we opened up on them with machine-gun fire and began to shoot them down. Those who survived the initial bursts from the machine guns scattered towards the shelter of the forest. In response we switched to HE from the 75mm, deliberately aiming high into the pines to create an airburst effect to cause more casualties. By the time we had finished firing, what remained of the slaughtered company lay in crumpled heaps of field grey at the foot of the pine trees.

Packed in close order and at a range of less than 400 yards, the enemy stood little hope of surviving the combined fire of the troop's machine guns and HE shells. But not all of the tanks had engaged in the destruction we wrought at the bottom of the valley below us. Alderson's Sherman had not opened fire and I remonstrated with him, reminding him that when under instruction he was to fire when I fired. He told me that he didn't fire because he thought that it was unsporting, given that the Germans hadn't stood a chance. I gave him a bit of a blast over the net and asked him where the hell he thought he was. I think I went a bit too far when I quoted the statistics of his chances of survival and that he would shorten them considerably if he didn't learn to follow instructions and behave in the same manner as those of us with more experience. Given my own day under instruction it was something I felt guilty about afterwards, not least when David later told me of the impact my comments had made on him.

As a recently joined subaltern, David Alderson was new to battle and was yet to develop the killer instinct so ingrained in the rest of us. He had not seen what a German MG42 section could do to our infantry as they advanced in open order across a field, or the damage their anti-tank weapons could cause to our tanks. Unlike the rest of us, he had also not engaged in the regular practice of machine-gunning enemy tank crews as they bailed out of a damaged vehicle; something the Germans applied in equal measure to us. Had David been exposed to such harsh realities of war, I doubt he would have had any compunction in joining in the shooting down of the enemy company. Judging the event by today's moral values, perhaps too many of our actions and attitudes may seem brutal. However, the circumstances of total conflict seventy years ago were very different. While the general laws of war applied, we were not troubled by the overly convoluted rules of engagement that are the concern of today's modern soldiers. We were placed on the battlefield with one clear mission, which was constantly reinforced by our senior commanders; and that was to kill Germans.

The enemy were equally determined to kill as many of us as possible. With their front line broken, they fought a series of small-scale defensive battles designed to cause maximum casualties and delay our advance. Where they could, they turned every village into a strong point and every exposed junction or stretch of road into an ambush killing area. Ahead of us C Squadron had a tough time taking La Bigne, which was defended stubbornly by fanatical soldiers from the 10th SS Division, who were reluctant to surrender. The village had still not been taken by the time the daylight had faded. But von Thoma was insistent that it should be captured and the squadron was ordered to put in a night attack. Working with the 7th Hampshires, the Shermans smothered the German machine-gun positions with

HE and then the infantry had to clear the houses systematically at the point of the bayonet. With La Bigne finally captured, we passed through C Squadron and led the advance to the regiment's next objective of Ondefontaine. Lying only ten miles to the northwest of Mont Pinçon, the ground became more difficult and our progress met with constant mortar and artillery fire called down by enemy observers positioned on its slope. Again the advance was conducted down a single narrow road that was flanked by high-banked hedges, providing little opportunity for a tank to manoeuvre off the road if we were engaged. The route of the advance was also exposed to the thickly wooded ridgeline of the Bois de Baron, which provided a barrier of forest that would also have to be penetrated before the village could be attacked.

None of the troop commanders relished the prospect of being the lead troop in such country and Semken shared and rotated the task between us. When my turn came it meant that I would always be the lead tank. In training, the RAC had taught us that the troop sergeant or corporal should be in control of the lead tank in the advance, so that the troop leader was located in the middle of the troop and better positioned to command in the event of a contact. Given the risk the lead tank faced in being brewed up first, the procedure in most troops was to rotate which tank led, sharing the task between the troop leader and the two troop NCOs. But RAC doctrine and common regimental practice did not take into account the fact that Harrison was my troop sergeant. There was no way that he was going to take a turn at leading and if the senior NCO wouldn't do it I could hardly expect Corporal Lane to. As a consequence I always put Aim at the front of the troop and each time I did it when leading the whole squadron it became a little harder.

Being the leading tank of the leading troop in the leading squadron advancing down the axis of a single road was, quite frankly, bloody dangerous. It dramatically increased the chances of being brewed up by a Teller mine, Panzerfaust, anti-tank gun or another tank, as you would invariably be the first Sherman to encounter them. It brought a dread expectation that every hill you crested or bend you turned might be your last, as you anticipated the ear-splitting crack and high-velocity whine of an 88mm round being fired at you. If you were engaged, you hoped that it missed and that you could get out of the line of fire and wouldn't be trapped in its killing area by high-banked hedges on either side of the tank. If it hit you, you hoped that it wouldn't kill or seriously maim you and that you would have the time and the strength to bail out before the second round arrived and before the tank turned into a raging inferno. If you managed to get out, you hoped you had the presence of mind to bail out over the back decks and prayed that you and the crew would be able to make it to the safety of the nearest ditch or solid piece of cover before the enemy bracketed you with machine-gun or mortar fire and cut you down.

My heart would sink when the squadron commander told me that 5 Troop would be in the lead. The crew hated it too, as they knew what it meant and they had seen what had befallen other crews. They would bitch and moan when I told them that we would be in the lead, constantly claiming that it was somebody else's turn and that it was 'Not fooking on'. If I knew that we were leading, I would deliberately not tell them the night before and would leave it to the last moment before we mounted up, as it was better to allow them a night of sleep without the worry of what might be awaiting us on the morrow. But they never hesitated to mount up and I admired them for it. For the ordinary crewman it was an exceptionally trying period. They spent most of their time sitting cocooned inside the steel confines of the tank, with little visibility of the outside world and little else to think about but whether the next round would hit them, main them or kill them. It must have played havoc with their nerves, but they never let me down. It was easier for the officers and to a lesser extent for the NCO tank commanders, as we always had plenty to occupy our

Me as an officer cadet before being commissioned into the Royal Armoured Corps.

omanry Shermans of the
ɪ Armoured Brigade packed
ɟht on the deck of an LCT
route across the Channel
Normandy on D–1.

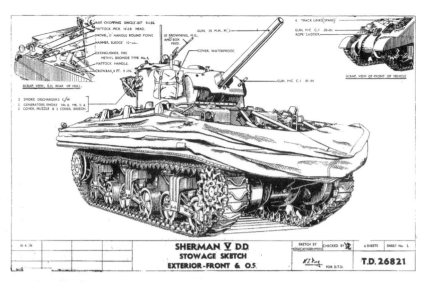

Top A DD variant of the Sherman tank that two of the squadrons of the regiment used to swim ashore on D-Day.

Above A Sherman M4A2 of HQ Squadron in a typical leaguer in an orchard in Normandy. Note the field grave of a German soldier, which suggests the position was formerly occupied by the enemy.

Left 'Semken's Tiger'. The first German Tiger Mark1 to be captured in Normandy after John Semken's frantic engagement with the 54-ton monster in the narrow streets of the village of Fontenay.

Right Sergeant George Dring MM and the crew of his Sherman 'Akilla'. Dring as the top-scoring tank ace in the Sherwood Rangers.

Below right Captain Jimmy McWilliam's Sherman knocked out in the fierce fighting to take Gheel in early September 1944. Despite the poor quality of the photo, the penetrating hole made by the handheld Panzerfaust is clearly visible.

Below Corporal Ken Mayo, my loader operator. Like the rest of the crew, he was a desert veteran. He was the one member of my tank who accepted me from the start.

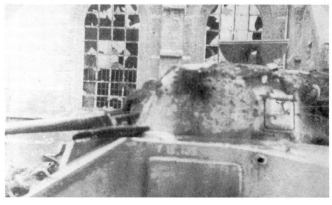

Below A Sexton 25-pounder self-propelled artillery piece of the Essex Yeomanry in the Nijmegen area in September 1944. Note the American glider in the background of the 82nd Airborne Division that the regiment fought with during Operation Market Garden.

Above American GIs of the 84th US Infantry Division march past the regiment's tanks outside Geilenkirchen in Novemb 1944. A Dingo (Humber Scout Car) is positioned between the two Sherman

Left Me standing on the back of my Sherman (commander in tank suit closet to the camera) duri Operation Pepperpot in February 1945, where 5 Troop fired over nine tons of 75mm HE shells.

Below left PBI (poor bloody infantry) riding on Sherwood Rangers' Shermans as the regiment advanced through a shell-damaged village on the Dutch–German frontier during the winter fighting

Right A Squadron officers on leave in Brussels in November 1944. I am standing on the left of Dickie Holman in the back row. John Semken and Ronnie Hutton area seated from left to right. It was a final foursome before the character of the squadron began to change.

Below right Major Bill Enderby in Germany, A Squadron Leader after John Semken, standing in the left-hand commander's hatch of his Sherman. Note the extra lengths of track on the front glacis plate that were positioned to provide additional protection.

Below Polished and repainted after battle, the Sherwood Rangers Yeomanry parade through German streets in May 1945 a week after the Nazi surrender.

Above One of the mass graves and some of the 30,000 unfortuna[inmates at the Sanbostel concentration camp in Germany that became known as 'Little Belse[which the regiment helped liberate in May 1945.

Left Padre Leslie Skinner, the Sherwood Rangers' chaplain, who preferred to operate at the sharp er and had the grisly task of extractin[the bodies of the regiment's dead from burned out tanks.

Right Lieutenant General B[Horrocks briefing troops of [regiment. A popular comman[he injected vital energy [enthusiasm into XXX Co[after he took command of [formation that the Sherw[Rangers regularly suppor[

ove Field Marshal Bernard Montgomery with Major General Ivor Thomas, the commander ↓3rd Wessex Division, who was nicknamed 'von Thoma', as most of his commanding cers were more scared of him than the Germans.

Below Stanley Christopherson, the regiment's third commanding officer after less than a week of fighting in Normandy after his two predecessors were wounded and killed. He went on to command until the end of the war and was a hugely popular CO.

Why die for Stalin?

In dying for Stalin your soldiers are not dying for democracy or the preservation of the democratic form of government—they are dying for the establishment of Communism and a form of Stalinist tyranny throughout the world. Furthermore, they are not dying for the preservation of the integrity of small nations (England's old war-cry) but are dying so that Poland shall be a Soviet state; so that the Baltic States shall be incorporated in the Soviet Union and so that Soviet influence shall extend from the Baltic to the Balkans.

Every British soldier who lays down his life in this war is not only a loss to his own country; he is a loss to the common cause of European civilization. Germany's and England's quarrel is a form of traditional rivalry. It is more in the nature of a private quarrel which Germany did not seek. The Soviet Union's quarrel, however, is a quarrel with the WORLD. It is a quarrel with our common heritage and with all those values—moral, spiritual, cultural and material which we have, all of us—Englishman and German alike—recognised, cherished and striven to maintain. TO DIE FOR THE DESTRUCTION OF THESE VALUES IS TO DIE IN VAIN.

Stalin, with all the diabolical power of Communism behind him, is seeking to profit from Britain's and Germany's preoccupation. The amount of influence which Britain can exercise on Stalin can be measured by the latter's undisputed claims to the sovereign territories of other nations. The only controlling influence left on Stalin is the strength and tenacity of the German Wehrmacht and of the European volunteers who support Germany in her fight for the survival of Europe, and its position as the cradle of our common civilization.

Every British soldier who dies for Stalin is another nail in the coffin of Britain's hopes of maintaining a "Balance of Power" in Europe.

Should the "Equilibrium" pass to Stalin then the equilibrium of the world is at an end.

THOSE WHO ARE ABOUT TO DIE—THINK IT OVER!

E113/3.44

An example of the German propaganda leaflets fired over our lines during the winter fighting, which was very helpful in supplementing our lavatory paper rations.

At the reception at the French Residency after France's Ambassador awarded me the *Légion d'honneur* in 2016. I am in the back row, far right.

minds. Taking orders, passing them on, organising the next day's operation, map reading, commanding the tank and the rest of the troop and working on the net to synchronise our movements with the other troops in the squadron were all welcome distractions from thinking about the fatal reckoning that might be waiting for us along the next stretch of road or around the next corner. Nevertheless, when it came it was frightening.

Covering 1000 yards of exposed road dominated by wooded high ground requires cautious movement. I advanced first in Aim under the static cover of Corporal Lane's tank and would go firm a tactical bound ahead of him. His tank would then join mine and we then repeated the process, with Harrison bringing up the rear with the Firefly. We had covered 400 yards when the first high-velocity AP round screamed past us at over 3000 feet per second, from somewhere in the trees above us on the right flank. I had just enough time to say 'What the fuck was that?' before my brain engaged and I yelled 'Anti-tank! Reverse!' into the microphone. Dixon slammed the tank into gear and pulled us back, slewing the tracks hard to get us off the road while avoiding putting us flank on to the likely location of the enemy. As Dixon maneouvred the tank, I was desperately trying to identify where the shot had come from. We were lucky that we could get off the road and into a hull-down position. We were luckier still that the second shot missed and that Lane had picked up where it had come from. He started pumping HE into the wooded edge of a sloping corner of a cornfield. I was calling out directions over the net and Semken was already feeding them back to the battery of Sextons that was in close support and moving to a position where he could adjust their fall of shot. Seconds later the air parted with the arrival of the first 25-pounder round, which exploded short and to the right of the corner of the wood. I heard Semken give a 'Right fifty, add two hundred' correction followed by the words 'fire for effect' over the command net, and less than a minute later the first battery salvo of eight artillery shells came in, followed thirty seconds later by the next batch. The gunners from the Essex Yeomanry had been with us since D-Day and as their feat at Gold Beach demonstrated, they were good.

An on target battery fire mission was enough to neutralise a concealed German 88mm anti-tank gun or an armoured vehicle. Although unlikely to destroy the latter, it would usually be enough to force it to pull out. But there were other tanks to deal with, which made for slow and dangerous progress. Mines also hampered the squadron's advance and engineers had to be called forward to lift them. The sappers had to be protected by infantry and tanks to take out the MG42s that were routinely positioned to cover the places where they had been laid, which made for further small-scale actions as we seemed to inch forward. With the Germans dominating the high ground, we were also under constant mortar fire. All hatches, except mine, had to be kept closed down and to leave the armoured safety of the tank was to invite serious risk of being hit by fragments. All bodily functions, therefore, had to be completed using empty brass shell cases, which we retained for the purpose. The pressure to keep driving on was relentless and if we weren't moving at night we slept in the tank during brief halts and cooked on the turret floor using the small primus stove.

There was no time, and it was too dangerous, to stop and get out to make a meal. We made do with hard tack biscuits, the contents of a tin and compo chocolate as we continually repeated the cycle of moving, reacting to a contact further up the road and fighting through the next village. Throughout it all we smoked like troopers and after six days of constant moving, fighting and living in the tank, we absolutely stank. It rained on occasion and our sodden clothes added to the stench as they dried out. But for the most part the weather was glorious, which added to the danger. The heat and our tracks churned the roads to dust and the clouds of fine-ground chalky powder our vehicles threw up provided another invitation for the German indirect fire observers to rain down more artillery shells and mortar bombs on top of us. C Squadron passed through us and Ondefontaine eventually fell, but the advance beyond the village continued. After nearly a week of living and fighting in such conditions, we were close to the end of our physical and mental endurance.

We were sick with fatigue. The constant pressure to keep advancing, the lack of rest and the inability to get out of our tanks was taking its toll. Our eyes were red raw with the grit that comes from lack of sleep and it became an increasing effort to stay awake and keep focused. I had to chide and cajole the crew to remain alert, but I could feel that my own span of attention was slipping. Ahead of us, Mont Pinçon had still not been captured and the divisional commander ordered repeated frontal attacks to be made up its steep slopes by the men of the Wiltshire Regiment. Von Thoma bullied his brigade commanders in 43rd Division and they in turn bullied the commanding officers of the infantry battalions. The men of the 4th Wiltshire suffered grievously for his insistence. They were cut to pieces on their start line and lost their CO when he went forward to get his battalion moving. Our own commanding officer was becoming concerned at our condition and the regimental medical officer had warned him that we would struggle to remain effective as a unit if we were not rested. Quite how he managed it I do not know, but on 7 August, after six days and nights without sleep, Stanley Christopherson managed to persuade the chain of command to withdraw us from the line for four glorious days of rest.

Two days later, Lieutenant General Brian Horrocks came to visit us at our leaguer at Beaumont near Villers-Bocage. Horrocks had recently taken over command of XXX Corps of which von Thoma's 43rd Division formed a part. But the new corps commander was a very different type of general to Thomas. Horrocks had recently returned to front-line duty after recovering from serious wounds sustained in the desert. He was well known in the army and, unlike von Thoma, he was popular. Horrocks could take a joke and enjoyed an easy familiarity with the troops, regardless of their rank. Most importantly he was courteous and made it clear that he cared about our welfare. Horrocks knew that we had been driven hard and made a point of congratulating the unit on its achievements. He then briefed the whole regiment on the general Allied situation from a large map he had brought with him on the back of a truck. Horrocks outlined how the Americans' drive from the southwest, combined with the British thrusts from the west and the advance of the Canadians in the north from Caen, was forcing the Germans into a constricting salient around Falaise. He told us that the enemy's forces in Normandy were being encircled; he explained how they were being pounded relentlessly from the air and that they were about to face complete destruction. I can't remember much of what our corps commander said. Like most of the men I was just glad to be out of the line and alive, but it was good to know that he cared and that meant something to us.

The Sherwood Rangers went back into the line to rejoin the advance of the 43rd Division on 12 August. Mont Pinçon had been taken and the 13th/18th Hussars had played a critical role in its capture when two troops of Shermans made a daring dash to the summit up a hidden track. But the final taking of the feature had been at great cost to the infantry and some of the assaulting battalions had been reduced to less than company strength. Von Thoma's men were still battling in a southeasterly direction as part of a new operation codenamed Blackwater. The intention was to capture the town of Condé, seize the crossings over the River Noireau and then swing northeast to join the advance on Falaise. Once again, the regiment would be supporting 130 Brigade and once more we would come under the relentless driving force of von Thoma. The 43rd Division's general had lost none of his vigour. On 14 August, A Squadron was tasked with supporting the 5th Dorsets' attack on the village of Proussy and

Thomas sacked 130 Brigade's brigadier for being slow in getting his units across the start line for the assault. He also sacked one of its battalion commanders and an infantry colonel in our own 8th Armoured Brigade for what he perceived to be a lack of grip. However, our assault on Proussy was a success. As we entered the village we put HE rounds through every building that might contain a sniper or an artillery observation officer. The infantry then flushed out the German defenders from each of the houses and rounded up over a hundred prisoners. B Squadron had more trouble in clearing their objective of Saint-Denis-de-Méré and lost two tanks before securing the village and taking more prisoners. The rest of the day was spent in conducting mopping-up operations, but a route to the home bank of the Noireau, north of Condé, had been secured.

The Germans had blown all the bridges across the Noireau, which is little more than a twenty-yards-wide stream that runs north to south through a deep-cut valley of wooded hills. The river is not deep, but its steep banks and the enemy mines, sown at likely crossing points, made it an impassable obstacle for tanks without engineer support. The sappers worked throughout the night of 15 August to prepare a way across for the regiment. Under constant enemy mortar fire, called down from the thickly wooded ridgeline on the opposite bank above them, they had completed their task by first light when C Squadron began to cross with infantry on the backs of their tanks. A Squadron crossed the river further north to support C Squadron's attack along the tracks that wound their way up the sharp incline of the ridge on the other side. But it was C Squadron that bore the brunt of the fighting. Co-operation with the infantry broke down as they pushed up through the steep wooded slopes that were thick with German snipers and paratroopers armed with anti-tank weapons. Six tanks were lost to Panzerfausts and six commanders were wounded or killed. With the slopes clear of enemy infantry, A and B Squadrons took the fortified villages of Le Hamel and Berjou and the capture of the ridge on the enemy's side of the Noireau was complete.

In eleven weeks of bitter fighting the regiment's breakout from Normandy and the drive to the Noireau had cost the Sherwood Rangers two hundred casualties, including fifty tank commanders, of whom thirty-six were officers. With the capture of the ridge above the Noireau, the German defences to our immediate front disintegrated and the regiment's involvement in the fighting in Normandy ended. We pulled out of the line on 20 August. The pleasure of being able to wash again, to be free of the mud and the dust and to be able to sleep without the dangers of anti-tank rounds and mortar fire on the morrow's dawn was immeasurable. After nearly three months of fighting in the bocage, I had beaten the statistical odds of survival and I was glad to be alive. A day later forces to our north closed the Falaise Pocket and the battle for Normandy was over. The pursuit to destroy the remaining German forces in the rest of France and the Low Countries was about to begin.

9

THE GREAT SWAN

Even as the Sherwood Rangers battled up the slopes of the Berjou Ridge on 16 August, the bulk of the German army was already on the verge of annihilation at Falaise. With Polish forces under Canadian command battling from the north, the British driving from the west and the Americans from the south, the jaws of the pocket snapped shut around them five days later and victory was declared. The remnants of approximately thirty thousand SS and Wehrmacht troops who had escaped encirclement were in headlong flight and Monty issued orders to defeat all remaining enemy forces in northeast France. He planned to use all four Allied armies in Normandy to drive as fast as possible to the Seine, cut off the retreating Germans and establish a bridgehead across the river. Once across the Seine, he planned to overrun the V1 flying bomb sites that were attacking England, clear the Channel ports, push into the Low Countries and then be in a position to bounce a crossing over the Rhine and drive into Germany.

The Canadian 1st Army would clear the area to the north along the Channel coast, with the 2nd British Army advancing on the Canadians' right flank in a direction that would take them to the Seine at Vernon. To their south the US 1st and 3rd armies would drive on Paris. As part of the British 2nd Army under General Miles Dempsey, Horrocks' XXX Corps was ordered to force a crossing over the Seine at Vernon using the 43rd Wessex Division and 8th Armoured Brigade. The assault across the river would be made by the infantry of the division's 129th Brigade with the 4th/7th Dragoon Guards in support. The Sherwood Rangers were tasked with supporting 214th Brigade and would be held in reserve during the operation.

The campaign in Normandy was a bloody battle of attrition, marked by the cost of 53,000 Allied lives, including over 16,000 British and Commonwealth troops; a figure that does not include the 9000 that went missing in 21st Army Group or the 58,000 that were wounded in action. But the final destruction of the German army at Falaise was an overwhelming defeat for Hitler's forces in the west. The precise statistics may never be known, but the Germans are estimated to have sustained casualties in excess of 200,000 troops killed, wounded or missing and a similar number taken prisoner. The panzer divisions that had been fielded at the start of the battle had virtually ceased to exist. With a deployment strength of over 12,000 men and 167 tanks and self-propelled guns, only 300 men of Panzer Lehr managed to escape across the Seine, leaving all of the armoured fighting vehicles either destroyed or abandoned behind them. The sheer scale of the German defeat became apparent to us when the regiment began its advance to the Seine on 23 August and our route took us through the small French town of Chambois, twenty miles to the south of Falaise.

It had been raining hard for two days and the squadrons moved through Chambois under a grey leaden sky that seemed heavy with foreboding. As we left the town to its northwest, we came across the killing fields of the Falaise Gap where the Allied air forces and artillery had wreaked absolute devastation among the 90,000 Germans who had been trapped inside the pocket. Packed tight in retreating massed columns, there was no need for the weapon-precision technology of today to cause utter devastation and carnage. Those that had not survived the onslaught by surrendering lay in a viscous mass in the meadows on either side of the road among smashed and burned-out tanks, guns and upturned trucks that spewed their contents across the ground. Teams of horses sprawled dead in the traces of their gun limbers and carts; many with their bellies ripped open by shrapnel, which had spilled their entrails on to the ground.* Among them thousands of German dead lay thick where they had fallen, like wax figures contorted into grotesque attitudes that captured the last moments of their death. Some had arms twisted out as if in supplication, others were burned black, their shrivelled bodies fused into the twisted wreckage of vehicles. One Wehrmacht soldier had been crushed by a concrete lamppost felled by an exploding shell or rocket. Incongruous as it seems, amid all that death and destruction his demise, resulting from a piece of concrete, struck me the most.

The entire area was pervaded by the stench of death and putrefaction. Whether human or animal, the carcasses had swelled and bloated in the heat and a blizzard of perhaps a million rapacious flies lifted as we passed. Most of the Germans killed on the road had been bulldozed to its sides along with their vehicles to allow the advancing Allied columns ahead of us to pass. But we couldn't avoid driving over some of them and our tracks ground their rotting bodies further into the road that was now a sea of grisly mud. The crew was quiet. There was none of the usual chat or banter over the intercom that had grown up between us as we became closer as a team. But while we recoiled in private horror at the graphic scenes around us, in truth we felt little compassion for the dead. We had endured weeks of bitter

---

* Only the panzer divisions were motorised fully and the vast majority of other German army formations relied heavily on horse-drawn transport to tow their artillery and move supplies.

fighting at their hands and we had seen our own gruesome sights of men with their faces blown off or burned beyond recognition in a brewed-up tank. As a consequence, the thousands of dead Germans that littered the countryside around us were no more than the remnants of an enemy that had been doing its best to kill us. Regardless of how we felt, it was a relief to leave behind us the foul concentration of death that the area around Falaise had become.

The sun eventually burst through the clouds and our mood improved as the regiment pushed on towards Vernon, although the progress it made was slow. The roads were congested with Allied vehicles all heading inexorably northeast. As the Sherwood Rangers were being kept in reserve for the Seine crossing operation we were not the priority and the unit spent hours waiting for a complete American corps to cross its axis of advance. A day ahead of us, the leading brigade of 43rd Division had reached the outskirts of the town on the afternoon of 25 August. Located on the west bank of the Seine fifty miles northwest of Paris, Vernon is connected to the village of Vernonnet on the east bank by a main road span and a separate railway bridge. In 1944, the railway bridge had been destroyed in a US air raid made before the D-Day landings. With the imminent arrival of the Allied ground forces, three members of the French Resistance blew up and severely damaged a span of the road bridge rendering it impassable to vehicles. In achieving what the British and American air forces had failed to do, it was a daring act of courage that met the Allied objective of denying the Germans passage across the Seine. By the time the British reached Vernon, the Resistance had also managed to eject the SS garrison. While it meant that the 43rd Division would not have to battle its way into the town, it also meant that they would now have to mount an assault river crossing over the Seine and then build their own bridges, before the bulk of British forces could begin to advance from the bridgehead the division had been tasked to create on the other side of the river.

By the time we drove through Vernon's well-manicured leafy boulevards and into its centre on the evening of 27 August, the 129th Brigade had managed to cross the Seine and had established a small foothold on the opposite bank. But their efforts had not been without cost. A 300-foot-high heavily-wooded escarpment cut by steep chalk bluffs dominated the east bank of the river and provided a natural defensive position for a screen of German machine guns and snipers. Crossing the river in collapsible storm boats, the assault by two of the battalions of infantry had met with mixed success. Although they eventually succeeded in making it to the opposite bank many of the densely packed boats grounded midway across the river and their occupants were cut to pieces by MG42 fire from the heights above them. They incurred further losses as they fought their way doggedly up the steep wooded slopes and cleared the village of Vernonnet. Tanks of the 4th/7th Dragoon Guards were ferried across on rafts to support them, but by the time the bridgehead was secured, 43rd Division had taken several hundred casualties.

Behind them the sappers of the Royal Engineers had worked tirelessly under shellfire to build two pontoon Bailey bridges across the river, losing several boats and men in the process. The first, completed by the late afternoon, was a Class 9 bridge, which was only capable of taking lighter soft-skinned vehicles. The second, a Class 40 pontoon bridge, was designed to take tanks and was barely ready for operations early the next morning. The whole operation to force a crossing over the Seine had been conducted in haste in order to take the Germans by surprise before they had a chance to consolidate their defences on the far side. But the building of the Class 40 bridge had been delayed by heavy traffic congestion along XXX Corps' route to Vernon. The corps' engineers had been forced to wait for several hours as endless columns of American vehicles cut across their axis. Consequently, they had to work hard and fast throughout the night to build the bridge and had no time to test it before 5 Troop were ordered to be the first armour to cross it.

The speed at which the operation had been launched had achieved its objective of catching the Germans off guard. But as their forward defensive screen among the forested slopes of the east bank began to collapse in the face of the assault by 129th Brigade, the enemy launched a regimental counterattack. Although the 150th Grenadier Regiment was a scratch German force it was supported by tanks and the thinly held bridgehead the British had established was under pressure. In response, Thomas ordered the 214th Infantry Brigade of his division across the river to reinforce its sister formation. However, in helping to fight off the German counterattack, A Company of the 7th Somerset Light Infantry had become separated from its parent battalion in the thick woods on the other side of the Seine and could not be raised by radio. Von Thoma was furious and wanted a troop of tanks sent across to find the lost company. The task had fallen to 5 Troop.

Made of modular pre-fabricated 180-foot steel trusses, each capable of carrying up to forty short tons, covered by decking and supported by floating shallow-draft open boats, the Class 40 Bailey bridge was a major feat of British military engineering. However, constructed under a pressing time imperative and the whip of an angry general, an untested construction was susceptible to a strong current or an unbalanced load, which could dislodge or break apart its sections or cause them to sink. The stretch of the Seine that runs past Vernon is 600 feet wide and fast flowing and I couldn't help noticing how the bridge bowed ominously at its midsection, as the muddy brown waters of the river surged against the pontoons and looked as if they might swamp them. As far as I was concerned the 840-foot metal structure we were about to cross looked decidedly dodgy.

Random shells and mortar bombs exploded in the water and on either side of the structure, but given our predicament I decided that the crew and I, apart from the driver, would be safer standing on the back decks of the tank. The Seine is over ten feet deep and we would stand little chance of surviving if the bridge collapsed or we toppled into the river. Being the only member inside the crew compartment was not a situation that Dixon was happy with. Determined to spend as little time on the bridge as possible, he took Aim down the approach ramp and then put his foot down on the accelerator as we levelled out with the line of the water. As we shot across the clanking decking at speed, the bridge creaked and groaned with the weight of the tank and I could imagine the fixing pins shearing under the pressure of the speeding Sherman and the drag of the current. The engineers shouted at me to slow down and I was already shouting into the microphone to tell Dixon to cut his speed; but fear is a strange motivator of men and he was having none of it. As soon as I reined him in, he picked up speed again and each of the sections we crossed swayed and bobbed alarmingly. We made it to the other side and jumped into our crew stations, I gave Dixon a bollocking and the rest of the crew called him a 'fookin twat', but I don't think it bothered him in the least; he was just glad to be back on firm land.

With the rest of the troop having safely crossed the bridge at a more considered pace, we set off to marry up with the headquarters of 7 SLI. Making our way up winding wooded tracks, we found their CO near a clearing at the end of a forest ride deep in the sloping woods. The ground was thick with trees and the forest floor at their base was a tangle of brambles and bracken, which made for ideal hiding places to conceal a German armed with a Panzerfaust. The colonel of the Somersets was clearly distressed about his missing company. Its commander was a new and inexperienced major and would not have been the commanding officer's first choice to lead the battalion advance. For some strange reason, though, the divisional commander had overruled him and Thomas had dictated that A Company should form the vanguard. I said I would push further into the forest to see if I could find the hapless major and his company.

The tall stands of trees blocked out the sun overhead and the wood ahead of us looked dark and forbidding. I could see how a company could lose its bearings in the confusion of rides and tracks, but it smacked of Briquessard all over again. A single troop advancing through a wood on its own, waiting to stumble into something. Gartside and Martin beaded and traversed the forest floor with their machine guns as we advanced forward in tactical bounds, with our guns made ready and the safety catches off. I heard the whine of its turret motor before I saw the Panther. A hungry mass of grey sloped metal peeking through the trees ahead of us. I saw the flash from its muzzle a split second before I heard the crack of its 75mm. The shot was wide and splintered the trunk of a tree a few yards to our right. Martin was already on him and we got one HE round away the instant I shouted 'Fire!' We hit him without causing any obvious damage and had our second round ready to go. The Panther roared into life and pulled backwards away from us at speed, in a cloud of blue-grey engine smoke. The closeness of the trees and the length of the Panther's barrel had prevented it from bringing its gun to bear accurately against us. Our much shorter 75mm was not similarly encumbered and I suspect my German opposite number knew it. I glimpsed the shape of a second Panther darting through gaps in the foliage to our left, as it also pulled out and quickly disappeared from view.

It was then I noticed that they had infantry with them, but the German grenadiers showed no desire to mix it with a troop of Shermans and also began to withdraw, following their own tanks. The enemy was clearly bugging out, but there was no sign of our own missing company, so I returned and reported the fact to the infantry colonel before moving to join up with the rest of A Squadron at a chateau located on the eastern edge of the wood. It later transpired that the lost company of the Somersets had overextended itself in the forest and had run into a hail of German machine-gun fire. Cut off from the rest of their battalion, they had surrendered and been taken into captivity. When he found out, Thomas sacked the colonel of the SLI, although the man held a DSO. The commanding general of the 43rd Division had clearly lost none of his vigour and it was classic von Thoma at his micromanaging and interfering best. However, the prowess of the men of 43rd Wessex Division who crossed the Seine and secured the wooded heights on the east bank of the river cannot be doubted. Supported by B and C Squadrons of the Sherwood Rangers, they went on to attack across open fields and clear the Germans out of the villages beyond the woods. In doing so the infantry took more casualties but with their blood, the loss of nearly 600 men, they had created the bridgehead the British needed on the other side of Vernon.

Once across the Seine, the ground east of Vernon opened up dramatically and allowed Horrocks to use the mobility of XXX Corps to fight a deep-penetration battle in the relentless pursuit of a defeated enemy. To meet the pace and style of operations the corps commander envisaged, the Sherwood Rangers had reorganised into a regimental battlegroup. All three tank squadrons would now work together, combined with an integral company of infantry mounted in Bren gun carriers from the 12th KRRC, a battery of Sexton 25-pounders from the Essex Yeomanry and two squadrons of reconnaissance cars from the RAC's 61st Recce Regiment. For the first time since North Africa, the regiment deployed in desert formation for the advance. The recce cars advanced in front of the regimental main body as a forward screen, with the task of finding routes and reporting the locations and strengths of any enemy positions. Behind them the lead squadron fanned out as a vanguard, with the other two squadrons moving in column slightly behind and on the flanks. The commanders of the subunits from the gunners and the infantry travelled in the centre with the four RHQ tanks, so that the colonel could deploy them instantly in support of the squadrons when needed. It was a far cry from being broken up as individual squadrons and parcelled out to support battalions in the infantry divisions.

The nature of the pursuit also differed radically from what we had become used to in the bocage. After Normandy, the Seine was the last obvious place where the Germans could really have made an attempt to stop us, but as an enemy in complete rout they had squandered the opportunity. Jerry was on the run and was being chased by four Allied armies of thirty-seven divisions advancing on a front of 200 miles. All organised German resistance had ceased to exist and where we did meet opposition it came in the form of isolated garrisons, or small rearguards clustered around a few anti-tank guns or the odd tank, which were easily brushed aside or bypassed. Most Germans were only too willing to surrender at the first opportunity, while the occasional fanatical desperado willing to fight to the last round for his Führer was easily dealt with. The new operational environment also suited the mobility, reliability and logistics support of the majority of the Allies' fighting vehicles and the Sherman came into its own. It could motor fast down narrow roads, cross a hastily laid Class 40 bridge and keep going with only the minimum of maintenance. Characteristics that stood in sharp contrast to the heavy, unreliable and excessively fuel-thirsty Tigers and Panthers of the German army. As far as we were concerned, once across the Seine the 'Great Swan' of the pursuit battle, as it was called, had begun and the race to the Rhine was on.

XXX Corps had an axis of advance that was set on crossing the Somme at Amiens and pushing on to Arras and then Lille before heading to the frontier with Belgium and then driving on to Brussels. On the first day we drove twenty-eight miles, meeting only minor opposition, which B Squadron and the KRRC infantry company dealt with easily. On the second day, 30 August, we travelled over fifty miles and then began to advance at an average rate of sixty miles a day. It was heady stuff as village after village slipped past as we travelled at top speed. We passed long straggling lines of German POWs trudging wearily westwards, looking sorry and dejected. They had spent weeks on the receiving end of bombardment from our artillery and air forces. They were probably glad to be out of it, as they saw the overwhelming might of massed Allied combat power streaming east in endless columns of tanks, guns and trucks. There was a general feeling of euphoria and optimism as we sped through the vast rolling landscape with the wind in our hair and the sun on our faces. The weather in Normandy had been capricious and un-seasonably wet, but now the late-summer sun shone high in a blue sky and tinged the surrounding fields of ripened corn a golden hue, heightening our mood.

The reaction of the French civilians to our arrival in Normandy had often been muted, which was hardly surprising given the death and destruction we had brought to their lives.* They knew that our presence spelt danger and would hide in their cellars or watch us passively from their doorways as we approached and drove through their towns and villages. But French attitudes changed the further we advanced away from the battlefields of the bocage. The country-side, towns and villages had been largely untouched by war and our arrival brought liberation without battle. They welcomed us with a spontaneous outpouring of jubilation. Flags flew from buildings and men, women and children cheered us with chants of *Les soldats anglais!* If we stopped they wanted to shake our hands, kiss us and shower us with gifts of food and alcohol. Their gratitude was deeply moving. But while jubilant at their liberation, occupation under the yoke of the Nazis had been hard and many French felt that they had scores to settle.

The women seemed to suffer the most, especially if they had

---

* French civilians suffered more than 15,000 casualties as a result of Allied operations in Normandy.

been accused of sleeping with the enemy. Distressing scenes where weeping women were roughly handled and paraded in public by the local toughs, who cropped off their hair and shaved their heads as a mark of collaboration, in front of a jeering crowd, were common and must have been happening all over France. Although distasteful and shaming, such incidents were generally considered as a matter for the French and we did nothing to intervene. The Maquis played a role in persecuting their own people and while often supporting the Allied purpose, as they had done at Vernon, the Resistance could also be a bloody nuisance. I am convinced that they shot at us as much as they did the Germans, likely as a result of poor military training and recognition skills. We were lucky that they were not generally armed with anti-tank weapons. They in turn were lucky that as officers we were expected to be more forgiving and to show restraint; if the blokes had had their way they would have shot back at them without hesitation.

On 1 September, the regiment advanced through the long shallow valley of the Somme. We crossed over the river at Amiens on bridges that had been captured intact and began to traverse former battlefields where the regular French army had been bled white in the defence of its nation more than two decades before. As we passed the war cemeteries of the British dead from the First World War, I thought of my father and the sacrifice his generation had made. I also thought of those of our own generation who lay behind us in temporary graves under the soil of Normandy. But there were lighter moments too. While John Semken kept a tight grip on us, as he did not want his troop leaders to go swanning off on their own, Harry Heenan, Dickie Holman and I played a game whenever we moved through a French street that was not filled with cheering crowds. It invariably happened in the early hours of the morning and involved a competition to see which of us could shoot out the gas-filled glass tabac signs from the turrets of our tanks with our Lugers as we passed underneath them. When we didn't think the squadron commander was on the radio net, we would place bets for packets of fags on who would hit and who would miss. We also took great delight in running our Shermans over abandoned cars and crushing them to the flatness of sheets of tinplate as a procession of tanks followed each other, one after the other. It was boyish high spirits that would have earned a Semken admonishment if he had known about it, but we were young, lived for the day and such pranks distracted us from the serious nature of the business that we were about. Bowling along flat roads running over gently undulating countryside, we were getting used to advancing at speed over long distances without meeting any enemy opposition. But the crack of an anti-tank gun could change all that and later that day we had a salient reminder that the battlefield could still be a deadly place.

The town of Doullens lies in the Authie river valley eighteen miles due north of Amiens along Route Nationale 25, which has made it an obvious point of interest on the path of marauding military hosts. Due to shifting frontiers and the historical fortunes of war, the town has been attacked by English, Spanish, French and German armies. Doullens' unfortunate strategic positioning is marked by the presence of a large fortified citadel on its southern edge and was reflected in the fact that a company of the Wehrmacht decided to make a determined stand there on the day that we arrived in the town. Had Harry Heenan been a better student of history he might have thought twice about the potential risk he faced in being the lead tank of the lead troop, as A Squadron advanced down the steep incline of the hill that leads into Doullens. The crew of the 75mm PAK anti-tank gun positioned on the bridge across the river would have spotted Harry's tank as soon as it crested the brow of the hill 400 yards in front of them. The first Harry knew about it was when the gun opened fire and struck the dome of his Sherman with a glancing blow, gouging a groove in the armour that glowed red-hot. The steep gradient of the hill and the angle of fire were probably what saved him, but it brought A Squadron's advance to a dead stop.

Taking rapid evasive action, Heenan reversed his tank hard back over the crest of the hill, causing the rest of the squadron to pile up in a nose-to-tail concertina behind him. Bringing up the rear with 5 Troop, the steel rim of the turret hatch almost took my teeth out as Dixon heaved back on the steering levers and brought Aim to an abrupt halt only a foot or two away from the Sherman that had suddenly become stationary in front of us. Surprised by the unexpected stop, I ordered my tank out of the instant traffic jam and pulled in behind the squadron leader's tank further up the column. Semken and I dismounted and gathered round a map at the rear of his Sherman to discuss the situation. With a German gun to our front covering our advance, the obvious answer seemed to lie in a troop making a flanking manoeuvre round the edge of the sunken citadel, which was a few hundred yards off to our left. Semken agreed and I set off to brief 5 Troop.

I left the Firefly in an overwatch position and the rest of the troop followed me as we broke through some trees and headed towards the citadel. It was an old seventeenth-century star-shaped fortification of thick-walled low-built ramparts topped with a wide, grassed glacis. I could see across the top of sloping turf-topped battlements as we motored round the western edge of the fort, using it as a cover to screen our advance. The little aircraft with stubby wings and some form of rocket motor on its back, mounted on a slanted rail, struck me as decidedly odd when I noticed the strange structure on top of one of the fortifications. There was another of the aircraft-like contraptions and some packing cases around the base of the long sloping metal rail. I hadn't a clue what they were, but they looked distinctly German, so we shot them up. Had I known they were V1 flying bomb rockets containing 1870 pounds of high explosive I might not have been so aggressive.

Conscious that we still had a job to do in taking out the German anti-tank gun, I pushed on and found a track that led into the outskirts of Doullens. Breaking right on to a narrow metalled road, we were suddenly accosted by a French woman who started shouting and gesticulating at us. I dismounted and approached her, but she seemed beside herself with worry and in broken English kept repeating, 'Good men. Don't shoot. No harm them.' I had no idea what she was on about, but she was pointing to a large wooden barn at the side of the road so I decided to investigate. The barn smelt of rotting straw and animal dung as Mayo and I entered with our Lugers drawn. To my surprise Harrison was with me and similarly armed. I was even more surprised when we discovered that the barn was full of fifteen to twenty Germans in the process of rolling up their kit, with their rifles stacked neatly against a wall. Pointing our Lugers at them, we told them to get their hands up and marched them out of the barn. I suspected they were in some way connected with the strange sight we had found in the citadel. I also wondered about the nature of the woman's relationship with the Germans and whether it would mark her out for rough handling by the local town thugs.

Lining the Germans up on the road we searched them quickly, relieving them of their pay books and the odd watch for the blokes. We were not equipped, nor did we have the time, to deal with prisoners, so I gave the German officer clear instructions that he was to march south with his men and surrender to the first Allied troops they encountered. Using broken German, my map and pointing in the direction of travel, I confirmed that the officer had understood what I had said and sent him and his men on their way. We mounted up and prepared to press on further into Doullens, when Lane called me on the radio. He told me that the Germans were making a run for it. I looked over the rear of the turret and the party that was meant to be marching south was sprinting north in the direction of its own lines. We turned the tanks' guns on them and shot them down, the last man staggering and falling backwards at the top of a small hill. I don't know what the French woman made of the incident, but we didn't hang around to find out.

From looking at my map, it told me that the road we had taken would bring us to a junction near the side of the bridge, which would put us flank on to the enemy anti-tank gun, but as we approached within a few hundred yards of the intersection we heard the sound of tank gunfire ahead of us. By the time we got there it was all over; the anti-tank gun crew lay sprawled around the 75mm PAK. Tired of waiting for me, Sergeant Dring had stalked forward with his Firefly and dealt with the German gun crew. Later that evening Harry Heenan ribbed me about my failure in coming to his rescue, but the chain of command were pleased when they discovered that we had overrun and destroyed a V1 rocket site. Having taken out the anti-tank gun on the bridge, A Squadron then advanced into the rest of the town with the attached infantry company of the KRRC in support. Together we knocked out four more anti-tank guns and took over a hundred prisoners, including the garrison commander. Our casualties were light, but ten miles to the south the crew of one of the regiment's reconnaissance vehicles had not been so fortunate.

The ability to manoeuvre as a unit in desert formation was subject to being able to traverse wide-open plains, or continuous tracts of large fields, unencumbered by woodland, hedges or river lines. When the ground closed up, as it did around the Somme valley area, we were forced to use the road network and tracks and travel in column. To provide flank security, the regiment's recce troop would often be deployed along a secondary road running parallel to the route being used by the main body. As A Squadron led the advance towards Doullens on the Route Nationale, Sergeant Leslie Cribbens was leading a section of three 'Honey' light reconnaissance tanks along an adjacent minor road on the left flank, which ran through the village of Flesselles. At around sixteen tons, with a crew of four

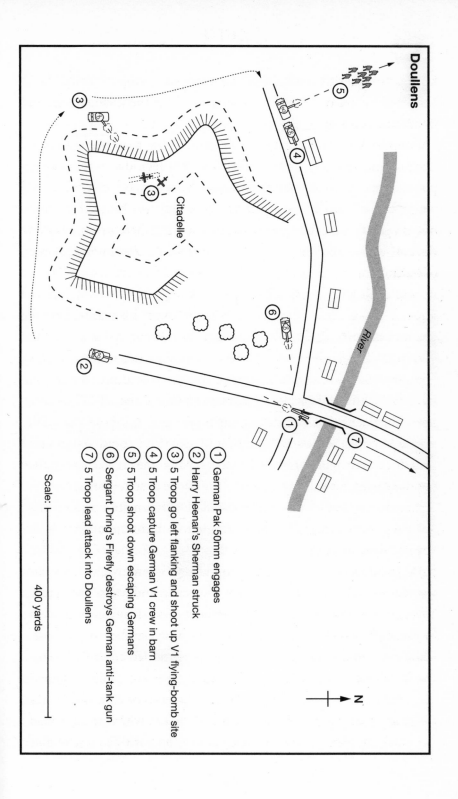

Doullens

Citadelle

River

① German Pak 50mm engages
② Harry Heenan's Sherman struck
③ 5 Troop go left flanking and shoot up V1 flying-bomb site
④ 5 Troop capture German V1 crew in barn
⑤ 5 Troop shoot down escaping Germans
⑥ Sergant Dring's Firefly destroys German anti-tank gun
⑦ 5 Troop lead attack into Doullens

Scale: ├───────────────┤ 400 yards

N

instead of five and equipped with a 37mm gun, the M3 light tank was half the weight of a Sherman and considerably less well armed and protected. However, its smaller profile made it ideal for the reconnaissance duties of identifying routes, warning of the presence of the enemy and reporting information back to RHQ. It also relied for its protection on observation and the stealth that came with its reduced signature. But on 1 September Cribbens failed to spot the Mark IV panzer lurking in the railway station at Flesselles. If he did see it, he saw it too late and the AP round it put through the lightly armoured vehicle killed him and Trooper Sharp.

Leslie Skinner heard about the incident as he travelled with the main body of the regiment, but it wasn't until a day later that the padre was able to go back and look for the bodies. By the time he got there, they had already been recovered by the local civilians and lay prepared for burial at the village presbytery. The German tank that had knocked out their Honey was also still there and had a clear view over the parish cemetery where the mayor and parish priest had decided to bury the two soldiers. The villagers persuaded Skinner that it was too dangerous for him to accompany them and the presence of the enemy forced him to watch the burial service they conducted from the safety of a window in the cleric's house. The vigilant crew in the panzer that had killed them watched too. Skinner then left by crawling back down the same ditch that he had used to enter the village unseen. It was typical Skinner and the fact that it got him in trouble with the Army Chaplain's Department was also typical. Military regulations dictate that soldiers on active service cannot be buried in consecrated ground, as it prevents their removal at a later date when an official war graves cemetery has been established. By allowing the villagers to bury Cribbens and his fellow crewman in their graveyard, our padre put the spiritual interests of our dead soldiers above army red tape and he was severely rebuked by the military chaplains' chain of command. Eventually the bureaucratic storm died down, but only after Stanley Christopherson stepped in to defend him.

Despite the sharp reminder at Doullens and the loss of two of our men at Flesselles, our optimism remained unbounded and there was an anticipation that we would soon be driving into the heart of the Third Reich and that the war would be over by Christmas. The advance continued and we motored through the bleak industrial area of Lille. On 4 September the regiment crossed the Belgian frontier at Tournai and the next day C Squadron shot up the rear of a retreating column of Germans on the outskirts of Ghent and A Squadron captured a hundred POWs. B Squadron and the CO used bluff, the assistance of a local priest and an appeal to a sense of military honour to persuade a garrison of 1200 Wehrmacht soldiers to surrender. Under negotiations conducted by Christopherson with the Germans' commander, they were allowed to march out of the Belgian village of La Pierre under a flag of truce with their arms intact, before surrendering in a formal parade where they shouted 'Sieg Heil!' three times, broke their weapons and then filed into captivity in an orderly Teutonic manner. However, our successes were surpassed when 11th Armoured Division captured the port of Antwerp before the retreating Germans could destroy its dock facilities.

Lack of serious resistance, retreating enemy columns, large volumes of prisoners taken and jubilant civilian crowds all reinforced our expectations, which were also shared by our senior commanders. On 7 September the commander of the 2nd British Army made a brief visit to the regiment's headquarters and told Stanley Christopherson that the surrender of the Channel ports was imminent and that once we started to advance into Germany there were likely to be very few enemy troops left to oppose us. The same day we entered Brussels, advancing behind the 6th Guards Armoured Division who took the honour of liberating the city earlier that morning without any fighting. The Sherwood Rangers passed through the capital in the early evening and the local population were still madly celebrating the end of four years of brutal occupation. We met a rapturous welcome from its people as they were overcome by the complete joy of the British arrival. Crowds lined the streets and mobbed our vehicles, showering us with flowers and wine. Pretty girls climbed up and kissed us and Dixon and Gartside were in their element as they enjoyed the full benefit of their crew station vantage point, seeing more flashes of legs and knickers than they had ever seen before; their appreciative grunts and less than clean remarks were abuzz on the tank's intercom as we made slow progress through the crowds of the liberated city.

The sun was setting in the west behind us as we leaguered for the night a few miles to the north of Brussels. We spent the next two days completing long-neglected maintenance on the tanks. Aim's milometer was showing 2000 miles since landing in Normandy and we had covered over 250 miles in less than two and a half weeks of swanning through France and into Belgium. Mechanically reliable as the Shermans were, they had suffered significantly. The speed and distances travelled had a tendency to wear out the rubber on the bogie wheels of the tanks' running gear. It had been a perennial problem throughout the advance and the mechanics of the regiment's Light Aid Detachment had done a remarkable job in replacing road wheels and changing engine packs to keep as many of the Shermans on the road as possible, but by now most of the tanks were in need of a major overhaul.

The pace of the advance had also been demanding on the body. Halts on the march were brief, time to sleep was often short and meals were taken on the hoof inside the tank. Usually bully and biscuits, or the contents of a tin; meat and vegetables eaten with a spoon that was then licked clean before being returned to a suitable cubbyhole for later use. If you couldn't find your own spoon you borrowed one of the crew's and the same thing applied to toothbrushes. Free of the everyday stresses of battle in the tight-knit countryside of the bocage, we had also become closer as a team. I maintained a necessary distance from the men, which was suitable to my position as an officer, lest familiarity breed contempt, and the blokes respected me for it. However, the banter and the jokes flowed more freely and we basked in the warmth of the shared experiences of having completed an adventurous journey, which included a collective sense of achievement and optimism for the future. As we rested in glorious weather, wrote letters home and washed from head to foot in cut-down fuel cans before letting our glistening naked bodies dry in the warmth of the sun's rays, all seemed well with the world. But to the north of us the fighting had started again, as the Germans began to recover from the shock of their defeat and consolidated their defences. The leaves of beech and elm had not yet lost their deep green of summer, but there was a hint of autumn in the air and the storm clouds were gathering once more.

10

POLDER LAND

In those first few heady days of early September of 1944, we seemed poised on the verge of victory. The German 7th Army had been chased out of France and thoroughly routed. What was left of it streamed in headlong retreat through the Low Countries towards the frontiers of the Third Reich. The advance of the Canadian 1st Army had eight battered divisions of the Wehrmacht's 15th Army pinned against the Channel coast. With the 2nd British Army in Brussels to their east, the Scheldt Estuary barred their escape route north along the coast. Ahead of us, large areas of countryside remained undefended. A fifty-mile gap opened up between the two German armies and with no more than an under-strength division, one Dutch SS battalion and a few detachments of Luftwaffe personnel to fill it, the route to the Rhine was all but open. We were in euphoric mood, the press was full of stories that the war was won and the prospect of it all being over before Christmas was on everyone's lips. The rapid advance following the breakout from Normandy had exceeded expectations, but the speed of the Allied drive through France and into Belgium had bred its own problems.

To our south, the two armies of the US 12th Army Group had

advanced to positions on either side of the Ardennes. The 1st US Army had almost reached the frontier with the Reich and the German city of Aachen lay tantalisingly close. Patton's 3rd US Army had established bridgeheads across the river Moselle and was threatening to drive east into the Saarland. But with some forty divisions, all hungry for supplies, the logistics chain for sustaining the British and American armies had become stretched to breaking point. The initial plan for supplying the four Allied armies, which were soon to expand to six as new American divisions flowed into northwest Europe, was based on the early capture of the Channel ports and the French railway system. But the majority of French ports would remain in German hands until the end of September and it would take weeks and months to repair the damage their garrisons had inflicted on the port facilities before surrendering. Dieppe was captured on 1 September and while it would only take a week to get its port facilities into operation, it could only deliver a trickle of the total tonnage of supplies needed. In turn Allied bombing, before and during the Normandy campaign, combined with demolitions carried out by the retreating German army, had rendered the French railway network virtually inoperable.

On 4 September, 11th Armoured Division captured Antwerp with its docks intact. But in focusing on seizing its port facilities, 65,000 German troops of the 15th Army were able to withdraw unhindered north across the Scheldt Estuary and the bridges of the Albert Canal on the northeast edge of the city. Allowed to escape, the Germans redeployed and dug into defensive positions along the north bank of the Scheldt. Capable of sweeping the estuary with fire, they were able to deny shipping access to the city's harbour from the sea, which rendered the capture of Antwerp ineffectual until its approaches could be cleared. The logistic dumps in Normandy now lay 300 miles behind the front line. Each Allied army needed between 4000 and 5000 tons of supplies a day, including fuel, and everything had to be brought forward by endless columns of lumbering trucks laden with fuel, rations, ammunition and equipment. As the lines of communication lengthened, and without the French railways and the ports that were so desperately needed, there was only sufficient road transport to keep one army sustained in the advance. Like the other three Allied armies, we were running out of fuel.

Following the liberation of Brussels, the order was given to halt all along the front. As we stopped, a difference of opinion broke out among the generals over who should be given priority for resupply. Montgomery demanded precedence and advocated making a single bold thrust with 2nd British Army. He argued that by driving north through Holland he could cut off the remaining enemy troops in the Low Countries, outflank the German frontier defences at the Siegfried Line, bounce a crossing over the Rhine, isolate the Nazis from their industrial heartland in the Ruhr and open the route to advance on Berlin before the onset of winter. Monty was optimistic that with the right resources his narrow-front strategy could still end the war in 1944. But he was no longer the senior ground forces commander and his former subordinates, such as Patton, were also insisting that they should be given priority. With the Americans providing the majority of divisions in northwest Europe, Eisenhower had assumed direct command of the land campaign on 1 September. While his strategic preference was for continuing to advance on a broader front with all four armies, he now had to decide between the competing demands of his commanders.

At a meeting on 10 September, Eisenhower agreed to back Monty's strategy as it also offered the advantage of overrunning the V1 flying bomb and V2 rocket launch sites. The larger V2 rockets had begun raining down on London from 8 September and had forced a political imperative on the Supreme Allied Commander. But Ike remained reluctant to commit all of his limited resources to Montgomery and allowed Patton to receive some supplies. It meant that Monty would be forced to rely on what the British trucks could bring up, which would only be enough to sustain one of his corps in the advance. To open up a route and cross the Rhine, Monty planned to use three airborne divisions, jumping ahead of XXX Corps, to seize and hold the bridges across three major rivers and five large canals that barred the advance to the north. The US 101st Airborne Division would seize the bridges across two canals at Eindhoven. To their north, the American 82nd Airborne Division would capture the bridges at Grave and Nijmegen over the Meuse and Waal rivers, while the British 1st Airborne Division and the Polish 1st Independent Parachute Brigade would seize and hold the bridges over the Lower Rhine at Arnhem. Spearheaded by the Guards Armoured Division, with 43rd Wessex and 50th Northumbrian infantry divisions following them, XXX Corps would then advance from northern Belgium and drive the sixty miles through Holland to link up with each of the airborne divisions to secure the route over the Rhine.

Operation Market Garden entailed risk. The nature of flat, low-lying reclaimed Dutch polder land made for poor tank country. Faced by terrain crisscrossed by numerous dykes and deep irrigation ditches and dotted with thick woods, Horrocks' complete corps of 20,000 vehicles would be restricted to moving along a single highway that ran through Eindhoven and Nijmegen and on to Arnhem. With little opportunity to deploy off the main road, the corps' flanks would be exposed and vulnerable to counterattack. Success would depend on surprise, good weather for airborne operations and the ability of XXX Corps to advance rapidly along a very narrow axis and batter its way through any opposition as fast as possible. Above all, success would depend on weak enemy resistance. But as the Allied armies had paused, argued and laid their plans, the Germans had used the time to recover.

Adept at forming ad hoc all-arms groupings of disparate units organised round a single commander, the Germans had stopped retreating and had begun to pull their fragmented army together into improvised battlegroups. Varying in size from a few hundred to several thousand troops, these scratch units, or Kampfgruppe, were being used to plug the gaps in the line and were beginning to dig in along the Albert Canal. They were also being reinforced with 20,000 troops of six German parachute regiments and 10,000 Luftwaffe personnel, who had been rapidly formed into the 1st Parachute Army. Although belonging to the Luftwaffe, and still in various states of training or reformation, the German paratroopers remained a body of elite troops that had equal status with the SS as a first-class fighting unit. Like the SS the 1st Parachute Army attracted the best recruits and received the best weapons, equipment and training. More importantly, its members were highly motivated and the majority of them were young and fresh to battle.

Sitting to the south of the Belgian–Dutch border, with a minimum width of eighty feet and running east to west for seventy miles between Maastricht and Antwerp, the Albert Canal is a significant water obstacle. When the Guards Armoured Division was ordered to resume the British advance on 7 September and cross the Albert Canal at Beringen in preparation for the start of Market Garden, it took the division four days to fight through ten miles of enemy-held territory and establish a bridgehead on the other side. In comparison, it had taken them six days to advance the 250 miles from Vernon to Brussels, which was a clear indication that the German forces had recuperated and the front line had begun to congeal again. As a lowly lieutenant, I was not party to the machinations of our senior commanders, their grand strategy or the bold moves of our enemy. But in the fighting the regiment was about to take part in, any aspirations we had that the war would be over by Christmas were about to be shattered.

Market Garden could not commence until a start line for the operation was established on the Meuse-Escaut Canal, which is a semi-circular branch of the Albert Canal running fifteen miles northeast from Beringen at its furthest point. While the rest of 8th Armoured Brigade were ordered to support the Guards Division in clearing the enemy from the area between the two canals, the Sherwood Rangers were ordered to support 50th Northumbrian Division in securing a second crossing point over the Albert Canal near the Belgian town of Gheel. Gheel is located two miles to the north of the canal and twelve miles west of Beringen and would be our objective. Orders for the attack were received on 8 September. A Squadron would be in reserve and the other two squadrons would lead the attack. But when B and C Squadrons crossed the canal on 10 September, the German paratroopers in Gheel were ready and waiting for them.

Although 50th Division had attacked across the Albert Canal on 8 September, the foothold its 151st Brigade held on the other side was tenuous. While C Squadron was sent north to capture Gheel with the 6th Battalion of the Durham Light Infantry, B Squadron was employed in supporting the brigade to reinforce the bridgehead. At 1400, C Squadron linked up with the infantry and advanced on Gheel following a preliminary artillery barrage. The leading infantrymen seemed few in numbers. Their numbers became fewer as the German Spandaus opened up with their characteristic *brrrp, brrrp, brrrp* sound and chopped into their ranks. Men were hit and fell. A platoon commander caught a full burst and was almost cut in half by the heavy automatic fire. Those not hit went to ground and began to dig. Hacking frantically at the earth with their picks and shovels, in a desperate bid to escape the bullets by creating a modicum of shelter below the earth's surface, they waved the tanks on. Clattering past them, the Shermans were impervious to the machine-gun fire, which rattled harmlessly off their sides. They fired 75mm HE at point-blank range into the German slit trenches, blasting their occupants into oblivion or surrender. But there was no time to take prisoners, which was a task left to the infantry as they pressed on into the town. Directing more HE fire into every house that might conceal the enemy, more Germans surrendered and as the tanks reached the town square the Fallschirmjäger began to withdraw. Belgian civilians started to emerge from cellars, national flags were flown from pock-marked buildings and resistance fighters appeared on the streets, but the inhabitants' sense of liberation was premature.

The bridgehead behind C Squadron was under constant counter-attack and the road from the bridge was cut. Listening to the radios in our tanks, we heard brief snatches of the action over the regimental net and from what we could glean from the radio, we knew that C Squadron was in trouble. As darkness fell, the German 6th Parachute Regiment used the cover of night to launch a counterattack on Gheel with the support of a company of Jagdpanthers, which made short work of one of C Squadron's troops with their 88mm guns. There was a blinding flash as the first tank was hit near the railway station to the north of the town. Flames shot from the turret hatch as fuel and ammunition began to burn. The survivors bailed out and stumbled from the blazing vehicle. Their clothes blackened and smouldering, they dragged themselves to the nearest cover. Provoked by the first explosion, the crews in the other two vehicles were already traversing their guns in the direction of the threat. A series of sharp cracks and near-instant almighty metal clangs rang out, as the crews lost the battle for speed with the German 88s and two more Shermans went up in flames. Within minutes a complete troop had been knocked out and their burning hulks cast flickering shadows against the walls of buildings around the railway station, as the German counterattack moved forward.

The Jagdpanthers and paratroopers then advanced on the town's square where Lieutenant Stuart Hills' troop maintained a lonely vigil. Losing one of their self-propelled guns to a shot from one of Hills' Fireflies parked in a side street, the German armour backed off and enemy infantry were sent in. Infiltrating through the cover of dark alleyways and gardens, the paratroopers fired flares to illuminate

Hills' troop so that the Jagdpanthers could shell them from stand-off positions. By the time morning came, the church in the town's centre was a burned-out ruin and Hills' Shermans were covered in bricks and dust. The troops of the Durham Light Infantry who might have protected them had melted away during the night. Without their own infantry to protect them, C Squadron's position became even more precarious, as the German paras began to stalk their tanks with Panzerfausts.

With only six tanks left and without infantry to support them, C Squadron's position was becoming untenable. B Squadron had been sent into Gheel to reinforce them, but lost seven of their own Shermans in the process. The consumption of shells for the 75mm guns had been prolific and, with the route to the bridgehead behind them cut, they were running out of ammunition. C Squadron's commander conferred with the surviving officers of his squadron and agreed to seek permission to withdraw. When the small conference broke up and Hills made his way back to his tank, there was a terrific explosion as the Sherman of Captain Jimmy McWilliam was turned into a mass of flames. The crew bailed out, McWilliam was badly burned and his driver was killed. No one knew where the shot had come from, but Hills suspected it was from an enemy infantryman armed with a Panzerfaust. His own Sherman was positioned close to McWilliam's tank on the northeast corner of the square, so that they could each cover off an approach to the town centre like two gunslinger partners back-to-back in a Mexican stand-off. But having seen what had happened to McWilliam and his crew at such close quarters, Hills decided to change his position and get away from the sides of the street, where enemy infantry could be lurking in the doorways. As Hills moved off, a terrific sheet of flame rose up as a Panzerfaust hit the forward right-hand side of his tank.

The molten copper slug of the shaped-charge warhead bored through a track plate and entered the hull compartment in a shower of sparks, before punching a neat hole through the gearbox assembly, but Hills' tank could still move. His gunner sprayed machine-gun fire in the general direction of where the shot had come from as the driver managed to crash the gears into reverse and the damaged Sherman backed furiously into the relative safety of the centre of the square. Hills and his crew were lucky. None of them had sustained serious injury and the tank had not caught fire. Had an AP round hit them, the tungsten shot would have ricocheted round the inside of the tank, severing limbs and pulping bodies and its white-hot tip would have ruptured shell cases and fuel lines, causing them to burn. They were also lucky that they had received permission to withdraw. Taking their wounded with them, the surviving tanks managed to extract from Gheel without further mishap, leaving the town in German hands.

The 50th Division was a spent force and the next day Gheel was retaken by the infantry of the 15th Scottish Division. A Squadron supported them and what was left of C Squadron came with us. Artillery fired us in and added to the significant damage the town had already sustained. We knew what had happened to the other squadrons and we didn't spare the place further injury. We pumped HE into any building that might house a sniper and hosed down every potential hiding place that might conceal an enemy equipped with a Panzerfaust. Resistance was slight, although Dickie Holman's tank was hit and his driver was killed. Dickie was OK, but the blast burst his eardrums. His survival, and that of McWilliam, highlighted how the crew in the hull of a Sherman tended to be more vulnerable to hand-held anti-tank weapons than those mounted in a turret. Lacking the optical sights of a tank or anti-tank gun, their firers aimed at the biggest mass of the tank. Stuart Hills was without his hull gunner when his tank was hit, but had the gunner been sitting in his crew station at the time he would undoubtedly have been killed.

We took no further losses in Gheel and the Belgian tricolours came out again; although the mood of the civilian inhabitants was more subdued, no doubt due to the damage caused to their homes and the Germans' removal of most of their male population between the ages of sixteen and sixty. Some of the Belgian resistance that had avoided the round-up reappeared, as they had done when C Squadron first captured the town. They drove about noisily in the odd car, wearing old French helmets, waving flags and toting Sten guns. Although we pushed the main body of enemy troops out of the town, the freedom fighters disappeared rapidly from the streets, taking their flags with them, when a few German paratroopers reappeared and made an attempt to stalk us with Panzerfausts. But there was no further concerted attempt by the Germans to contest Gheel and by the end of 13 September the town was firmly in our hands. Later that day the tanks of the City of London Yeomanry relieved the regiment and our much-depleted squadrons moved ten miles to the east to rest and refit at a leaguer 8th Armoured Brigade had established at Bourg-Léopold.

A Squadron's role in the fighting at Gheel had been limited and B and C Squadrons had borne the brunt of the action. With eleven Shermans destroyed and two damaged by enemy action, the tank losses at Gheel were the worst the regiment had sustained since landing in Normandy. They were also the most significant losses the Sherwood Rangers had suffered since the North African campaign, where seventeen tanks were knocked out at the battle of Wadi Zem Zem. The unit also lost forty-six men, including six officers, and the toll was once again heaviest among the tank commanders. The streets that we left behind us were littered with the dead of both sides. As we pulled out of the line, Leslie Skinner remained behind to complete his grisly role of recovering the dead and burying their bodies. He searched the ash of burned-out tanks for the remains of crewmen and stitched what was left into grey army blankets, chain smoking furiously in an attempt to ward off the stench of charred and putrefied flesh. The padre had been given two medical orderlies to help him, but when the frightful nature of the task became too much for them he worked on alone. Some of those killed in Gheel were buried in a mass grave near the church, alongside the Belgian civilians who had died in the fighting. The town was still within the range of the German guns and Skinner was forced to conduct the burial service for the British casualties from inside the shelter of the grave as shells crashed down about him.

The level of casualties also stretched the regiment's medical officer. While Skinner focused on dealing with the dead, Dr 'Hilda' Young had been busy attending to the wounded. Captain Charles Young had joined the Sherwood Rangers in the desert. With a tall, stooping frame and greying hair, he left his practice in Somerset, lied about his age to join the army at the outbreak of war and was awarded an MC during the fighting in France in 1940 before being evacuated from Dunkirk. During operations, his job was to run the unit's Regimental Aid Post. Consisting of two lightly armoured half-track vehicles and some medical orderlies, the RAP travelled with RHQ during a battle and was designed to receive, triage and stabilise casualties prior to their evacuation to advance dressing stations behind the front line. Unlike the infantry, the regiment's RAP didn't have stretcher bearers. Consequently, casualties were brought back to Young's medical post on the back of a Sherman or by the stretcher bearers of the infantry unit that we were supporting. But Young often insisted on going forward himself to attend to the wounded of a knocked-out tank and had to be restrained from doing so. Young was a man who had both moral, as well as physical, courage. He was not averse to making a direct approach to either the CO or the brigade commander when he felt that the regiment was being pushed too hard. He did it twice during the fighting in Normandy and on both occasions his intervention resulted in us being pulled out of the line to rest.

The loss of tanks and men, dead and wounded, underscored the vulnerability of armour in an urban area when not properly protected by infantry. Although they had also taken significant casualties, the battalions of 50th Division that had attacked Gheel had not covered themselves in glory. But I felt that we could hardly blame them. Since landing on D-Day, their numbers had been badly depleted. Those original members of the infantry companies who had assaulted across the beaches and survived through the bullets and shellfire of the bocage and through the rain, the mud and their own fatigue and fear, could be counted on the fingers of one hand. Their numbers had been made up by new drafts and battle casualty replacements, but while accounting for only 15 per cent of the 2nd British Army, the infantry sustained 63 per cent of the total casualties in Normandy. It was a high rate of attrition, which often exceeded the casualty levels of the First World War, and it meant that the infantry were always in short supply. Lacking the protection of armour, the infantry were often reluctant to advance with us and a common excuse they gave us was that they didn't have enough men. Another reason was that we were dangerous to be around or, as Martin put it, 'because we attracted tha shite'. When pinned down by a Spandau, the infantry were happy for us to go forward and blast out the enemy machine-gun post with HE. But we were often invited to piss off when located close to them, as our presence attracted mortar and artillery fire.

The fighting prowess of the German soldiers we faced was another reason for the high level of casualties. The Fallschirmjäger were highly motivated members of an elite unit; they had an average age of seventeen and a half and many were prepared to lay down their lives for their Führer. The paratroopers who surrounded C Squadron in the square were heard calling out in the darkness that they were prepared to die for Adolf Hitler.

Like the majority of men serving in the British Army during the war, those men that joined the ranks of the infantry were neither pro-fessionals nor volunteers. Conscripted into the service, they formed part of a citizens' army. Their primary motivation was to survive and return to the civilian lives that they had been wrenched from. The bulk of the paratroopers we fought in Gheel were also conscripts, but they were a very different product to our soldiers, who came from a liberal democracy in which the rights of the individual were respected. In comparison, the German paras were born of a totalitarian state and had been brutally institutionalised by Nazi militarism as schoolchildren. They were also considerably better equipped than our infantry. MG42s, MP40s and Panzerfausts were superior weapons to their British equivalents. While the Panzerfaust provided the German infantryman with a one-shot, disposable, highly portable, effective light infantry anti-tank armament, the British Projector Infantry Anti-Tank bazooka, or PIAT, was anything but. The Heath Robinson-looking projector had a similar range to a Panzerfaust, but while it was reusable it was heavy and cumbersome. It required the Herculean effort of a man lying on his back to cock it by pulling back a huge metal spring, which propelled a small spike-pointed bomb out of the weapon. The projectile regularly bounced off the armour of a tank; that is, if the firer was lucky enough to survive the loading process and hit it.

The mass conscript army, of which the British infantry formed part, was also in its fifth year of war and we were on the borders of the Third Reich. Most of us who fought it knew that it was no longer a conflict of national survival but a matter of beating the Germans and forcing them to surrender, which was an imperative that made one's own personal survival all the more acute. In contrast, the enemy were now defending their *Heimat*; in simple terms, they were fighting to protect their homeland. As we roared triumphantly into Belgium, we thought that it was a fight that was largely finished. The experience of Gheel was a powerful demonstration that the Nazis were far from beaten and our sense of optimism evaporated as we began to realise that much bloody fighting still lay ahead and the odds of making it through were once again stacked against us.

Despite the increasing German resistance, the commander of 21st Army Group did not reflect the pessimistic mood of his troops. I can't remember the precise time or date when Montgomery spoke to us, but his address to all the officers of XXX Corps took place in the large theatre at Bourg-Léopold before the commencement of Operation Market Garden. I can recall what he was wearing, what he said to the several hundred assembled officers, the prickly manner in which he said it and the catcalls he provoked. Surprisingly, Monty was not wearing his trademark non-regulation items of clothing. There was no usual black RAC tank beret with double cap badges that he was not entitled to wear, or sheepskin jacket. I suspect that he might have made an effort for us, as the wearing of another regiment's emblem or item of distinctive unit dress caused significant chagrin among those that had a right to wear such marks of a particular affiliation. Instead, Monty wore standard service dress with a red-banded peaked cap. We stood up as he entered, to a clatter of banging theatre seats. He strode up to a stage and placed his hat and cane on a table in front of him. Montgomery then told us in a haughty lisp that we had a minute to get our coughing and sneezing done before he started to speak. The assembled crowd milked his prim, uptight schoolmaster-like instruction for all it was worth. The place erupted in a cacophony of nasal-orientated sound, as virtually every young officer took it upon himself to make as much noise as possible.

The schoolboy-like behaviour over, the field marshal started to speak. When Montgomery asserted that the enemy was beaten and that 'we' would go forward together, his remarks met with an isolated outburst of derision and I am sure I heard the use of the word 'bollocks' echoing from somewhere at the back of the theatre. He ignored the heckler who questioned his use of the word 'we', as he ignored the subsequent jeers when a wider group of the younger cohort of officers in the audience joined in. Like us, I suspect that many of them had witnessed the reality that Jerry was far from defeated. For me it shattered any newsreel illusion I had of the popular image of the darling of the 8th Army who had restored the morale and offensive spirit to a once-defeated army. I have no doubt about the contribution Monty made both there and in northwest Europe, but to the majority of us he was certainly no Alexander the Great or Julius Caesar. Being good chaps, the Sherwood Rangers officers remained in embarrassed silence. But Montgomery didn't miss a beat, as he told us of his belief that in making one more daring bold thrust we would be on the Rhine in a week, that Germany was on its knees and that the road to Berlin was open. If he expected a rousing cheer, he certainly didn't get it. I doubt he said anything to his staff officers when he left, but I bet he didn't ask them if they thought his speech went well.

The briefing Horrocks gave for Operation Market Garden on 16 September in the same theatre, to all the commanding officers of the units in XXX Corps, was an altogether more dignified affair, which was given a reasonable portrayal in the famous scene in the film *A Bridge Too Far*. Horrocks was a favourite of Monty, but the two men could not have been more different in character. Men like Montgomery and von Thoma are testimony that generals are not generally well-loved by their soldiers, but Brian Horrocks had retained the popularity he enjoyed on assuming command of XXX Corps seven weeks into the battle of Normandy. Horrocks was charismatic. His enthusiasm and energy were infectious and they had transformed the divisions under his command. Horrocks' conference and the orders that followed it confirmed the regiment's role in the operation. While the rest of 8th Armoured Brigade would support the corps' advance to the bridges seized ahead of them by the Allied parachute divisions, the Sherwood Rangers would act as an independent battlegroup. Once the Guards Armoured Division had started to blast its way up the road that led to Arnhem, we would be used to picket a stretch of narrow corridor between Eindhoven and Nijmegen. The unit was also warned off to be ready to support the US 82nd Airborne Division in operations to protect their bridgehead at Nijmegen.

At lunchtime on Sunday 17 September the sky to our west became filled with the throbbing drone of engines, which grew to a mighty roar as a vast air armada of transport aircraft and gliders flew over our heads, taking the first wave of 34,000 British and American paratroopers towards their targets. At precisely 1435 hours, the rolling barrage of 350 guns started to lay a curtain of fire along Highway 69. Ten minutes later the lead unit of the Guards Armoured Division crossed its start line and began to proceed up the road to Eindhoven. Within two minutes nine tanks of the Irish Guards were knocked out by German troops dug in on either side of the road ahead of them. We didn't start moving up what became known as the 'Highway of Death' until 20 September. The same day the lead units of the Guards Armoured Division were preparing to break out of the US 82nd Airborne Division at Nijmegen and continue the advance to Arnhem, where a single parachute battalion of the British 1st Airborne Division was desperately clinging on to one end of the bridge over the Rhine. It had taken three days for the Guards to get to Nijmegen. The British paratroopers had been told that they only needed to hold on for two days, perhaps four at the most, and time was running out for them.

It took the Sherwood Rangers a full day to travel the seventy-two miles to Nijmegen. With several hundred tanks, guns, trucks and Bren carriers in the regimental column moving along a single two-lane highway, we were also competing for space with thousands of other XXX Corps vehicles. The narrow width of the axis of advance meant that it could be easily cut by enemy action and B Squadron were forced to rush one of the bridges across the canal at Son when the enemy mounted a local counterattack against it. The Germans had also mined the verges on the sides of the road, which made it more difficult to overtake or recover a broken-down vehicle. All of this added to the delay and was an indicator of what it must have been like for those units forward of us that were having to fight their way along every yard of road. As we left Eindhoven and approached Nijmegen from the south, we passed the airborne landing zones, which were littered with gliders. Snatches of white silk billowed from the odd parachute canopy caught up in bushes or trees and I wondered what had happened to the men that had used them to jump into battle. It was evening by the time we drove into Nijmegen. The evidence of the fight for possession of the city was marked on its streets, which were covered with severed and twisted cables that had once provided power to the city's trams. Some of the fires caused by bombing and artillery still burned and the light of their flames reflected off the broken glass that lay everywhere. The large grey girder-span bridge that crossed the Waal had been knocked about, but the paratroopers of 82nd Airborne had captured it intact. What we didn't know at the time was the manner in which it had been taken a few hours before the Sherwood Rangers arrived in the city.

The division captured the bridge over the Meuse at Grave on the first day of the operation along with two canal bridges in the area. After some bitter fighting, they also secured the Groesbeek ridge to the southeast of Nijmegen, a ten-mile spur of elevated ground that dominates the approaches to Nijmegen from the east below the river Waal. However, due to strong resistance the city's bridge was only taken on 20 September, after the 3rd Battalion of the division's 504th Regiment had made a daring river assault across the Waal in twenty-six collapsible canvas boats. Using their rifle butts to assist them, they paddled across 400 yards of fast-moving water in a hail of bullets that sank over half of their boats. Those that made it to the other side assaulted the northern end of the bridge. After a series of fierce engagements, the US 82nd Airborne forced the Germans to withdraw and enabled the bridge to be captured intact before the enemy could blow it up. Having linked up with the Americans, our job was to help them secure the area they had seized from German counterattack, as the rest of XXX Corps continued to battle up the remaining nine miles of road to Arnhem. But as the Americans captured their bridge at Nijmegen, the last remnants of the British Paras holding the northern end of the bridge over the Rhine had run out of ammunition and were overwhelmed by the superior SS forces ranged against them. What was left of the 1st Airborne Division had been surrounded in a shrinking perimeter in Arnhem's suburbs and was still holding out desperately, waiting for relief.

Like their British paratrooper counterparts fighting for their lives only a few miles to the north, the US 82nd Airborne Division was an all-volunteer unit and their tough training, combined with their martial prowess, made them an elite formation. Despite three days of intensive combat, the light of battle was still in their eyes when we met up with them. But there was plenty more action to be had, as the Germans made repeated counterattacks in an attempt to interdict the route to Arnhem and cut off the advance units of XXX Corps from the American airborne divisions behind them. To prevent the enemy from achieving these aims, the bulk of the 82nd Airborne's troops were committed to holding the Groesbeek ridge. Anchored at its southern end by the small town of Mook, the ridge touches the border with Germany where it meets the Reichswald Forest. The American lines stretched across the ridge from Mook and then curled approximately eight miles north to the town of Beek on the eastern edge of the suburbs of Nijmegen. Having linked up with the 82nd's commander, the CO set up the Sherwood Rangers' RHQ with General Jim Gavin's headquarters in Groesbeek. Stanley Christopherson agreed to support the division's regimental positions centred on Mook and Beek at either end of the ridge feature with a squadron apiece, with one squadron being held back in reserve at Groesbeek. Each of the squadrons would then be rotated between these roles and locations.

At daylight the next day, A Squadron moved into the southeast sector of the bridgehead around Mook and struck up an immediate rapport with the US paratroopers they were tasked to support. It was helped by the fact that the Americans construed that having 'Rangers' in our title meant we were some form of armoured commando unit, no doubt helped by connotations of Sherwood Forest and Walt Disney's portrayal of Robin Hood. While we did nothing to disabuse them of their misconception, the fact that our tanks had 75mm guns and could carry several days of rations also helped cement a strong sense of empathy between us. Airborne operations are barebones affairs. Paratroopers jump into battle carrying everything they need and fight on their feet without vehicle support. The Germans' ability to cut the main supply route meant that the Americans had to rely on resupply by air for food and ammunition, with the priority being placed on the latter. As a consequence the American troops we linked up with around Mook were starving. We gave them all our spare ten-man ration boxes and they loved us for it. In turn we were taken in by their cocksure attitude, as they strolled around in their baggy field pants, tucked 'Airborne style' into their rubber-soled jump boots. Most of us had never left England before embarking for Normandy and we loved their easygoing manner and the way they spoke with their Texan drawls and the accents of men that came from seemingly glamorous places like New York and California. The Americans appeared to be equally taken with the way we spoke, but I can never be sure if they ever understood a word of what the likes of Dixon and Gartside said.

I was surprised that the Americans weren't better at living off the land, which was something that we had been doing since Normandy. It was a matter that I was discussing with David Alderson, as we looked round a deserted Dutch farm for chickens. The Germans had ransacked the place, but we hoped that the odd bird might have escaped their clutches. The place was absent of poultry, but our presence must have attracted the attention of a German observation post. Suddenly, the cobbled farmyard was full of exploding shells and we dashed for cover into a hen-house. Its flimsy wooden sides offered scant protection from the shrapnel that tore about the place. David questioned the wisdom of our choice of shelter, as we lay on the chicken shit-covered floor of the coop. I quipped that if he had a better suggestion he was welcome to take his chances outside. We lay there for a while after the shelling had abated with the intention of extracting ourselves once the artillery spotters had lost interest in our presence. Lying prone in the muck, we had little else to do but wait and David brought up the subject of being under my instruction and when I had told him about the life expectancy of a new troop leader in battle. It made me feel guilty, as he also told me that he hadn't slept for two weeks as a result. A few days later, Alderson's tank took an AP round through the turret, which wounded him and two of his crew.

Although surprised by their lack of prowess in foraging for food, we were generally impressed by the way the US paratroopers fought. They were tough buggers and they seldom went to ground. They weren't used to working with armour, but once we had suppressed a dug-in German position, they were ferocious in the assault. They also had something of a reputation for rarely taking prisoners. A hapless German soldier who survived the initial infantry fight would be lucky if he got sent to the rear with little more than a few blows from the butt of a rifle and a kick to his backside. The ground around Nijmegen favoured the defender and when we supported the Americans' patrols and local attacks the paratroopers took significant casualties. As a consequence, not unlike Normandy, an enemy soldier who decided to surrender at the last safe moment when his position was being overrun might expect little quarter from the buddies of the men he had killed just a few moments before.

The terrain in 82nd Airborne's sector was not much better for tanks. Dotted with woods and orchards, the Dutch polder of marshy reclaimed land, intersected by dykes and ditches, restricted our mobility to long straight high-banked elevated roads. There was limited opportunity to deploy off them and they channelled our movement and skylined our Shermans for the benefit of any 88mm set up in a defilade ambush position in an adjacent copse or a German infantryman equipped with a Panzerfaust lurking in an irrigation ditch. The whole area was also under enemy observation. Any movement on the east side of the Groesbeek ridge or on the flatter land at the foot of its slopes between Mook and Beek invited being bracketed by German artillery and mortar fire. Given the nature of the ground, it was hardly surprising that the proposed armoured dash to Arnhem had slowed to a crawl. On 25 September, XXX Corps lost its race to reach the beleaguered British paratroopers encircled on the other side of the Rhine. That night what was left of the 10,600 men of 1st Airborne Division who had jumped into Arnhem or flown in by glider nine days previously were withdrawn back across the river. By early the next morning, when the evacuation operation ended, just over 2000 British soldiers had reached the safety of our own lines. We knew that the British Paras to our north were in trouble, although we were not party to the extent of their peril. But on that fateful day when the decision was made to end Operation Market Garden, I had enough problems of my own.

While the generals began to count the cost of the failure to bounce the crossing over the Rhine at Arnhem, A Squadron was working in the Beek sector of the bridgehead around Nijmegen, where the north-east edge of 82nd Airborne's perimeter touched the German border. The sector extended south for a few miles adjacent to the frontier and then crossed over into the dark mass of the Reichswald Forest on the other side. The Germans had been launching attacks from the forest to cut the road links to the bridges and our job was to help the US 508th Parachute Infantry Regiment consolidate their positions and push back any attacks. The precise area in which we were operating on 25 September escapes me, but I can remember the exact layout of the defensive position of the battalion of US paratroopers we were supporting. Their forward companies were dug in along the bend of a high-banked elevated road that straightened out as it ran towards the German front line located in a wood line 300 yards away. The enemy's position is also etched upon my memory; not least the low sloping silhouette of the Hetzer Jagdpanzer self-propelled gun that was clearly visible on the right-hand side of the edge of the trees. The 75mm gun faced back down the dyke-topped road towards us. Looking through my binoculars, I could also make out the coal-scuttle shapes of the helmets of the enemy infantry dug in along the foliage on either side of the armoured vehicle. The Germans must have had an equally good view of the American positions and they must have been aware of our arrival, but there was little discernible activity from their side of the line.

I sought out the battalion's CO, but the American major in command of the unit displayed a notable lack of aggression compared to the rest of his counterparts in the 82nd Division. When I asked him about the tactical situation, he mentioned something about an unofficial policy of live and let live existing between the two sides. The Germans a short distance across the fields in front of his forward companies were not bothering him, so he was not about to bother them. He didn't take too kindly to my pointing out that we couldn't leave such a clearly identified enemy position unmolested and I suggested we put in a joint attack with his unit. He obviously saw me as some upstart young Brit swanning in to upset things when his troops had just survived a parachute jump into combat and had experienced several days of tough fighting. He responded to my suggestion by telling me that if I planned to attack his men wouldn't be coming with me, but if I wanted to be a 'crazy cock-sucking son of a bitch' then I could be his guest. I would have preferred to deal with the German position with the support of one of the major's companies. However, I had my orders and I knew that John Semken wouldn't tolerate my troop hanging about doing nothing when there was a bunch of highly visible enemy sitting untouched a few hundred yards to our front.

I took a dekko through my binoculars. The ground to the right of the high-banked road looked boggy; not great ground for tanks to advance across. The field on its left looked firmer and its appearance suggested that it might give us a more covered approach. I had a brief conference with my tank commanders and sketched out my plan of attack. First, I would take out the Jagdpanzer with an AP round. It was much smaller than the Jagdpanthers we had encountered to date, so I presumed that it had thinner armour and one armour-piercing shot would do the trick. Having fired, Aim and Arrow would then make a fast dash up the road in order to close half the distance to the enemy positions before dropping off the bank and into the field on the left to avoid being skylined on top of the dyke. Using the cover of the bank we would then advance line abreast and blast out the German infantry from the dugouts with HE and machine-gun fire. Archer and the Sherman Firefly would hang back and cover us from the forward edge of the American lines. I asked for any questions. Sergeant Harrison confirmed he was happy with this arrangement and we synchronised watches and mounted up. I briefed the crew over the intercom, but thought better of telling them that the US paratroopers wouldn't be coming with us.

The Jagdpanzer was the one tank that I can claim my Sherman took out on its own during the entire war. It was a one-on-one shoot and we had the advantage of surprise that came with a willingness to break the unofficial local ceasefire. Martin hit it with his first round and the armoured panzer brewed up in a ball of black smoke and flames. At the time I didn't spare a thought for the crew inside it. If it was manned no one bailed out, but we were already moving. Dixon worked fast through the gears and the tank picked up speed in a spray of dust and gravel as we shot down the road. We had made roughly a hundred and fifty yards when Dixon braked as I barked 'Half left, now!' into the intercom. The tank slewed round with the locking of tracks, the steel of the hatch ring biting into my ribs, as Dixon yanked back on the left steering lever and we dropped down the bank with a thump. I had a sense of movement off to my right that suggested that we had stirred the enemy into life. What I didn't realise was that the German commander of the 88mm hidden in the trees had sited his anti-tank gun in anticipation of such a manoeuvre and had a direct line of sight along the left-hand side of the dyke.

I felt the pressure wave as several pounds of high-velocity tungsten steel, moving faster than the speed of sound, whip-cracked over my head. I heard the almighty crash of a gun's retort a split a second later, which confirmed that my visual reconnaissance had been less than complete. I hadn't spotted the ground-mounted 88mm gun or realised that the open field we had dropped into was saturated and swampy. Without a stitch of cover to our left, the only way out of the killing area was to get back up the bank. I shouted frantically into the microphone and the engine squealed in low-gear, high-revving protest, as Dixon hauled the tank round in an effort to get back up the steep incline of the bank. The tracks slipped in the soft churning mud and failed to gain purchase, as Dixon continued to push the engine hard. Our attempted flight put us in the wrong attitude to return fire and we were a sitting duck. The second round arrived in a long screaming shriek, ploughing a furrow into the ground next to the Sherman and showering me with earth, as the German gun crew adjusted their fall of shot. Caught broadside on to an enemy zeroing in on us with a lethal anti-tank gun was a tank commander's worst nightmare and I was about to order the crew to bail out when the next shell came in and everything went black.

I slumped back into the tank with my hands clamped to my eyes. My face was burning and I was yelling that I couldn't see. I was incapacitated and the crew were frozen with fear; as the commander, I was blind and so was the tank. Martin and Gartside were shouting at

Dixon to get us 'tha fook out of here'. Dixon was screaming back at them that he was 'doin 'is fooking best' and that they should 'shurap the fook up'. It was all happening in an instant, but it felt like the end. Then Ken Mayo reached across and prised my fingers away from my face. He cleared the gunk of dirt from my eyes and started shouting at me that I was all right. My sight came back in a blurred watery haze and I realised that I could still see. But my relief was short-lived, as my brain re-registered the predicament that we were in. Stuck fast on the side of a dyke and about to be brewed up. I hauled myself back up into the hatch ring, anticipating the crash of the next round and the devastating impact as the enemy gunners found their range. But while the 88mm crew had been slow, the commander of 2 Troop had been quick. A voice cut through the mush of static in my headset.

'Hello 5. Bet you thought you were a gonner there?' It was Harry Heenan.

Harry's troop had been operating two fields away to our left and had been screened by a long thick stand of poplar trees. He had spotted the anti-tank gun and saw it engage my tank. Knowing that he couldn't risk firing HE through the trees, Harry had dismounted and walked his own Sherman into a firing position where his 75mm gun could be brought to bear. His gunner then pumped out three rounds of HE in rapid succession. Only protected by an armoured plate shield on the front of their gun, the 88mm crew didn't stand a chance against the exploding rounds from Harry's tank and they lay dead among its broken carriage wheels. Surviving such a close shave was something akin to the feeling you get when you have just survived a near-miss collision with another car. Although far more intense, especially when mixed with the abstract notion that someone has just been doing their deliberate level best to kill you. I called him back on the radio, my voice charged with emotion and relief. Harry said something else, about me owing him a beer; then there was a click and the net went dead.

Anti-tank Ambush, Nijmegen

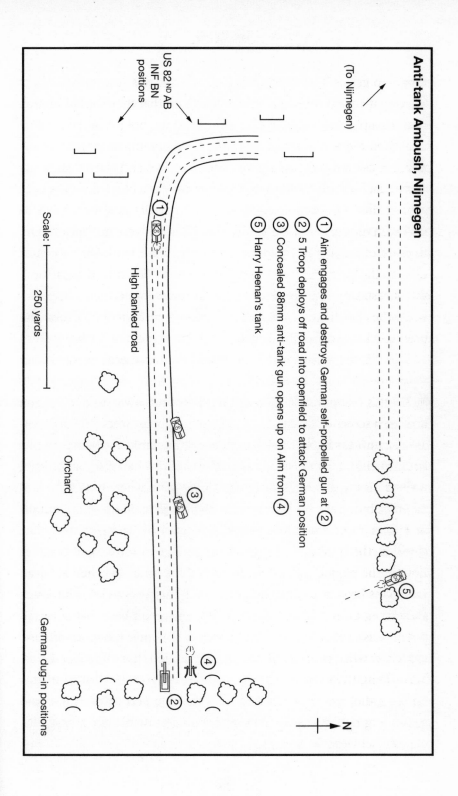

(To Nijmegen)

US 82ND AB INF BN positions

Scale: 250 yards

High banked road

Orchard

German dug-in positions

N

① Aim engages and destroys German self-propelled gun at ②

② 5 Troop deploys off road into openfield to attack German position

③ Concealed 88mm anti-tank gun opens up on Aim from ④

⑤ Harry Heenan's tank

I still had a dull headache from the effect of the shockwaves of the AP round that passed close enough to take my head off, as Corporal Lanes' Sherman towed us back up onto the top of the bank. He rolled his eyes at me when we were back on the road, but said that he was relieved that we were all right. Lanes had tried to get a shot in at the 88mm, but the position of Aim had obscured his line of fire. He was not the only one who thought we were dead meat. But what the Yanks thought about it I don't know and I didn't bother to find out. Darkness was approaching and I was glad that we could pull back out of the line; we had had enough excitement for one day. I sought out Harry as soon as we returned to the leaguer later that evening. I wanted to clap him on the back, ruffle his fair hair and thank him for what he had done. But I couldn't find him. Perhaps I should have read something in the eyes of his crew when I went up to his tank and asked where he was. I still couldn't believe it when John Semken took me gently aside and told me that Harry Heenan was dead.

In his elation at taking out the eighty-eight and saving our lives, Harry had leapt back into his tank and grabbed his mike to call me up on the radio. In the process he dropped his Sten gun. As the butt of the weapon hit the floor of the turret it fired off its action. The bullet it discharged hit Harry in the thigh and stomach. His wounds were fatal and he bled out in minutes, covering his crew with his blood. Harry Heenan had become another grim statistic among the thousands that had already paid the ultimate price in a vast army at war. In four months of fighting I had seen many men die. Men I had got to know, men I liked and respected. But death was all around us and there was seldom time to grieve. It was a constant of battle. You had to put each loss behind you and get on with the job at hand. But Harry Heenan was different. He had become my best friend in the regiment and I was shattered by his loss. I found it difficult to comprehend; one minute he had been there and now he was gone. Only a few days before we had been shooting out tabac signs and ribbing each other over our prowess, or lack of it, with a Luger. Harry had always been there at the end of a day in action to share a brew, talk and laugh with. Even after Semken had given me some rum and had spoken some kind fatherly words, which I have long since forgotten, I still expected Harry to appear round the side of a parked Sherman with his boyish grin, ready to rib me about the eighty-eight or a tabac sign that I had missed and he had not.

It was a friendship that had made the rigours of war more bearable and with Harry's loss I found myself having to cope with emotions I had never experienced before, which were hard to control in the company of others. Harry's troop had been cut up by his death; he was respected and liked across the squadron and a small cohesive unit feels it keenly when a popular young officer is killed. But as his closest friend I found the pain of his loss hardest to bear. John Semken had lost a number of good friends in North Africa and knew what I was going through. I suspect that the whole of A Squadron did; they knew Harry and I were close. I can remember registering their kindness and understanding, especially from my crew who squared the tank away for the next day's action without me having to utter a word. There was food and a brew for me when I got back to Aim, but all I wanted to do was be alone with my grief. I disappeared for a few hours into the darkness around our billets with a lump in my throat and my eyes welling with tears. Even today, looking back over all those years, the acute memory of the pain that came with Harry's death is still there.

The shock of the day's fighting and Harry's loss were still with me when I reflected on the weird geometry of chance in battle, which is no discriminator of rank or circumstance. I had survived being stuck fast on the side of a dyke, flank on to a deadly full-bore German 88mm anti-tank gun and Harry Heenan had been killed by the accidental discharge of his own cheaply manufactured weapon, having just saved my life. Harry was twenty-one years old and I had just reached my twentieth birthday a few days before. But the last vestige of my youth and the innocence that went with it seemed to die with him, just as the last hope of ending the war before Christmas had died with the forlorn British Paras at Arnhem. The canopies of the trees were daubed with the yellow and russet red of autumn, as if in a sad salute to the final passing of summer and optimism. Winter was coming and the war would go on. There would be tough fighting ahead of us and it would be even harder without my best friend.

11

SLOGGING IT

Operation Market Garden was the last major British offensive drive towards Germany in 1944. The failed attempt to capture the bridge at Arnhem left a thin sixty-mile salient that jutted into the enemy positions in Holland. Monty described it as a 'dagger pointing at the heart of Germany'. In reality the front line in the British sector would not move appreciably east for almost another six months, as it began to stagnate in the blood and the mud of the worst winter in thirty years. Various plans were conceived to advance on the German defences of the Siegfried Line, which stretched down the length of the western borders of the Third Reich. Also known as the West Wall, the construction of the Siegfried Line had started on Hitler's orders before the war. Its concrete pillboxes, anti-tank obstacles and thick belts of barbed wire extended the length of Germany's western frontier for some 350 miles from Switzerland to where the Rhine touched the Dutch border near the German city of Cleves. However, the approaches to the port of Antwerp would not be cleared until the end of November and with the continuing supply problem Eisenhower placed his priorities elsewhere. Behind us, the Canadians fought to clear the Scheldt Estuary and the Americans to our south pushed forward, as the Supreme Allied Commander sought to bring the US forces into line against the German border.

The Sherwood Rangers remained in the Nijmegen area as the US 1st, 3rd and 7th Armies battled slowly forward towards the enemy frontier to begin conforming on the right flank of the 2nd British Army. Although there were no major operations in our area of the front we were far from inactive. The squadrons continued to rotate between Mook and Beek in support of the 82nd Airborne Division. We supported their patrols and minor attacks to strengthen the bridgehead and fought off local German counterattacks. We shelled their positions and they shelled ours. But it was hardly a war of movement and gains were measured in terms of a wood line or a field won or lost. For the most part the opposing sides remained static. Often we were close enough that our wireless frequencies overlapped and the Germans would tune into our net. They would refer to us as Tommies and tell us that we were *Schweinhunde* and they were coming to get us. I couldn't resist the temptation to get back to them on the radio and tell them they had better hurry up, as we would have a cup of tea on the go for them when they arrived. My crew liked that. Harry Heenan would have seen the funny side of it too.

The enemy made repeated bombing raids against the bridge at Nij-megen. They also attempted to destroy the large steel structure using floating bombs, midget submarines and, on one occasion, frogmen, who managed to damage the bridge severely with explosives. But while there were no major ground offensives, there were still some small-scale tank actions. At the end of September, C Squadron broke up a German attack around Beek, when they caught a number of Panthers and Jagdpanthers, along with their supporting infantry, in the flat open ground to the southeast of the town. C Squadron's Shermans ambushed them at first light and had a field day, knocking out at least four of the enemy tanks. We were in the south at the time operating around Mook, but when we moved up to relieve

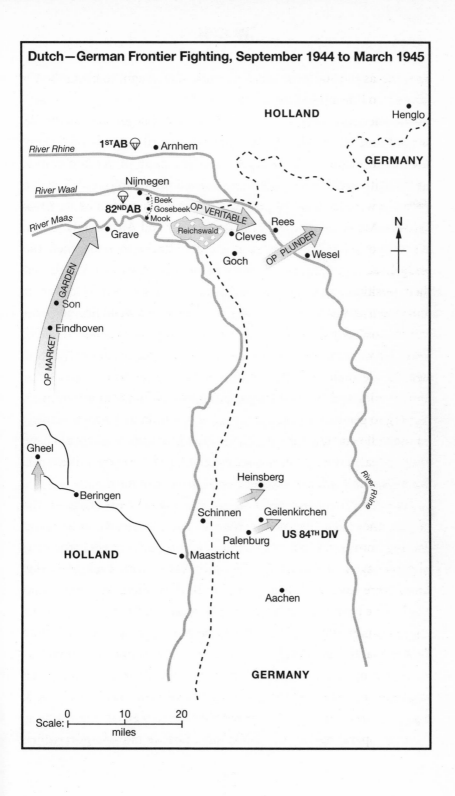

Dutch—German Frontier Fighting, September 1944 to March 1945

HOLLAND

Henglo

River Rhine 1ST AB Arnhem

GERMANY

Nijmegen

River Waal

82ND AB Beek OP VERITABLE

River Maas Gosebeek

Mook

Grave Reichswald

Cleves Rees

Goch OP PLUNDER Wesel

N

GARDEN

Son

Eindhoven

OP MARKET

Gheel

Heinsberg

Beringen

Schinnen Geilenkirchen

Palenburg US 84TH DIV

HOLLAND Maastricht

Aachen

River Rhine

GERMANY

Scale: 0   10   20

miles

C Squadron in the Beek sector the next day, the blackened shells of several German armoured vehicles still lay abandoned between the dykes and the orchards. The large inert hulk of a Jagdpanther was located close to our troop position, the barrel of its eighty-eight hanging down at a lopsided angle across the front of its sloped, armoured glacis plate. The self-propelled gun showed none of the signs of being hastily abandoned, as the ground around it was absent of the usual scattered items of equipment that tended to be dropped by a crew when bailing out from a stricken vehicle. Motivated by curiosity and the lure of looting another enemy pistol, I couldn't resist the temptation to look inside it. I was particularly keen to get my hands on a German Walther P-38 pistol, which was even better than a Luger.

The Jagdpanther was a giant of a beast compared to a Sherman and was liberally provisioned with external armoured stowage bins, which provided protected storage space for the crew's kit, putting our storage arrangements to shame. Lashed under nothing more than a canvas tarpaulin, our personal gear was forever being shot up. The cargo bins were also an obvious place to look for booty, but the only thing I found of any interest inside them was a large red-and-white Nazi flag with a black swastika emblazoned in the middle. I made my way forward to the top of the vehicle and prised open one of the heavy steel-plate crew hatches. The foul stench of decomposition and cooked human flesh hit my nostrils even before the hatch had locked home into its open position. The inside of the vehicle was a charnel house. What was left of the crew had been incinerated into charred black lumps and the intensity of the inferno that had raged inside the Jagdpanther when it was hit had fused the bodies into their seats. I recoiled back from the ghastly sight, my stomach churning over, as I grabbed the Nazi flag and scrambled down off the vehicle. I vowed that I would never be tempted to look inside a knocked-out tank again.

A week later, the regiment was pulled out of the line. After three days' rest we were sent to support the infantry formations holding an area on the northern side of the Nijmegen Bridge known as the 'Island'. Nestling in the Y junction where the Waal and Lower Rhine meet, the Island is a flat spit of land lying between Nijmegen and Arnhem. Enclosed by the split of the two rivers as they flowed east towards the sea, the Island represented the high water mark of XXX Corps' advance during Market Garden and the bridge the corps had failed to capture lay temptingly close on the other side of the Rhine. Each of the three armoured regiments in 8th Armoured Brigade rotated through a ten to twelve day tour of duty, supporting one of the two infantry divisions on the Island. Initially, the Sherwood Rangers supported the US 101st Airborne Division. The American paratroopers of the Screaming Eagles were as famous as their counterparts in the 82nd Airborne Division, but we saw little action with them. The second rotation on the Island was equally quiet and we worked with 43rd Wessex Division. Von Thoma's men must have been similarly relieved that there was no significant operational activity, beyond intermittent shelling, sniping, patrolling and the odd skirmish. But the most significant enemy was the weather.

By late October, the last of the leaves had been stripped from the trees and the flat, dreary, grey landscape seemed all the more bleak. The temperature dropped and the rain started to fall incessantly. We were issued tank suits. An all-in-one light stone-coloured garment, they were good pieces of kit and had a zip down the middle and copious map pockets. They were also showerproof and fleece lined, which helped against the cold, but they couldn't keep us completely dry. The large fan that cooled the tank's engine sucked in huge amounts of freezing air through the turret hatch and pulled in every icy droplet of rain with it. Working its way through the seams, the water pooled in the crotch of my suit and dripped down the backs of the loader and the gunner. While it made life in the turret pretty miserable, as usual it was the poor bloody infantry who suffered most. We were fortunate in that we still pulled back to leaguers at night. Additionally, the crews were billeted in the homes of local civilians, where we could get dry and prepare a meal under cover. In comparison, the infantry stayed forward and lived in the waterlogged slit trenches dug into the flooded low-lying ground. With little more than sodden greatcoats and the odd blanket to keep them warm, they had to tramp back into the rear areas to pick up their food before taking it back to their dugouts, where they ate it under the inadequate cover of a gas cape stretched over their muddy holes in a vain attempt to keep out the rain. In such conditions, it was hardly surprising that the old First World War scourge of trench foot came back to haunt them.

Apart from dry billets, the static nature of operations also had other advantages. We usually had four to five days between rotations and the time away from the Island allowed us to take leave in Brussels. In mid-October, 8th Armoured Brigade established a rest camp at the town of Leuven, which was located fifteen miles to the east of the Belgian capital. It took six hours in the back of a freezing army truck to get to Leuven from Nijmegen, but it meant that we could enjoy a two-day pass in the city. Brussels provided ample opportunity for the blokes to pursue their primary off-duty predilection for booze, food and women, or what the men referred to as 'bints' or 'crumpet'. Recently liberated and still suffering from the strictures of rationing, the majority of the population found food in short supply. However, the black market was thriving as it was fuelled by the influx of thousands of Allied soldiers, all ready to trade compo rations, loot and issued cigarettes for the pursuit of pleasure. The officers were no exception, but our desires tended to be less racy and were gratified by staying in grand hotels like Le Plaza, located near the famous Grand Place. We could blow the best part of a month's pay staying there, enjoying endless hot baths, fine dining and the luxury of sleeping between crisp, clean white sheets. During one forty-eight hour leave period, I met up with my brother. All the hotels in Brussels reserved for officers were full and we were directed to accommodation at 8 Rue de la Place. The mirror fixed to the ceiling above the large double bed in the room we were sharing indicated that we were staying in a less than salubrious establishment. Being a little more worldly-wise than me, Geoffrey suggested that we were staying in a brothel. As if on cue, a knock on the door confirmed his suspicion and my brother politely informed the Madame that we would not be requiring her services or those of her girls.

While the halt to major operations in the north provided us with the occasional opportunity to take leave away from the front line, on 8 November the Sherwood Rangers received orders to support American operations in the south. XXX Corps had already handed over the Nijmegen sector to Canadian troops at the beginning of the month and had taken up new positions at the southern end of the British line near Maastricht, where it met the northern boundary of the 9th US Army.

On the afternoon of 9 November, we loaded our Shermans on to tank transporters and began the long journey through the night to the small town of Schinnen, ten miles from Maastricht, which lies close to the Dutch–German border. The 9th Army was a new American formation and had only recently arrived in Europe. To their immediate south, their more experienced countrymen in the US 1st Army had spent October battling towards the German frontier to capture Aachen. The American attack had driven a significant dent into the German defences of the Siegfried Line. But while the German front line had sagged under the pressure of the American attack it had not broken and it had left a twenty-five-mile wide bulge. In order to straighten the defences, maintain pressure on the Germans and set the conditions to continue the advance to the Rhine, 1st and 9th US Armies were ordered to push the bulge back. Codenamed Operation Clipper, a key 9th Army objective of the operation lay in pinching out a thin salient of the Siegfried Line around the German town of

Geilenkirchen. As a recent addition to the Americans' growing order of battle, the 9th US Army lacked experience and it was agreed that XXX Corps would be placed under their command to assist them in taking Geilenkirchen. The attack would require two divisions. Horrocks would use 8th Armoured Brigade and von Thoma's 43rd Wessex Division, but as it was the only British division available his corps was reinforced with the US 84th Infantry Division. While the other regiments of 8th Armoured Brigade would support the British infantry battalions of the 43rd Wessex, Horrocks directed that the Sherwood Rangers would be used to support the US division allocated to his command.

Nicknamed the 'Railsplitters', because of their divisional insignia – an axe splitting a rail – the American soldiers of the 84th US Division were also new to theatre, having only recently arrived from their training camps in Texas. They were the product of an impressive industrialised process that could train and equip a complete homogenous division of 14,000 men made up of infantry, artillery and specialist units, which would allow it to fight as a single joined-up formation. Like their counterparts in the 82nd Airborne Division, the 84th US Infantry Division wore distinctive olive-green field-jackets and carried the same Garand .30-calibre semi-automatic rifle, known as the M1. They also wore the typical American Doughboy helmet, but unlike the American paratroopers it lacked the characteristic airborne camouflage netting cover and they wore gaiters instead of tucking their combat pants into the tops of their boots. In contrast to their airborne cousins, they were green and untested. As they lacked the experience that only battle can bring, Horrocks decided that, as his most experienced armoured regiment, the Sherwood Rangers should be used to support them. It was a worthy accolade, but it also meant that we would be involved in a six-day slogging match in the most atrocious conditions against prepared defensive positions that would test us to the limit.

No longer needed in the wake of the Nazi victories in 1940, the Siegfried Line had been left neglected and stripped of most of its guns. With the collapse of the German position in Normandy, over 300,000 civilians had been conscripted to improve its fortifications. Since late August they had been employed in the desperate process of building new bunkers, digging trenches, deepening minefields and erecting new barbed-wire entanglements. Capitalising on the pause in Allied operations during the autumn, the Germans had strengthened the defences further, which now lay, better prepared and menacing, just a mile ahead of us beyond the bleak mining town of Palenberg, which would be our jumping-off point with the Americans.

Palenberg had been smashed to pieces by artillery fire and we spent six miserable days there sheltering in the desolated remains of its buildings and cellars, among the ugly slag heaps that surrounded the town, as we waited for the weather to clear and the bombers to arrive. On 16 November, the rain finally stopped for long enough to allow 2500 British and American aircraft to drop 9400 tons of high explosives on the enemy's positions. The artillery then added several hundred tons of shells to the bombardment before the US 2nd Armoured Division began to advance on the right flank. Our own attack with the 84th US Infantry Division started two days later, in the early hours of the morning, once the American armour had taken its objectives. The 43rd Wessex Division advanced on our right, but the task of taking Geilenkirchen and the high ground around it would fall to the regiment and the American infantry that we were supporting.

Geilenkirchen is a nondescript drab German town that sits on the northern bank of the river Wurm. It was once a minor rail and road hub for the surrounding mining district, but in 1944 its importance stemmed from the fact that it formed the forward bastion of the portion of the Siegfried Line that jutted furthest into the Allied lines. Recognising its significance, the Germans had made good use of the available time and the surrounding terrain to enhance its defences. The embankments and cuttings of the railway line running on the southern side of the river had been turned into a substantial anti-tank obstacle, forming the first line of defence in front of the town. Every obvious breaching point had been heavily mined and covered by the interlocking fire of numerous pillboxes and gun casements. Trenches had been dug between the bunkers, which would allow the defenders to move unhindered and unseen between threatened strong points. Additionally, the fields of fire to their front had been systematically cleared to ensure that the lethal effect of their machine guns and anti-tank weapons could be maximised. Designed to withstand artillery and tank fire, each concrete fortification would have to be dealt with in turn. Geilenkirchen itself was held by a Volksgrenadier Division. Behind Geilenkirchen lay more defensive positions spread out in depth and extending for several miles in and around the surrounding villages. To the rear of these defensive positions, the tanks of the 9th and 10th SS divisions lay waiting in reserve, ready to be launched forward to conduct counterattacks.

It was pitch black when we married up with the infantry of the Railsplitters' 333rd Regiment on the morning of 18 November. We waited cold and wet in heavy falling rain, as our artillery opened up and pounded the ground in front of us with a terrific barrage that lasted for ninety minutes. It was still dark when the order came to advance, but the brilliant beams of a battery of searchlights reflecting off the clouds illuminated the area. Known as 'Monty's moonlight', the searchlights turned the world around us into a blue-black monochrome, in which we could make out the dark outline of the specialised armour as it began moving forward to the first line of obstacles. It was led by Sherman flail tanks that would beat a path through the minefields and these were followed by Churchill engineer tanks, which were equipped to create gaps in the obstacle belts and blast out bunkers with their short, stubby 290mm Petard spigot mortars. We were also supported by Crocodile tanks, which towed tanks of fuel behind them and belched liquid jets of flame from their hulls. Moving like some form of mythical armoured dragon, they made for a terrible sight as they hosed down the embrasure of a concrete bunker and covered its occupants in blazing petroleum. Ultimately, they forced the defenders to flee from the fiery confines of their bunkers, often ablaze and in agony. The supporting tanks or the infantry would then shoot them down. But first we had to get there.

A Squadron set off through the first minefield in column behind John Semken's Sherman, which followed one of the flail tanks, while the American infantry moved off on foot on the right flank. The heavy steel chains on the giant rotating drum of the flail tank flayed deep into the oozing mud. They sent up a continuous spray of sticky wet pieces of earth and fountains of water, as the round metal weights on the end of the chain links sought out the Teller mines buried beneath the quagmire the ground had become. As the flail tank beat through the minefield in a whir of spinning metal and mud, the first mines began to explode in a shower of oozing debris. But its progress became slower and more laboured as the morass of mud became deeper and thicker. The specialised tank was two thirds of the way through 200 yards of minefield when it became bogged in up to the top of its tracks and stopped. With the troops of his squadron strung out behind him, Semken made the practical but courageous decision to take over the lead in his own Sherman. The column was being bracketed by German artillery fire and the infantry needed our support. Pushing past the stricken flail, he pressed on through the sea of mud. There were fifty yards to go. As the mud became deeper the tank's engine laboured hard to maintain forward movement. Semken and his crew held their breath, waiting for the inevitable detonation beneath their tracks as they ground agonizingly through the mire. It looked as if they would make it when an almighty series of explosions lifted the tank bodily into the air.

The force of four exploding Teller mines stripped the running gear from the tank's bogie wheels and tracks and it thumped back down unceremoniously into the mud. Miraculously, none of the crew was seriously injured, but the tank was a write-off. The rest of the squadron pushed past the destroyed vehicle and we made our way unscathed out of the minefield to continue the advance towards the enemy positions with the infantry. The area we had just crossed was still under artillery fire and Semken ordered his crew to split up and make their way back to our own lines. Under the direction of the squadron's second in command, we pressed on to close up with and cover the movement of the other specialised armour as they set about dealing with the pillboxes and remaining obstacles. With gaps made in the line, we pushed through the breaches accompanied by the American infantry. Then the MG42s opened up from the firing ports of the bunkers located in depth and GIs began to fall.

While the Shermans were impervious to the German machine-gun fire that ricocheted off their steel sides, their 75mm and 17-pounder guns could not punch through the four or five feet of concrete that protected each pillbox. But we could suppress the firing-point embrasure with HE to allow the surviving infantry to pull themselves out of the oozing mud and get close to the offending bunker, where they could then lob grenades through its firing port. The Germans often closed their embrasures to keep out our HE fragments and the Americans' grenades, but in doing so they rendered themselves blind and inert, which allowed the infantry to get round behind them and blow in the steel entrance doors at their rear with satchel charges of explosives. The Yanks would then clear the interiors with automatic fire and more grenades, just as they had been taught to do on their training ranges in Louisiana. What the Americans lacked in experience, they certainly made up for in eagerness and their skills were improved and refined through the hard teaching of battle. However, the cost of such learning was measured in the lifeless forms stuck face down in the mud and the frantic cries of 'Medic!', which went up as a clarion call after every heavy burst of German machine-gun or mortar fire.

The process of clearing each defensive line was painfully slow and the sequence of suppressing, blasting and clearing was repeated as we came across more positions in depth beyond the railway bank. The quagmire of liquid mud that we struggled through was proving almost as effective in hindering our advance as the subsequent mine-fields, anti-tank guns and bunkers that we came across during our painstaking crawl towards Geilenkirchen. However, with the crust of the forward defences broken, the defenders of the town put up only light opposition and we followed the infantry as they once again put their training into practice and systematically cleared its streets building by building. Like so many of the towns and villages we had advanced through in Normandy, Geilenkirchen had been pounded by Allied aircraft and artillery and was a shattered ruin. Unlike France, the authorities had evacuated most of the German civilians before the fighting started. But it was still enemy territory and we took no chances as we supported the infantry's advance through the rain-sodden rubble-strewn streets that were littered with abandoned equipment and enemy dead. The slightest hint of opposition met with almost point-blank fire from our 75mms, although most of the Germans appeared to be second-rate troops and were only too ready to give up. Files of prisoners were soon emerging from bunker positions and cellars, some waving white flags or approaching us with their arms raised.

With Geilenkirchen taken, we pushed on northeast beyond the town to support other companies of the American 333rd and 334th regiments, as they attacked positions in the surrounding villages located along a five-mile stretch of the Wurm valley. The village of Prummern lies a mile to the east of Geilenkirchen on the south side of the Wurm River and was A Squadron's next objective. As we left the town behind us, we ran into the depth positions of the Siegfried Line. German resistance stiffened and we found ourselves repeating the process of slogging forward pillbox by pillbox with the infantry. B Squadron advanced on our right and made equally slow progress. The ground was atrocious and several tanks became irrevocably bogged down in the mud, forcing their crews to abandon them. As we pushed deeper into the defensive layout and reached the outskirts of Prummern we encountered enemy tanks concealed among the houses of the village. An armoured duel ensued, as we traded anti-tank shots with a half-company of Panthers. A German tank was knocked out and then one of our Shermans was hit by an AP round that penetrated through the top of the tank, killing its commander and one of the turret crew. Sergeant George Dring employed his celebrated tactic of dismounting to seek out the remaining enemy panzers on foot and walk his 17-pounder equipped Firefly into a killing position. But his luck ran out. When Dring approached a Panther he thought had been destroyed the German tank suddenly burst into life and engaged him with its main armament. The round landed sufficiently close to him to wound one of his hands badly and remove three of his fingers; a direct hit from the 75mm gun would have blown him to pieces. Although the injury was not life threatening, Dring's tank-stalking days were over.

The eastern end of the village was still in enemy hands when C Squadron finally relieved us and we pulled back to Palenberg. While the Sherwood Rangers could claim to be the first British unit to create a breach in the Siegfried Line, the regiment had not broken through it. We had taken a day to advance just three miles and the depth positions of the German defences remained intact. A Squadron had taken losses in men and tanks, but Dring and the members of the crew killed outside Prummern were not our only casualties, as John Semken had also been posted as missing in action. When his tank was blown up in the minefield and his crew made it back to our lines, it had been assumed that John had moved on to assume command of another tank to continue the battle. When Semken's call sign failed to come up on the regimental net, he was posted as missing and the padre went forward into the battle area to look for him.

Leslie Skinner eventually found Semken sitting in a small captured pillbox reading poetry. Semken appeared to be in a confused state, which was often described as being 'bomb happy'; a colloquial term for someone suffering from extreme battle fatigue or shock. As the fighting raged around them, Skinner sat with him and the two men talked about poetry until they decided to walk back to RHQ. When he reported to the CO, Semken was still in a state of shock. He was stood down from action for a twenty-four hour period, which was the normal policy in the regiment for a commander that had just survived having his tank knocked out from under him. But it was an ominous sign of the mounting stress that the man we had considered to be indomitable was under. A Squadron spent the next day resting and reorganising in Palenberg, which I suspect might have had something to do with what had happened to John Semken. We returned to the battle the following day in support of the rifle companies of the 333rd Regiment, as they launched an attack on the village of Kogenbroich, which lay two and a half miles beyond Geilenkirchen on the west bank of the Wurm River.

It was still dark and raining hard, as we waited on the start line with the American infantry, who sheltered in the ditches at the side of the road, as our artillery opened up. They felt the warmth of their early morning rum ration in their bellies, a benefit of being under British command. We sat in our tanks and counted the minutes to H Hour, the allotted time when the firing would lift and the attack would begin, as the shells shrieked overhead. The expectation of battle is often worse than the battle itself and the crew were pensive and quiet. Each one of us was wondering how many times we had done this before, whether our luck would hold out and what would be waiting for us when we moved against the fixed line of defences, which the enemy had had ample time to prepare. Although no one spoke of it, the thought of hitting a mine was ever present in our thoughts, as was the risk of getting bogged in the mud, stuck fast and disabled, an easy target for an AP round. Throughout, the luminous minute hands of our watches ticked relentlessly on and H Hour came, the artillery lifted and we started to advance.

The infantry moved off on our flanks across the flat, waterlogged fields. They had been churned into a sticky morass of deep boot-sucking mud that forced us to keep to the single-axis road that ran towards the village. It was an obvious approach route for tanks and we shot up the ground ahead of us as a precaution against mines. The Americans pushed on across the open ground without cover, crouching and hunched in anticipation, as they slowly closed the distance to the first buildings ahead of us. Then the German machine guns started, whipping up sheets of water in front of them as they sought shelter in flooded shell holes and folds in the earth; anything that might offer them a modicum of refuge from the murderous fire. They risked getting cut to pieces if they stayed where they were, so I dismounted from Aim and ran over to tie up with a squad of GIs crawling in the mud. I think they were somewhat taken aback at my appearance and sudden arrival. I wore my beret instead of a helmet, my tank suit must have looked pristine compared to men covered in the saturated filth of three days of fighting and my offer to go forward and take out the offending MG42s that were causing so much bother might have seemed overly polite, given the circumstances. But they were right up behind us after we had put three rounds into the first house. Twenty-odd Germans came out with their hands up, unwilling to face an assault by the infantry having just been blasted by HE. Then the enemy put a stonk right on top of us and a heavy concentration of shells crashed around us. Some of the German prisoners ran in panic and the Americans shot them down.

We pressed on across more open fields as soon as the shelling abated. The pillboxes in the next line were covered in earth and blended in against the bleak landscape they defended. A series of muzzle flashes betrayed their presence, as did the men who spun and splashed into the mud as they were hit. The infantry sought cover in the muck once more, as we moved up and suppressed every flashing embrasure. Then the Yanks pulled themselves out of the squelching filth and crawled and dashed forward to work their way round the pillboxes and take them out from the rear. And so it went on. Men fell as we cleared one field then another, met the next line of resistance and repeated the process until the light began to fail. But the village had not been taken and with darkness approaching we were becoming increasingly vulnerable and could no longer support the infantry with fire. The Americans didn't like it when we pulled back, but they knew that we were becoming increasingly exposed and needed to withdraw to 'gas up' as they put it. I felt guilty about leaving them, as they began to dig into water-filled holes to spend the night shivering in the cold and the rain. It was dark by the time we headed back towards Geilenkirchen, guided by the light of the searchlight battery established behind the town. Where we could, we stopped to pick up wounded and dead GIs and brought them back on the decks of our tanks.

The rain was still falling as we reached the leaguer long after dark. We were dog-tired, cold, wet and hungry, but we still had to complete the lengthy process of refuelling, replenishing with rations and water and bombing up each of the tanks. Even with the assistance of the fringed edge of artificial illumination from the searchlight battery it was hard graft, as we worked in the cold biting rain and the darkness with numb fingers to strip off the cardboard casings of ammunition boxes, slip off the safety clips from the fuses and load the brass-cased rounds of HE, AP and smoke shells into their racks inside Aim one by one. The .30-calibre ammunition belts had to be inspected to check that the rounds were sitting properly in their links before each box could be stowed. Dixon had to complete essential maintenance amid the thick clay mud that had congealed in the tracks, while Ken Mayo sat cramped in the dripping confines of the turret as he replaced wireless valves and checked that the radio was working. It was gone midnight by the time we had finished, received orders, had something to eat and then slumped exhausted into our billets. We would be up and out of the leaguer long before daylight the next morning, ready to repeat what we had done the day before as we slogged up the narrow, miserable flooded valley on the other side of Geilenkirchen once again. The process continued for another three bloody awful days and the relentless effort and fatigue began to take its toll.

On the sixth and final day of the attack, 23 November, I committed the cardinal sin; I was late for H Hour. For reasons that I can only put down to being utterly shattered, I had overslept. I woke with a start to the sound of tank engines outside the billet, as the squadron formed up and moved out of the leaguer. Pulling on my tank suit over my pyjamas, I raced down the stairs of the billet, shot through the door of the building and scrambled into Aim. The rest of the crew were already mounted in the Sherman and we sped after the rest of A Squadron. They had already crossed the start line for the attack by the time we caught them up. John Semken's voice was loud in my headset, his voice laced with invective, as he asked where the hell I had been, told me to get a move on and to push forward to support the leading American platoon that had come up against an enemy pillbox. Daylight was already creeping over the horizon as we headed up the single road towards Kogenbroich and I told Dixon to step on it. We hurried past a few shell-damaged farm buildings and I saw a squad of infantrymen flat on their bellies in the middle of a field. A machine gun flashed from the embrasure of a bunker a few hundred yards to their front, pinned them down and kicked up the mud around them in vicious little fountains. Haste in military operations is a dangerous thing and I might have paused to shoot up the road in front of us, but with the infantry caught in the open and an angry squadron commander on my case, I pressed on to get into a fire position as fast as possible. We were barely level with the American squad, and had started to open fire, when the tank rocked to a bone-jarring halt. There was a blinding flash of yellow light and a deafening bang. A sheet of bright stabbing sparks lit up the inside of the tank and in an instant it was full of thick, choking black smoke.

The crew of a tank might survive an encounter with a Teller mine relatively unscathed if it only blasted off a track or smashed the running gear. But if it penetrated the armour of the belly plate, the consequences for the driver and the hull gunner at the front of the tank could be devastating. I ducked into the turret and squirmed past Mayo, my mouth and nose filled with the acrid taste of burned explosive, as I sought to assess the damage. The crew checked in amid their coughing and a multitude of expletives. Dixon was worryingly quiet. The mine had detonated under the right track and its blast had deflected off the bogie wheels to penetrate the floor of the tank at its weakest point. The force of the explosion had turned the heavy plate escape hatch, located behind the hull gunner, into a lethal projectile. Miraculously, it had missed Gartside, but it had smashed into Dixon's back, killing him instantly. I clawed my way back into the hatch, just in time to see a group of Germans wheeling an anti-tank gun round the side of the pillbox. Disabled and unable to fight back, it was time to go and I ordered the crew to bail out.

Grabbing the radio code books and my Schmeisser, I shouted at Martin and Mayo, 'For God's sake, dismount over the rear decks and keep to the tank tracks!'

The last thing I wanted was to set off any more mines. We doubled back up the road at a crouch, as the inevitable machine-gun bullets smacked into the ground round our heels and cracked over our heads. There was a loud crump and crack around the tank, as Jerry attempted to get us with his mortars. My heart was thumping with the effort of running and the adrenaline that coursed through my body, when we came across a wounded GI sheltering in a ditch. We stopped briefly, grabbed his arms and pulled him along with us, his feet dragging in the mud. With an injured man in tow, we needed to get into cover quickly and we made for one of the buildings we had passed before we had been blown up.

Stanley Christopherson was somewhat taken aback as four tank men, coal-black from burned explosive, and an injured American burst into the farmhouse he was sitting in with the commander of the 8th Armoured Brigade. As my commanding officer, he was probably even more dumbfounded as I proceeded to tell him that I had been blown up, needed a new tank and demanded to know what he was going to do about it. I was in a highly agitated state and no doubt still suffering from the shock of what had just happened. I noticed a bottle of wine on the table, although I stopped myself short from telling the CO that I could also do with a drink. Perhaps it was the absurdity of the situation, but training and military discipline has its place and before he could answer me I snapped to attention, saluted and sharply turned about. Stalking out of the house, I stomped off to find my troop corporal, turfed Lane out of his tank and went back into action.

I never knew what Christopherson thought of my outburst. I expect he took it in his stride, which was a reflection of the type of man he was. Stanley Christopherson had been a troop leader himself, before commanding a squadron and then taking over command of the regiment. Having had five tanks shot out from under him in North Africa he knew what it was like to be in the forefront of battle with all the risks and stresses it entailed. Conversely, as a lowly lieutenant, I never realised the pressures he was under as the CO. He had to deal with shits like von Thoma, send his men into action again and again and keep the unit going in the most demanding of circumstances. Christopherson was not a regular officer, but he was cool and calm in combat and I am convinced that he kept us performing when other units faltered and that we lost fewer men as a result of his professional leadership. Throughout he balanced his competence with compassion and consideration for those he commanded. He could level with his soldiers and officers in a way that made him popular with all ranks. Shortly after joining the Sherwood Rangers, I can remember him standing by the side of my tank in Normandy in full view of the enemy, asking me how I was getting on, as shot and shell rained down around us. To us, nothing appeared to faze Stanley Christopherson and he always seemed to be smiling and laughing, but he felt every loss in the regiment with a keen sense of personal guilt, which troubled him deeply to an extent that none of us ever knew at the time.

The particular responsibility for the regiment's dead and wounded must have weighed heavily on Christopherson's mind after the fighting around Geilenkirchen. Later on 23 November the Sherwood Rangers were pulled out of the line and we handed over to a US battalion of tanks. The attack up the narrow sector of the Wurm valley would go on, but it would be someone else's battle. Six days of near-constant combat in the rain and mud had cost us sixty-three men. Fifteen had been killed in action, including poor Joe Dixon. We lost nine other Shermans along with our trusty tank Aim, which had pulled us faithfully all the way from the beaches of Normandy and now lay a broken hulk on some desolate muck-covered road. Five other tanks were damaged and another five were so badly bogged down in the mire of the valley that they were beyond recovery. The American infantry had also suffered; the US 84th Infantry Division lost 169 men killed and over a 1000 of its GIs were wounded. Although Dixon was just one life among so many, as a crew of five we felt his loss. Closed down in an environment restricted to a narrow slit of vision, a tank driver's lot is not an enviable one. His connection to the wider world is limited to the voice of the commander giving him instructions in his headset and the backbreaking work of maintaining the vehicle when out of it. But the quiet young man from Nottinghamshire had driven us with skill and had kept Aim on the road from France to the frontiers of Germany and we would miss him. However, we had to put his passing behind us. Death was all around us and to some extent we had become numb to it. We would get another driver, we would be issued with another tank and the war would go on. But someone's else's universe would be shattered by his death, which would be announced by a short official telegram from the War Office regretting to inform his next of kin that their beloved Joe had been killed in action.

The whole squadron felt the loss of its leader. In war, every man has a finite bank account of endurance and John Semken had been spending heavily. Like Stanley Christopherson, I never realised at the time the huge pressure he was under. While we slept for a brief few hours, as the squadron leader Semken would be up long into the night after we had gone to bed, studying maps and thinking through his orders for the next day's battle. He would be constantly rechecking his plans, asking himself if he had done it right, if he had done enough to prepare us and whether his decisions would save or cost lives on the coming morrow. All John's friends who had been so important in keeping him going as a troop commander had been killed in the desert. One had been blown to pieces right next to him as he sat on the turret of his tank, covering Semken in his grisly remains; which was why he became sensitive to anyone climbing up on to his tank and sitting next to him. The tank that he had lost at Geilenkirchen had been the third that had been destroyed under him. He had so desperately wanted to command A Squadron, when he could have held a safer job on the regiment's headquarters staff, but ultimately his willingness to continue to serve at the front had cost him. His injury was not physical, but poor old John had come too far and seen too much and after Geilenkirchen he had passed the limit of endurance and the constant exposure to combat had just become too much.

Today John Semken's condition would be referred to as post-traumatic stress disorder or PTSD, but then it was recorded as 'battle fatigue' and it was severe enough for him to be posted away from the Sherwood Rangers to a training job back in England. John Semken did not leave immediately, but stayed on long enough to attend an investiture on 30 November, where Field Marshal Bernard Montgomery pinned the Military Cross* on to John's breast. It was a richly deserved mark of his gallantry and a fitting way to end his last few days in the unit. But John had been our rock. We worshipped him and loved him in a way that only soldiers can love one another. The circumstances of his departure meant there was no time to say goodbye, but regardless of how he left we knew that we would face a more uncertain future without him, especially in the weeks and months that lay ahead, as the Germans seemed willing to fight to the end.

---

* John Semken was also awarded a Silver Star by the Americans for his leadership and gallantry during operations at Geilenkirchen.

12

ADVANCE TO THE RHINE

I was at the brigade leave camp near Brussels, acting as the regiment's imprest officer, when news of the Ardennes flap broke. After Geilenkirchen, the Sherwood Rangers had been moved out of the line with the rest of XXX Corps to prepare for an all-out advance on the Rhine. The Scheldt Estuary had been cleared by the end of November and with the port of Antwerp now finally opened the Allies were bringing in sufficient supplies to build up their forces to resume large-scale offensive operations across the front. The attack would begin as soon as the incessant rains of the autumn had given way to the freezing temperatures of winter, which would harden the ground and improve the going for tanks. As we waited for the big push to begin, the rest centre at Leuven had reopened and I had been sent there to issue pay to the soldiers to spend on their forays into the Belgian capital. But Hitler took advantage of the weather before we did. On 16 December 200,000 men of the 5th Panzer, 6th SS Panzer and 7th Armies crashed through the lightly held sector of the Ardennes forest, catching the Allies by surprise, just as they had done in May 1940. The intention was to split the American and British armies and capture Antwerp. It took two days for the news of the enemy breakthrough to reach us.

By the time it did, the leading panzers had already penetrated twenty miles into US lines.

The leave camp was rife with rumours and speculation of an imminent collapse at the front and of SS soldiers dressed in American uniforms and German paratroopers operating in our rear. There were even fears that Brussels might fall. Despite the alarm and anxiety, there was no direction as to what we should do, but I knew that in such a situation I should get back to the regiment as fast as possible. In the absence of orders, or any other Sherwood Rangers officers to defer to, I commandeered a 15-cwt truck, packed it with as many of the unit's blokes as I could find who were on leave in the camp and set out for Schinnen. The small Dutch town where the regiment was quartered is 150 miles due east of Brussels; if I put my foot down, I knew that I could get back there in less than eight hours of hard driving. We did it in seven, although in my haste I managed to turn over the truck on an icy, cambered stretch of road. Fortunately I did so without causing any serious injuries to my passengers or significant damage to the truck and we reported back for duty expecting to be sent straight into action.

Despite the initial panic, the Battle of the Bulge was largely an American affair. The Sherwood Rangers were put on notice to act as a mobile reserve, but we were not needed. By the beginning of the final week in December, Hitler's last gamble was already petering out and we were able to celebrate Christmas at Schinnen. The deep covering of crisp, even snow, tank-drawn sleigh rides and presents of sweets from our ration packs for the local children, plus an all-ranks dinner of tinned turkey and bottles of beer served by the officers to the men, should all have added to the festive mood. But despite the glee of the Dutch children and the traditional celebratory fair, the prospect of an imminent return to action was uppermost in our thoughts.

Schinnen was in a relatively quiet sector of the line. Most of the action was taking place to our south in the freezing forests of the Ardennes, as the American forces drove back the bulge the German offensive had driven into their front. But it didn't prevent the enemy facing us from making their own local attacks against us. As ever, our own infantry were thin on the ground and on 28 December two Wehrmacht companies used the cover of night to infiltrate into the villages of Vintelen and Kievelberg. One of our Shermans in Vintelen got a bloody nose from a Panzerfaust and I ended up retaking Kievelberg with 5 Troop, killing a score of Germans and capturing about thirty more. It was a minor action that was typical of the occasional small-scale skirmishes that took place around Schinnen in the severe weather of one of the hardest winters on record. Keeping warm soon became our major preoccupation, as it snowed heavily and the temperatures dropped to well below freezing. Each regiment of 8th Armoured Brigade rotated through the forward positions, where the engine fans of our tanks sucked in every snowflake that fell within two feet of the turret. The ground froze as hard as iron and the steel sides of our tanks became cold enough to strip the skin off an ungloved hand. When not in the line, we built raging fires in our billets, huddling round them to dry out our soaking tank suits and absorb their heat into our freezing bodies, as the snow continued to fall outside.

We spent New Year's Eve on the line and 1945 dawned bitterly cold. With the focus of the fighting in the Ardennes there was little activity in our area, save for the occasional shelling and the firing of artillery rounds containing propaganda leaflets. We fired ours and they fired theirs, each side's flyer containing more or less the same messages foretelling death, but offering the alternative of safe passage for surrender. About the size of a notebook page, the leaflets fluttered down over the forward lines, where British and German soldiers alike used them to supplement their supply of lavatory paper. The terrain around our sector of the line was dead flat and I often wondered why the Germans didn't attempt to stage a more concerted attack in our area, rather than fight through the dense wooded mass of the Ardennes. Looking across the open fields of the front, we occasionally saw columns of enemy tanks and trucks moving in the far distance towards the south. We suspected that they were heading to where the fighting was raging against the Americans. By the end of the first week in January the Battle of the Bulge had been contained and the US forces were pushing the Germans back to their start lines and punishing them severely for their daring audacity. However, after the brief excitement of retaking Kievelberg, the only movement towards our positions came in the form of a German Shepherd dog.

We were back in the line, and I was shivering in the sleet-driven downdraught of the turret, when the long-legged creature came bounding through the snow towards us. I half expected it to set off a mine as it zigzagged its way across the large expanse of open fields. Gartside shouted a warning and told me that he had the dog covered with his machine gun; his logic being that it was 'a Jerry mutt and was cumming from tha side'. I told him not to be so stupid and not to open fire. The dog stopped a few yards in front of the tank, cocked its head to one side and looked at me quizzically. I climbed down from the turret and called it over. It dropped its head and wagged its tail as it came to me and I reached in my pocket for a fluff-covered biscuit. I made a fuss of the fella and we took to each other, so I decided to take the animal with us when we pulled back to the leaguer. The dog found no difficulty in jumping up on to the hull and following me into the tank. Using the topside of the breech as a step to get down into the crew compartment, it licked Mayo and Martin before making itself comfortable in one of the storage sponsons running alongside the hull under the turret ring, which was to become 'Fritz's' home for the next two months. The name of the dog may have lacked imagination, but it seemed apt in the circumstances and played to Gartside's suspicion that Fritz had a canine allegiance to the enemy. Interestingly, he was the only member of the crew that the dog barked at, apart from the chickens when they were in residence, which also were less than amenable to having a new member of the crew in their midst. I later found out that Gartside was right. Fritz was a German 'mine dog' that had been trained to find paths through minefields, but he seemed more than happy to stay with us.

With the exception of the hens, Fritz was a welcome distraction for all of us from the privations of the weather and the inevitable prospect of returning to action. The cancellation of all leave to Brussels and orders to paint our tanks white were the first indication we had that operations were about to resume. On 18 January the regiment was sent to complete the business we had started at Geilenkirchen of pushing the Germans back to the Roer. It involved more slogging through the defensive positions of the Siegfried Line and more mud, but it was also more successful and our casualties were lighter. It took just over a week to capture our objective of Heinsberg, situated ten miles inside the German border. But after months of constant fighting, the fatigue, privations and stress of battle were beginning to tell. A soldier's attitude to combat changes with continuous exposure to it and I knew that I was dicing against the mathematical odds as the war went on. The law of averages dictated that my luck could not last. I had long ago resigned myself to the probability that I was going to get killed, but as each day passed I had to dig a little deeper within myself every time I climbed back into the tank and went into action.

The colonel was alive to the pressure his squadron and troop commanders were under. Stanley Christopherson had seen what had happened to John Semken and knew that, after several months of near-continuous action, the margins between sticking it or breaking down were thin. As a consequence, he had an unofficial policy of periodically giving his subalterns a break from leading their troops during an offensive by assigning them a less dangerous role, either in RHQ or with the unit's logistic echelon elements. It was not something that he ever discussed with us, although I suspect that Hilda Young, the unit's medical officer, was in some way involved. After the operation to take Heinsberg the CO had probably recognised that my time had come and I was informed that I would be acting as his liaison officer during the coming offensive, to drive to the Rhine as part of the initial advance into Germany.

Delayed by six weeks due to the need to deal with the Germans' unexpected attack through the Ardennes, Operation Veritable was part of what became known as the Battle of the Rhineland. It was a two-pronged affair that involved the 1st Canadian Army and XXX Corps attacking south from Nijmegen and the US 9th Army attacking north across the Roer from the area above Geilenkirchen.* We would be part of XXX Corps, which was attached to the Canadians. The pincer movement of the two armies under Monty's command was designed to breach the northern end of the Siegfried Line on the Dutch border, by clearing the Reichswald Forest, capturing the fortified German towns of Cleves and Goch and then linking up with the Yanks. In doing so, the intention was to eliminate all German forces on the west bank of the Rhine and set the conditions for subsequent operations to cross the mighty river. It would involve attacking through waterlogged polder land, made worse by deliberate enemy flooding, and the sinister wooded mass of the Reichswald in the depth of winter. If I had gained a better appreciation of the bigger strategic picture, I would probably have been glad not to have been leading my troop. But although the colonel ultimately had my best interests at heart, his decision to give me a temporary break from front-line

---

* The US part of the offensive was codenamed Operation Grenade.

combat command during Operation Veritable was a compassionate gesture that nearly cost me my life.

The offensive started on 8 February with a massive preliminary bombardment of 1000 guns, which was supplemented by the tank fire of the armoured regiments. At maximum elevation, the 75mm gun of a Sherman can lob one of its shells several thousand yards. Although we couldn't see the targets that we were firing at, the regiment's tanks were formed into a straight line and each one was issued with 300 rounds of HE that were fired on co-ordinates given to us by the gunners. The use of the tanks in the artillery fire plan was known as Operation Pepper Pot and added to the hundreds of tons of explosive that were plastering every known enemy position ahead of us. The noise was terrific. All along the front gun crews and tank crews sent a storm of steel towards the German positions. The air above us was screaming with shells and inside the turret Martin and Mayo were sweating and grunting as the breech shot back between them, spat out an empty brass case, was reloaded and was fired again in accordance with a strict timetable that we had been given. The targets had been marked in Chinagraph pencil on a map trace. Each tank fired in a relay at a rate of two rounds every minute for approximately forty-five minutes. My job was to co-ordinate which tank fired when and I estimate that between us the troop fired nine tons of HE shells. Interestingly, Fritz didn't seem to mind a bit and remained curled up in his sponson throughout the shoot.

I completed Operation Pepper Pot with the troop before I left them to start my temporary assignment during the operation as the CO's liaison officer, the next day. On arrival at regimental headquarters, I was pointed towards a Daimler Dingo scout vehicle and was told that my job was to follow the CO's tank and be prepared to run errands for him and liaise with the brigade that we were working with. The Dingo was a low-silhouetted four-wheeled armoured car and with a top speed of fifty miles per hour, it was fast and nippy. But the advance of the regiment's sixty-odd tanks was anything but, as we joined a vast column of over 1000 other vehicles that started out towards Cleves later that evening. Attacking with 1st Canadian Army to our right, Operation Veritable involved four British divisions of XXX Corps that had swelled to over 200,000 men. The 53rd Welsh Division and the Jocks of the 51st Highland Division had already begun their attack into the Reichswald Forest, while the 15th Scottish Division had been tasked with breaking through the German defences to the northeast of the forest. The 43rd Division, whom the Sherwood Rangers were supporting, would follow them and then take over the lead to capture Cleves.

By the time the attack started a thaw had set in and the snow had turned into heavy sleet-filled rain. Within the first few hours of the offensive, the armour of the leading division had become bogged down, as they attempted to traverse the waterlogged ground. By opening the sluice gates of the local river systems to flood much of the low-lying area, the Germans had denied us the ability to move cross-country and restricted the axis of the advance to a single narrow road. As a consequence, progress was painfully slow. As the Dingo was open topped, there was little to do except sit next to the driver and get wet, as we crawled behind the colonel's Sherman in a nose-to-tail line of vehicles. Infantry from the 43rd Division sat on the tops of the regiment's vehicles. Riding on the tanks spared their feet, but it made for a precarious form of transport. There are few places to gain satisfactory purchase on a Sherman. The heat from the engine made the metal of the back decks too uncomfortable to sit on for any length of time, while riding on the smooth sides of the turret and the sloping hull on either side of the gun entailed the risk of slipping off the sides of the tank and being caught in the tracks. Ahead of us, the rumble of artillery sounded in the darkness as we drove slowly and inextricably forward. When the rain stopped, the clouds parted and the moon came out briefly to reflect its silver light off the surface of the flood water that glistened shiny black in the fields on either side of the road. To our right I could make out the dim outline of the Reichswald Forest. I pitied the men of the Welsh and the Scots units that were fighting there. Perhaps the poor bloody infantry of the West Country regiments that clung on to the sides of our tanks in the soaking miserable weather were better off after all.

Although the congestion caused by the sheer volume of troops competing for limited space in our narrow sector of advance made for sluggish movement, initial enemy resistance was light. In the early hours of 10 February, 15th Scottish Division reached the outskirts of Cleves and reported that the way into the city was clear. However, the attempt to pass through the rear brigade of 15th Scottish Division resulted in one of the worst traffic jams of the war. True to form, von Thoma blew his stack, as he tried to get 43rd Division's vehicles forward through the packed columns of stationary trucks and armoured vehicles in front of him. It resulted in a less than cordial exchange between the two divisional commanders and it was good to know that the foulest of language was not just the preserve of troopers like Gartside and Martin. Had the commander of the Scots division not been of equal rank, von Thoma would undoubtedly have sacked him. Once through the gridlock, B Squadron led the advance into the devastated remains of the birthplace of Henry VIII's fourth wife. Anne of Cleves' less than appealing looks may have saved her from the chopping block, but the RAF had not been so kind to her native city. By destroying 90 per cent of Cleves' buildings in a massive raid on the night of 7 February, it looked as if Bomber Command had done our job for us, as we advanced unopposed through the obliterated city of rubble-strewn streets and shattered ruins. But then the inevitable shots of sniper fire began to ring out and the German paratroopers began emerging from the cellars.

We were strung out in a line of vehicles along one of the roads running into the city centre when the fighting started. I was still with the CO's tactical HQ, which had pulled up close to 129 Brigade headquarters of 43rd Division. We had been on the move all night and I got out of the Dingo having been tasked by the adjutant to find the suitable remains of a house in which to get a brew on. When mortar fire started to land any thoughts of tea were quickly forgotten. I made my way back to the relative safety of the scout car. Up ahead, B Squadron encountered an enemy roadblock and there were reports of enemy self-propelled guns as a melee of street fighting broke out between the Fallschirmjäger and the 4th Wiltshires. As the infantry battled it out among the bomb craters, shells of shattered houses and streets blocked with piles of bricks and smashed furniture, small-arms fire began to crackle around our own position. I saw the tanks of A Squadron and my own troop move up past us, but there was little I could do, apart from sit in the Dingo and await instructions from the CO. The German paratroopers were beginning to work their way around the column and put in an attack against the brigade headquarters. It was beaten off, but not before some of the staff officers had to draw their revolvers to defend themselves, and one of them was killed and another wounded in the process. Throughout, snipers firing from upper-storey windows kept up a steady fusillade that threatened anyone caught out in the open or exposed in a turret. I felt somewhat helpless sitting in the Dingo, although if I kept my head down below its rim the armoured shields of the vehicle were sufficient to keep out the bullets and my job was to stay put until called for.

The information about the precise location of the enemy was confusing and vague. Around me I could hear the solid bangs of tank fire, the occasional blast of a Panzerfaust and the stutter of machine guns. Further up the column, I could see that Shermans from RHQ were attempting to engage a Jagdpanther. The German self-propelled gun was using the cover of the façades of wrecked houses and the gaps between them to jockey in and out of fire positions. It would suddenly appear in the spaces between the ruins, fire one or two rounds and then pull back out of sight, before appearing at the next gap to fire again. I could hear the growl of its 12-cylinder Maybach engine and the heavy squeal of its tracks, as the forty-five ton monster moved behind the ruins looking for more fire positions. Popping my head up over the armoured plate of the Dingo, I squinted across at the gap between what remained of two houses next to our vehicle. Suddenly I found myself looking down the barrel of a bloody great 88mm gun, as the Jagdpanther reappeared less than twenty yards away. It had a clear line of sight to where we sat immobilised, with only a rather inadequate 12mm-thick section of the vehicle's armoured shield to protect us. There wasn't even time to think about bailing out.

It was like something out of a slow-motion film and I think I might have got as far as saying 'shit', before I was stunned by the flash of the trace in the back of the armour-piercing round that shot less than a foot over the top of my head. It filled the compartment of the armoured car with a blinding light and I felt its heat before I heard the deafening report of the gun that had fired it. At 4 feet 11 inches, the top of the Dingo is significantly lower than the height of the average tank. Built with stealth in mind, it was a design feature that saved the driver and I from being atomised by the tungsten slug, which broke the sound barrier as it whipped over our heads. Given the range of the engagement, I have always suspected that the Jagdpanther was unable to depress its gun sufficiently to hit us. Fortunately, it did not hang around to prove me right or wrong, or to switch to an HE round that would have finished us.

It took until the evening to clear the city finally, although a number of enemy paratroopers held out stubbornly on the high ground behind us for a further day. In retaliation for losing Cleves, the Germans breached some of the dykes along the Rhine, which added to the level of the flood water. At one stage the single road that stretched all the way back to Nijmegen, where the attack started, was under several feet of water and we could only receive supplies brought forward by amphibious DUKW vehicles. With virtually no buildings left standing, we were forced to find billets in the cellars. The majority of German civilians had been evacuated from Cleves and we took advantage of what they had left behind. Most of the basements we occupied were surprisingly well stocked with jars of preserved fruit, sugar and coal and it didn't appear that the inhabitants had been suffering overly from the lack of provisions. The distinctive smell of German soldiery, which seemed to permeate all their dugouts, vehicles and barracks, also pervaded the cellars. The stink of Jerry was something that we all commented on and it seemed to emanate from a combination of sweat, leather, the strong black tobacco they smoked and the carbolic soap that they washed with. I have often wondered what we smelt like to them.

Operation Veritable was to last for another month. It involved tough fighting through appalling weather, as XXX Corps advanced slowly towards the Rhine through the torrential rain and the mud. The rate of advance rarely exceeded a mile a day as the remnants of a score of German divisions fought desperately to prevent us from reaching the river. The Sherwood Rangers spent a week fighting to clear the villages and woods around the immediate area of Cleves, which was to remain our base location for the duration of the offensive. With the departure of John Semken, Ronnie Hutton had badgered the colonel for a combat command and Christopherson had finally relented by making him the interim commander of A Squadron. Two days after taking Cleves, A Squadron captured the village of Louisendorf, which included the local mental hospital. Ronnie reported on the radio that he had detained 'three doctors, thirty female nurses and 1300 lunatics'. The colonel replied that he could keep the doctors and the patients, but that he could '. . . send back the nurses to Regimental Headquarters'. The reply was typical of Stanley Christopherson, who continued to display a sense of humour regardless of the circumstances. But our role in Operation Veritable had a harder edge to it and the regiment lost fourteen tanks in the fighting and suffered thirty-one casualties.

In some cases the Germans fought fanatically and as we pushed closer to the Rhine some units were prepared to fight to the death. Most of the rearguard covering the river consisted of small groups of enemy paratroopers. Although the majority had not completed their parachute training, they were still imbued with the collective airborne spirit of the volunteer and were tough fighters, indoctrinated with the cult of their Führer. B Squadron ran into a group of young Fallschirmjäger holding out in a farm on the west bank of the river near the village of Weele. The tanks pounded the Germans with HE and infantry mortar fire, but instead of surrendering, the enemy formed up with their rifles and Panzerfausts to launch a last-ditch charge against the tanks facing them, shouting their willingness to die for Adolf Hitler. It was a desperately brave but fruitless action and B Squadron obliged them to a man. Other larger German formations were also suffering grievously. Panzer Lehr, that once proud formation that had been nearly destroyed in Normandy, rebuilt for the Battle of the Bulge and then re-equipped to fight in the Rhineland, had virtually ceased to exist. As it was pushed back to the Rhine, the division was caught in the open by the rocket firing Typhoons and the RAF blasted most of its remaining tanks to extinction.

I resumed command of 5 Troop soon after the operations around Cleves had been completed, but the character of the A Squadron I returned to had begun to change. I had a new troop sergeant in the form of Dennis Webb. Sergeant Harrison had taken advantage of the Python leave programme that had been introduced in the closing stages of the war in Europe. Under the scheme, any soldier who had served for five years, with less than six months spent in England, could elect to be posted to a unit stationed at home. Over a hundred men in the regiment qualified, but most opted for the alternative of taking a week's leave in England. Many did so because they feared being sent to a unit that would then be dispatched to finish the war against Japan. Sergeant Webb was a very different cut to the man he had replaced. Of medium height and with a friendly disposition, Webb joined us just before the Pepper Pot shoot. He was instantly supportive and saw it as his job to back me as the troop commander. Webb had certainly looked after 5 Troop in my absence and I noted how he had automatically taken on the traditional administrative responsibilities of the senior troop NCO, which would leave me to focus on the leadership aspects. With the arrival of Webb, I felt that all was finally well with 5 Troop. But I was less certain about the squadron as a whole.

The biggest change to A Squadron came in the form of the new squadron leader. Ronnie Hutton's command had only been a temporary arrangement to fill the void left by John Semken's departure after Geilenkirchen. On 18 February, Bill Enderby rejoined the regiment at Cleves, having recovered from the wounds he had received on his landing craft on D-Day. Officially, he had been medically downgraded as a result of the injuries to his arm, but by January 1945 he had managed to convince an army medical board that he was fit enough to return to active duty. Enderby was a pre-war regular cavalry officer who had been commissioned into the 2nd Dragoon Guards, although he had seen little active service with them. By the time he joined the Sherwood Rangers in North Africa in 1943, the fighting in the desert campaign was over. Like Makins before him, tenure in combat command was important if Enderby wanted to further his career as a regular army officer. Fearing that his desire to see action might never be fulfilled, Enderby was desperate to rejoin the regiment before the war against Germany finished. Through no fault of his own, Bill Enderby had missed the intense learning experience of Normandy and was joining a close-knit squadron of veterans that had been led and trained by a man who would be an exceedingly tough act to follow. Given his circumstances, had I known them, I might have had more sympathy for him. However, on my own return to A Squadron I found that he had already made a decision that meant my new squadron commander and I were unlikely to see eye-to-eye with each other.

I was pleased to be back with 5 Troop; acting in my capacity as the colonel's liaison officer I had missed the easy banter and close comradeship that comes with being part of a crew and a small unit. I had also missed the better protection of a tank and, more importantly, the ability to have something to fight back with when under fire. The dog was overjoyed to see me and I think that the rest of the crew were pleased to see me too, but my delight at being back with the blokes and Fritz quickly evaporated on discovering that the tank that had replaced Aim was a petrol variant. When I asked why I was told that it had been a decision made by the new squadron leader. I agreed with the crew that it was 'not fooking on'. The Sherman Mark 4A4 was powered by a Chrysler multi-bank engine system consisting of four ordinary car engines that had been mated together. A contingency design to overcome the high demand for diesel-driven engines, the petrol variant had some distinct disadvantages. Driving a tank filled with 160 gallons of highly flammable petrol made for a greater fire hazard. The petrol engine also lacked the pull of a diesel. Additionally, two of the Chrysler engines were mounted upside down, which made the engine prone to stalling due to the effect of gravity. If a petrol engine stopped, unburned fuel had a tendency to collect in the bottom cylinders and made for the devil when trying to get the thing started again. Speed, power and reliability were essential to a troop commander on the battlefield and it made absolutely no sense to be given a petrol-driven tank. Sergeant Webb agreed with me and I set off to have it out with Enderby.

That first meeting I had in the cellar of a bombed-out house in Cleves with my new commander was not all that it could have been. I was just twenty, but I had nine months of hard-won combat experience under my belt. I had also just narrowly missed being blown to pieces by another 88mm gun. I was clearly agitated and, looking back on it, I was missing John Semken. Needless to say, it resulted in a row. My initial deference to senior rank dissolved rapidly when I realised that Bill Enderby wasn't prepared to listen to my arguments. While we never questioned John Semken's orders, he was always keen to hear our point of view as troop commanders, especially when it was based on logic and made sense. Perhaps it was a reflection of Enderby's status as a regular officer finding his feet in a command position and an environment with which he was unfamiliar. Regardless, he didn't take too kindly to being taken to task by a relatively junior officer and was having none of it. After telling me that diesel tanks were in short supply and that he wasn't prepared to consider a reallocation within the squadron or countenance my questioning of his authority, he told me to get on with it and then dismissed me. I was fuming as I stalked back through the rubble-filled street to the troop leaguer position. When I got back, I was swearing like a trooper and found myself in good expletive company when I passed on Enderby's final decision to the rest of the crew.

The weather remained incredibly cold and it was trying hard to snow, but by 10 March the west bank of the Rhine had been cleared of German troops. The British 21st Army Group had closed up to its proposed crossing points opposite Rees and Wesel and the link-up with US forces advancing in the south had been achieved. What remained of the Germans' vastly depleted divisions had either been withdrawn across the river or were now part of the 50,000 enemy soldiers who had gone into the bag as Allied prisoners of war. The Jerries had blown the bridges over the Rhine behind them and they had lost another 40,000 men dead and wounded. The US 12th Army Group had also closed up to the Rhine all along their sector of the front. Three days earlier, the Americans had seized the one bridge across the river that the Germans had failed to destroy, at Remagen, and had quickly established a bridgehead of four divisions on the east bank. Clearing the approaches to the Rhine had been a long hard slog, but the traditional German frontier had been reached. Once the bulk of the Allied armies crossed the river, the enemy would have little left in the way of cohesive forces that could offer comprehensive resistance. We were on the brink of crossing the last barrier that protected the Third Reich and once across the Rhine the route to the heart of Nazi Germany would be open.

Looking back seventy years, it is easy to think that there must have been some euphoria surrounding the fact that we were on the edge of victory. But it didn't feel like that then. We knew that the Germans were beaten, but it had cost XXX Corps 15,634 men to advance to the Rhine, without even accounting for the considerable losses the rest of 21st Army Group and the Americans had suffered in the south. Although their defeat was imminent, the enemy showed no signs of giving up and gave every indication that they would make us pay dearly for every yard of ground we gained once across the Rhine. My fatalism remained and I believed that the odds dictated that I would probably get killed. But the end was in sight and there was a chance that one might just make it through. In many ways, compounded with the accumulative degrading effect of months of bitter fighting, the prospect of becoming one of the last casualties of the war made things worse. For me, finding myself in a petrol-driven tank with all the increased risks that entailed and having a new squadron commander who lacked experience and understanding did not help. To some extent I felt a greater sympathy for how

Sergeant Harrison must have felt. But regardless of the circumstances, I was determined that I would not allow myself to be found wanting.

13

LAST BATTLES

Codenamed Operation Plunder, the British 21st Army Group began its assault crossing on the Rhine on the night of 23 March. Just before 2100 hours, DD tanks of the Staffordshire Yeomanry and four infantry battalions of the 51st Highland Division mounted in tracked Buffalo amphibious troop carriers, slipped into the river's steady current and began to swim the 600 yards to the other side. The attack had been preceded by three days of bombing, which unleashed 29,000 tons of high explosive on the German positions, and an artillery bombardment prior to the start of H Hour that had involved over 1000 guns. The massive use of firepower assisted the first wave in getting across with little opposition and they began to establish a bridgehead on the east bank near the small German town of Rees. Under the command of XXX Corps, the assault at Rees was one of three Allied crossing operations made in 21st Army Group's sector. A second British corps crossed twenty-five miles upstream at Wesel, while 9th US Army made a further river assault to their south.

Operation Plunder was another product of Monty's meticulous planning and represented a huge build-up of men, equipment and materiel. Since 12 March, the regiment had been stationed in Goch, which was on the west bank, a few miles short of the Rhine where it flowed past Rees. Preparations to cross the river had begun soon after our arrival and included sending all the tank drivers back to Nijmegen to witness a vehicle rafting demonstration on the Waal. It was not a great success and did little to boost their confidence in what lay ahead, as all of the rafts sank as soon as they were launched into the water. While it was obvious that an assault crossing of the Rhine was afoot, the particulars of the operation were only shared with the squadron commanders and I was not party to the details for the assault until the day it began. Although tasked to support 51st Highland Division, we were allocated the role of the reserve armoured unit and would not cross the Rhine until called forward a few days later. Until then we waited in our assembly areas and listened to the rumble of artillery as the battle progressed on the other side of the river.

The first morning of the operation dawned bright and clear and we watched hundreds of troop-carrying aircraft and gliders stream over us towards the Rhine. Between them they carried 10,000 troops of the British 6th Airborne Division on their way to drop in front of the leading assault troops on the far bank of the river. It was an overwhelming sight and testimony to the might of the Allied forces ranged against the Germans. But the blue skies over the distant drop zones were soon thick with the menacing dark airbursts of anti-aircraft fire. It was ample evidence that the enemy still had some bite left in them. I saw a large Hamilcar glider cracked open by the shell of an 88mm gun and watched in horrified fascination as it split in two and spilled its contents of a light tank and its crew a few hundred feet from the ground. The surrounding air was a blossom of white dots as thousands of parachute canopies popped beneath their aircraft. Occasionally a small dark dot dropped away more quickly than the rest and accelerated to the ground, as a chute malfunctioned or was shredded by enemy ground fire. It was an awesome spectacle and I took my hat off to the men who were brave enough to parachute into battle or fly into action in flimsy gliders made of balsa wood. Like the American airborne that we had worked with in Nijmegen, the British Paras were all tough professional volunteers and every bit as good as their American counterparts. The airborne troops would take significant casualties in the fighting to establish the bridgehead, as the Germans began to resist stubbornly on the east bank of the Rhine.

On the evening of 25 March the Sherwood Rangers were called forward to join the battle. Having been told about the results of the demonstration at Nijmegen, the crew were not overly impressed to learn that we would be rafting across the Rhine. Sid Martin was particularly unimpressed, as he was a non-swimmer. He made the usual expletive-laden remarks about how unfair life was, especially as some of the other units were using the floating Bailey bridge that the engineers had managed to construct across the river. Martin remained in a state of high anxiety and kept up his moaning throughout the time spent in the marshalling area until we began crossing on the tank ferry early the next morning. I dreaded to think what he would have been like if the task of swimming the river in DD tanks had fallen to us instead of the Staffordshire Yeomanry. Each raft could take one Sherman and was ferried across by means of giant lengths of steel cables. The sun was up and there was a strong hint of spring in the air, as we drove on to our ferry. There was some occasional shelling that threw up columns of water, but we crossed the Rhine without mishap in glorious weather. Fritz ran round the side of the tank and barked at the current of the river as it surged against the raft and even Martin perked up.

By the time the Sherwood Rangers commenced operations on the far side of the Rhine, the bridgehead around Rees had been expanded to a depth of twenty miles, along a thirty-mile-wide stretch of the east bank. But the Germans were still fighting desperately to contain it.

The regiment was ordered to support the battalions of 51st Highland Division and punch a hole in the enemy defensive line that would allow the Guards Armoured Division to drive northeast to the North German Plain. Once we had broken out onto the more open ground of Westphalia, Monty believed that the route to the Elbe, and the tantalising prospect of Berlin beyond it, would be open. Montgomery still saw the German capital as the main prize, although inter-Allied politics and the closer proximity of Soviet Forces on the Eastern Front dictated that the Red Army would take it. As far as we were concerned the Russians were welcome to it. But even the prospect of reaching the Elbe was a long way off and our field marshal still had a tendency to underestimate the opposition we faced. The Germans opposing us in our sector of the bridgehead came mainly from the 1st Parachute Army and although seriously depleted in numbers they had lost none of their fighting prowess.

We went into action the next day supporting the 1st Gordons and the 2nd Battalion of Seaforths, as part of the Highland Division's efforts to create a breach in the German line, where Holland's border bends back towards Germany at the Dutch town of Dinxperlo, which is located ten miles north of Rees. We advanced with the initial objective of taking the modest-sized town of Isselburg that lies a few miles to the south of Dinxperlo and immediately ran into heavy mortar and sniper fire. The German paratroopers had turned the high banks of an uncompleted autobahn in front of the town into a defensive feature and pinned down the infantry with the ubiquitous fire of their MG42s. Approaches to the position were also covered liberally with Teller mines. As we moved forward to support the Jocks, Dickie Holman's tank was blown up by a mine, which wounded his driver. He dismounted and removed the remaining mines from the road, which allowed the rest of his troop to get through and deal with the Spandaus. Dickie was later awarded an MC for this action, but the German mines caused us more problems the next day when we pushed on towards Isselburg. As the advance resumed at first light, Sergeant Major Hutchinson was killed when the tank he was directing on foot detonated a mine. The blast also wounded Neville Fearn in the head. As the squadron's senior NCO and battle captain, Hutchinson and Fearn had been two of the men that I had got to know since joining A Squadron in Normandy and their loss was a further blow to the original character of the subunit.

A day later, on 29 March, the regiment supported another battalion of the Seaforths to capture Dinxperlo. Intelligence reports suggested that the Germans were beginning to pull out of the town, but our infantry insisted on stonking it heavily with artillery before they began their assault. With hindsight, it could be argued that firing a weighty concentration of high-explosive shells against a Dutch urban area that was believed to be lightly held was unnecessary. However, like the debate about bombing civilian areas before attacking them, I fall on the side of the unprotected infantryman, who will always argue against taking the chance of increased casualties when high explosives can do some of the work for you. By the time A Squadron entered Dinxperlo the place was a shambles of shell-damaged buildings and roads. We worked with the infantry to clear its houses and turned out a large number of prisoners, some of whom may have decided to snipe at us or take us on with Panzerfausts had we not battered them with artillery. The POWs were also an indication that resistance was slowly beginning to slacken, as more and more Germans seemed to be willing to take the opportunity to surrender. It was also a sure sign that the enemy front that sought to contain the bridgehead had begun to fracture.

With Dinxperlo taken, the Guards Armoured Division passed through us and began their breakout to drive deeper into the northeast of Germany. On 1 April, with our initial Operation Plunder task completed, 8th Armoured Brigade swapped formations again and was ordered to advance directly north back across the Dutch border in support of 43rd Wessex Division. Their task was to liberate the areas of Holland that were still under occupation to the east of the Rhine. With the collapse of the German position around the bridge-head, the regiment was once again reorganised as a battlegroup in order to begin the pursuit battle. Equipped with our own battery of self-propelled guns from the Essex Yeomanry, and a company of infantry in Bren carriers from the 12th/60th KRRC, the regiment also had a squadron of Kangaroos under command to carry an infantry company of the 4th Wiltshires. Driven and commanded by the RAC, the Kangaroo was a Canadian-built variant of the Sherman that had had its turret removed to allow it to carry a ten-man infantry section. We had first seen the personnel carriers in use during Operation Veritable and they finally provided the infantry with protected mobility and an ability to keep up with the armour, without having to engage in the highly dangerous activity of riding on the top of our tanks.

After five and a half long months of attritional slogging through flooded polder land of thick mud, extensive waterways and fixed defensive lines, we were finally moving at pace, as the cohesion of the German forces began to disintegrate. On the first day of the pursuit, the regiment advanced over twenty miles. The Kangaroos were immediately put to good use in attacking an enemy rearguard that had established a roadblock on the northern side of the Dutch village of Ruurlo. With the support of the fire from our tanks, the Kangaroos were able to drive the infantry straight on to the German position. Although the men of the Wiltshires were still vulnerable at the moment they tumbled over the sides of the vehicle's open turret rings, the Kangaroos enabled the infantry to contribute to the rapid shock action of battle that had been missing during much of the previous fighting in France and the Low Countries. But despite the improvement in all-arms co-operation, we only had one company of Kangaroo-mounted infantry and the war of rapid movement into

Germany and the immediate borderlands of the Third Reich had a very different edge to it from the pursuit battles of the summer. We were advancing into the fatherland of the enemy. Our purpose was one of invasion, not liberation, and far too many enemy soldiers had a greater reason than before to resist us, as they fought for their homes and among their own people. It was a difference that brought me into another open conflict with my new squadron commander.

Following the action at Ruurlo, A Squadron was ordered to continue to advance five miles north to Lochem and seize a crossing point over a canal that cuts through its northern edge. Once claiming the medieval rights of the status of a small city, Lochem is a prosperous Dutch market town that had been under attack many times in its history. Bounded by a wide canal and a railway line to its north and the river Slinge to its immediate east, and flanked by small forests on three sides, its topography made it an obvious defensive point in 1945. We knew that the Germans loved to dig in along water features and the wooded areas offered numerous firing points for any enemy soldier equipped with a Panzerfaust. It was good ambush country and the nature of the ground demanded that the approach to Lochem should be undertaken with caution, although Bill Enderby had other ideas. No doubt, as the squadron commander, he felt the pressure of a senior command, where his superiors were always pressing for faster progress. Consequently, he was probably doing his best to meet their intent to advance quickly. However, I took issue with his orders, which entailed splitting up each troop in order to complete a wide sweeping manoeuvre to take the town from the northeast. The squadron would be operating independently, as the infantry were not available to support us, and I argued that all of the four troops should operate together and that we should plaster the approach route with fire before moving in mutually supporting tactical bounds. The plan smacked of rigid RAC training orthodoxy and ignored the hard schooling of the bocage and the polder land. But Enderby ignored my protests and told me to get on with it. The friction between the two of us at the O group was obvious. Before we folded our maps and mounted up Peter Mellowes, who had taken over 2 Troop after Harry Heenan had been killed, told me that I was my own worst enemy when it came to dealing with Enderby.

My tank commanders shared my concern when I briefed them on the plan. Sergeant Webb sucked his teeth and offered to lead. I shook my head and said 'no', as I knew that it was my job to lead. However, I decided not to share my concerns with my own crew as we mounted up and each of the squadron's four troops set off on their individual routes. It started to go wrong soon after we split up. We were pushing round a large block of forest doing our best to keep out of the range of any Panzerfaust-wielding infantry that might be hiding among the trees, when I heard over the squadron net that the leading Sherman in 2 Troop, which was operating out of sight behind me, had been hit by a 'bazooka'; the common term for a Panzerfaust. I assumed that it must have been Peter Mellowes' tank. I subsequently discovered that it was his troop sergeant. Hidden to our rear, the German paratroopers let Sergeant O'Pray's tank go past them before they hit it at close range with their launcher. The shaped charge of the Panzerfaust must have struck the midriff of the turret, as it caused severe head injuries to most of the crew, who were unable to bail out when the tank started to burn. Although badly burned, the driver managed to get out and charge the firing point with his Luger, killing two of the enemy. The others fled. The four men left in the tank were later recovered but succumbed to their wounds. When Mellowes' remaining tanks shot up the undergrowth that had concealed the offending Panzerfaust, they flushed out over half a company of Fallschirmjäger.

The loss of a tank behind us made me even more nervous as we broke out into a more open area and pushed on towards Lochem.

The troop was flank-on to the line of the river on our right, we were devoid of cover and I could sense that the Germans were watching us. It had rained during the night and the ground to our front looked soft and marshy. I was keen to cross it quickly to minimise our obvious exposure and ordered the driver to speed up, but the pull from the petrol engine was sluggish and it began to labour as the tracks slipped and sank into the boggy earth. I was mentally willing the blasted Sherman on as the relative safety of the outskirts of the town became visible a few hundred yards ahead of us, when the engine spluttered, stalled and the tank stopped. There was a desperate attempt to restart the engine. The sickening, frantic, high-pitched mechanical whir of the starter motor was loud in our ears as it fought a losing battle against the fuel that had flooded into the inverted cylinders and it failed to spark the tank back into life. We knew we were in trouble and my mind raced as I scanned the ground to our right trying to spot the likely hiding place of a concealed anti-tank gun, pointless though the exercise was. Then intuition and survival instinct kicked in and I shouted into the microphone and ordered the crew to bail out.

They didn't wait to be told twice, as the two forward hatches were flung open and Martin, Mayo and Fritz followed me out of the commander's cupola. I yelled at the crew to get away from the damn tank and make for the safety of the trees 300 yards away in the forest to our left. I didn't bother to look back, but I knew that the stutter of machine gun fire that had opened up from the direction of the river was meant for us. As we pumped our arms and legs as fast as we could in a desperate bid to reach cover, I shouted at the blokes to spread out and not to bunch, which is a natural human inclination when a group of men are under fire. We were halfway to the sanctuary offered by the wood when I heard the whistle of shells, which indicated that we were about to be bracketed by artillery fire. A split second later, 105mm rounds began to land around us in a series of almighty bangs that sounded like the crack of doom, as they smacked down around the abandoned Sherman. We were still close enough to feel the blast of their pressure waves. My lungs felt as if they were about to burst, but the alluring safety of the trees was still over fifty yards away when the next volley of shells crashed in. I felt the air above me split with the sound of heavy metal moving at terrific speed. Suddenly, the pines in front of us were cleaved flat in a blizzard of splintering timber and broken branches. One of the high-explosive rounds had scored a direct hit on the tank. The kinetic force of the impacting shell had smashed off the cupola and turret hatches, turning the steel frame into a spinning solid disc of over a hundred pounds of metal, which had scythed into the treeline just as we reached it.

We scrambled past the remains of the shattered stumps of pine and pushed deeper into the wood for cover. Each of us gasped for breath with our hands on our knees, as we stopped among a small clearing of pines. The late-afternoon air of the forest was thick with obscenities, as we contemplated the near miss we had just experienced. In our haste to bail out, nearly all of our kit had been left in the tank and the only things I had brought with me were my Luger and my map. Any sense of relief that I felt was quickly replaced by anger. But there was still a battle to be fought and I ordered the crew to make their way back to our lines and then set off to find the rest of the troop. The one casualty from our near miss was Fritz. He had been running with us, but I lost sight of him as he reached the wood line. He disappeared into the trees and didn't come back.

My anger turned to something approaching rage at the end of the day, when Enderby informed me that he was going to have me court-martialled for abandoning the tank. He accused me of having done it deliberately in order to avoid having to command a petrol-driven Sherman. It was a preposterous suggestion. Fortunately, Ronnie Hutton, who had stayed on in the squadron as the second in command, intervened and used his Northern Irish charm on us both to cool the situation. He then took Enderby aside and filled him in on some of the facts of life concerning the nature of armoured operations. Later that evening, with Lochem secure, we returned to salvage what we could from the tank. It lay smashed and broken where we had left it. The inside of the vehicle was a shredded mess of ripped seating and dangling wires. Had we stayed a minute longer in the Sherman we would have been killed. Having recovered what we could from the vehicle, I walked into the woods and called for Fritz. The rest of the crew joined me and even Gartside was troubled by the fact that we couldn't find him. But night was approaching and we had to give up the search.

Following the incident at Lochem, A Squadron went back across the border with the rest of the regiment to make an attack from the east on the much larger Dutch town of Hengelo. Advancing from the German side of the frontier, we caught the German garrison by surprise, as A and B Squadrons carried out a pincer movement in support of an assault made by three infantry battalions of 43rd Division. There was little resistance and the enemy began to pull out as we entered the town. Our ability to engage the retreating Germans was hampered by the rapturous reception of the local inhabitants, who were finally free after five years of Nazi occupation. It was like a mini version of the liberation of Brussels all over again. The population broke out into collective celebration, swarming around the tanks and proffering gifts and kisses. Gartside was once again in his element, enjoying the ringside seat of the hull gunner's position as Dutch women clambered up the front of the tank and kissed him and kissed me. Ken Mayo squeezed up through the hatch next to me and was also able to appreciate some of the attention from the fairer sex. Stuck inside the confines of the turret, Martin grumbled about the unfairness of it all. We spent just under a week in Hengelo enjoying the gratitude and warm hospitality of the local people and the fact that we were billeted under the roofs of proper houses for the first time in nine days of action.

The six days the Sherwood Rangers spent in Hengelo were a welcome interlude from operations, but we knew it would not last and that we would have to cross back over the border again and resume the advance into Germany. Although the newspapers from England that had caught up with us were a few days out of date, they spoke of the imminent collapse of the Third Reich, and even the more timely bulletins on the BBC hinted that the war in Europe was all but over. However, the recent fighting and intelligence reports indicated that the enemy were far from finished and had plenty of fight left in them. There was a growing mood of war weariness among the regiment and we wondered how long it would go on for. Back home, our families waited and worried. They read the same newspapers, watched the newsreels and listened to the radio. The newsreaders' announcements must have weighed heavy on their hearts, as they spoke of the latest advances in clipped tones, using phrases such as 'heavy fighting' and some 'losses have been incurred', provoking fear for the safety of their menfolk and hope that they were not involved. Those waiting in England could do little but wait for letters from the front reassuring them that their loved ones were all right, while at the same time dreading the telegram that would tell them otherwise.

On 9 April we received orders to move. The regiment's ultimate objective was Bremen and whatever else lay beyond that. However, first we had to get there. The port city lies astride the Weser, thirty miles south of where the mouth of the river flows into the North Sea. Reaching Bremen would require us to advance through 150 miles of hostile territory. The Dutch people of Hengelo had shown us great warmth and kindness, but as we prepared to cross the border again we were in no doubt that the reception we would receive when we entered German towns and villages would be of a very different nature.

The trees were beginning to sport their first buds of green, and some were alive with a profusion of blossom, as we started up our engines and prepared to move. But while the grip of winter was finally passing, it was still bitterly cold, as our column of tanks and supporting vehicles clanked on to the road running through the centre of Hengelo, faced east and headed ineluctably towards Germany again.

Travelling as a battlegroup, the regiment made good progress, covering over forty miles in the first two days. Initially we met little opposition, but the speed of our advance once again entailed risk. As we advanced further into Germany we passed hastily filled-in road craters with piles of mines lifted by the engineers stacked neatly beside them and marked off by white tape. Along with the remains of what had once been German soldiers, lying among the traces of the odd smashed anti-tank gun and the occasional hulk of a burned-out British tank, they were salient markers that recent fighting had already taken place along the route. The regiment ran into the first roadblock at the halfway point to Bremen. They tended to consist of felled tree trunks lashed together to form a rough triangular abatis. The obstacles were nearly always laid in conjunction with mines and required engineer support to clear them, but invariably they were also covered by fire. When we came across one, the column would stop a few hundred yards short, as the commander in the lead tank stared through his binoculars, scanning the road ahead for any sign of the enemy. If we saw them before they opened fire, we might call artillery down on them before launching a quick attack with the infantry. Once the opposition was dealt with the advance would resume.

If Germans were spotted in a wood or a farm building that couldn't directly threaten the road, we might bypass them and leave them for follow-up troops to deal with. However, far too often the lead tank being hit by a Panzerfaust or going up on a mine was the first indicator of the enemy's presence and their determination to fight us on the line of advance. As had been the case in Northern France, no troop commander relished the prospect of being in the lead tank. When A Squadron led the regiment, John Semken maintained a strict schedule of rotating the role between the troop leaders and gave clear instructions on which one of us would be the lead troop for a particular phase of an operation. Bill Enderby's O groups lacked clarity on the issue and the matter of which troop would lead where and when became something of a debate, which was not helpful. After ten months of combat, and with the increasing onset of combat fatigue and the prospect of the war's end being tantalisingly close, no one was going to volunteer and in such circumstances firm direction from the squadron commander was required.

But it was not A Squadron that was leading on 11 April, when the regiment ran into a roadblock at Löningen. B Squadron had the un-welcome task on this occasion and they lost two tanks and ten men killed in the lead troop when they were hit by Panzerfausts fired by Germans hiding in the village. I read after the war that in Normandy the hand-held rocket launcher had accounted for 6 per cent of British tanks lost to the enemy, but in Germany that figure jumped to 34 per cent. With the Germans' own heavy losses of tanks and self-propelled guns, which they could no longer replace, the Panzerfaust was an increasingly obvious weapon of choice. It could be produced and distributed in large numbers and was simple to operate; making it an ideal weapon for the boys and old men who were increasingly recruited into the Germans' equivalent of the Home Guard, called the Volkssturm, as the Nazis scraped their manpower barrel to boost their rapidly diminishing fighting strength. Frequently, the firer lost his life if he missed, or was shot down by the tanks supporting the vehicle he managed to hit, but in the brutal arithmetic of Germa-ny's last-ditch effort to resist us, the life of one man was a reasonable trade for an Allied tank. Mines were another highly effective means of impeding our advance. If we detected them they took time to lift and clearing them was a dangerous occupation. They were often booby-trapped and wired together to increase their explosive force. The mutilated bodies of the British soldiers by the sides of numerous road craters were testimony to their lethal effect.

I cannot recollect how we resolved the issue of who would command the lead tanks when A Squadron took over the advance to the next village, but it wasn't 5 Troop. Lastrup had been reported as being clear of enemy, so the squadron's leading tank got a rude shock when it had to run a gauntlet of machine-gun, Panzerfaust and sniper fire as it entered the village. Amazingly, the Sherman got down the main street unscathed before pulling a hard right turn at top speed to exit the village by a side-track and loop back to join the rest of the squadron, when it put in a hasty assault with C Squadron and the supporting infantry. Fortunately, the countryside of the North German Plain was good tank country. It was flat, naturally well-drained and lacking hedgerows, which meant that we could deploy off the road quickly and use the ground to put in rapid flanking attacks against positions established in the villages. We would then continue the advance, leaving a blazing cluster of buildings behind us, the smoke from the fires smudging the horizon and adding to the oily black plumes that belched from our knocked-out Shermans. While often still costly, the opposition of a scratch force in a small village could be overcome relatively quickly. However, countering resistance in the better-established environs of the towns we advanced through was a different proposition.

A Squadron was back in the lead again when we came up against German paratroopers in the town of Cloppenburg, located thirty miles to the southwest of Bremen. As we approached the outskirts, a series of large explosions signalled that the enemy had blown the bridges over the river Soeste, which runs through the town's centre. We also came under fire from two of the enemy's few remaining self-propelled guns, which succeeded in knocking out the leading Sherman. The tank brewed up, but the crew managed to bail out and bolt for cover as we fired back furiously and forced the German SPs to pull back further into the town. The 7th Hampshires from 43rd Division were ordered to launch a deliberate attack with B Squadron, as we continued to fire at the enemy infantry dug into the forward edge of the town. As our attacking force advanced up the main street, the German armour reappeared and harassed the forward company and the B Squadron tanks, which quickly became separated on either side of the river due to the absence of bridges. Discovering one bridge still intact, a crossing was forced, but not before the lead tank was brewed up by a Panzerfaust. The commander and a crewman lost their lives and two other members of B Squadron were killed by machine-gun fire when trying to rescue them. With a crossing point secured, A Squadron pushed into the town to cover the captured bridge, as the subsequent fighting broke down into a melee of close-quarter actions among the warren of streets and ruined houses, lasting long into the night.

While it took nearly two days to clear Cloppenburg, which was virtually destroyed in the process, other smaller towns and villages that we passed through surrendered without a fight. White sheets fluttering from street windows were the usual indicator that the inhabitants were willing to surrender. Although some areas were utterly devastated, many were untouched by the physical signs of war. However, the more abstract scars of five long years of brutal conflict were there when you went into the churches. The name of one village we leaguered in for a night has long since fled my memory, but I can remember going inside the church that was centred among the orderly lines of thirty or forty neat red-brick houses nestled in the surrounding countryside of well-kept farmland. There were no enemy troops in the village when we arrived. I suspect the locals had managed to convince any German soldiers stationed there of the futility of further resistance, in order to spare their homes from destruction. Evening was fast approaching when I decided to enter the modest whitewashed nave. Through the gathering gloom, I could make out two or more score of laurel wreaths fixed above the altar, each one denoting the sacrifice of one of the village's menfolk. It explained the lack of men of fighting age, who had long since departed to add to the huge toll of Germany's losses in godforsaken places like the deserts of North Africa and the steppes of the Eastern Front. I had gone into the church to seek some sort of solace. Padre Skinner used to say that there were 'no atheists in a foxhole', but I questioned my own religious faith when I looked at the memorial to so many fallen in such a small place and contemplated the fact that both sides claimed to believe in the same God and the righteousness of their respective causes.

The attitude of the remaining civilians varied. Few Germans we came across were outwardly hostile. Most bore a muted sullen resentment towards us as an enemy that had inflicted so much destruction on their country, although most seemed to be glad that the war for them was over and they had survived. Their general attitude was also one of servility; they appeared to be a people used to authority and accepting orders. The army issued strict instructions regarding how we should conduct relations with the civilian population and had a paranoid fixation with the issue of fraternisation. We were prohibited from talking to Germans unless in the course of duty. Laughing with them, shaking hands, sharing a house with them or giving them cigarettes or food, even sweets for the children, were all absolutely forbidden. Regardless of the regulations, they had little impact on the blokes' obsessive pursuit of crumpet. Given the privations of war, the general absence of German males and the high value attached to tobacco when traded on the black market, there was plenty to be had. If we were in a town or village, and there was time, most of the blokes would head off to the nearest cellar to seek gratification and comfort in the arms and between the legs of any frau willing to surrender herself for the price of a few fags. At the time, the promiscuity of my soldiers shocked me. But while I had lost my innocence as a soldier on the battlefield, I had little advanced experience of the opposite sex and my chastity remained intact. At the time, it seemed deplorable to me that Sergeant Webb often had to round up the crews from the dark confines of a basement before we moved off. But for men who were expected to risk life and limb on a near-daily basis, it provided relief from the stress of battle, as well as meeting a normal and very basic human need.

The army also had rules about the looting of German possessions, although what constituted loot was difficult to define. The regiment generally followed an unofficial policy that it was acceptable to help ourselves to articles that would make our lives more comfortable, such as bedding and clothing. This included items that we felt the Germans could do without, such as eggs and alcohol. By the end of our drive into Germany, I was sporting a very fine pair of German knee-length boots that I had taken from a Wehrmacht officer. They were the devil to get on and off, but I wished I had had them when we were fighting through the mud and the wet of Holland. Chickens continued to be added to the crew as temporary members and the occasional pig was commandeered and slaughtered by the squadron; the difference was that in Germany we neither asked nor bartered for what we took. We applied a similar approach to commandeer-ing German houses as billets. Giving the occupants a few minutes to gather a bundle of clothing and their personal possessions, we waved them out onto the streets without ceremony, sparing little thought for them. If our new quarters were undamaged, we took great delight in discovering working electricity, hot water and flush-ing lavatories. Most of the homes were well stocked with food and alcohol, which stood as an incongruous contrast to the rationing and shortages we knew that our own people were experiencing in England.

The signs of plenty and the lack of damage in the German homes that we occupied were less apparent as the advance towards Bremen continued. Drawing closer to the outskirts of the city, we passed the mutilated remains of German soldiers and horses lying alongside the remnants of smashed, burned-out vehicles that had been caught from the air by marauding Typhoons. Often, it was hard to avoid the miserable fragments of what had once been a German soldier, sprawled across the road. In some places the route was choked with files of dirty, dejected prisoners of war, with only the officers at the front showing any semblance of bearing, as they tramped wearily past us heading to the POW cages in the rear. They competed for space with straggling columns of German refugees, clutching suitcases, pushing prams and pulling handcarts, as they headed away from the fighting. But among the vast tide of humanity that was driven by the unforgiving energy of conflict, it was the 'displaced persons' that stood out the most. Recently freed Dutch, French, Russian and Polish slave labourers, released from their camps as the Nazi edifice collapsed around them, wandered in groups, clutching their pathetic bundles of possessions as they headed east or west, depending on their nationality. Others squatted at the side of the road picking through discarded German rations or feasting off the flesh from dead horses. They made for a pitiful sight and I wondered what stories of hardship and woe lay behind each emaciated and wretched individual we passed as we ground relentlessly on towards Bremen.

On 18 April the Sherwood Rangers attacked into the southern suburbs of the city on the west side of the Weser, under the command of the 3rd Infantry Division. The division had been one of the leading assault formations on D-Day, but it was the only infantry division of the 2nd British Army that we had not worked with before. In the week since crossing back into Germany, the regiment had conducted a war of rapid advances against isolated rearguard positions. But as we pushed into the outskirts of Bremen our progress slowed in the face of more consolidated opposition, as the German forces in the area regrouped to mount a last-ditch defence of the city. The attack met with considerable artillery and mortar fire, as well as shells from enemy gunboats moored in the harbour. Some of the resistance remained fanatical, but most Germans were eager to surrender when we closed with them and gave them the chance to capitulate. Peter Mellowes' troop was asked to deal with an 88mm anti-tank gun by a platoon commander of the Royal Ulsters, who had spotted it dug into an embankment covering a crossroads. The enemy gun emplacement was supported by machine guns and mortars, which would have made for a costly frontal assault. But the position was poorly sited; Peter managed to get his troop in behind the Germans without being detected and then obliterated them in a hail of HE and machine-gun fire. On climbing out of his tank he was sickened to discover that most of the dead were teenage boys. Their relative youth may have accounted for their poor defensive positioning, but had they been given the chance they would have killed us all as surely as any properly trained adult soldiers.

The biggest danger came from mines. Advancing into an urban area canalises armoured movement and the defenders dug in large sea mines designed to sink ships under the road, setting them to detonate after several vehicles had passed over them. One blew up a Kangaroo travelling in front of Stanley Christopherson's tank. Containing around a thousand pounds of high explosive, the mine atomised the twenty-ton armoured vehicle and the ten-man section of infantry travelling in it, leaving absolutely nothing behind. None of us spent too much time dwelling on the thought that our tanks had probably driven over it before it exploded. B Squadron lost one tank to a concealed 88mm. The AP round penetrated the turret, killing the troop commander, Lieutenant Denis Elmore, and fatally wounding his gunner and loader. Denis Elmore had been wounded in Normandy before rejoining the regiment at Schinnen just after the

New Year. He was the unit's last officer casualty and it seemed the cruellest fate to be killed so near to the end.

Four days later, we transferred back under the command of 43rd Wessex Division and crossed over the river Weser to join the final attack into the heart of Bremen. No one relished the task of battling into the centre of a modern city prepared for defence. Its substantial buildings and large network of gridded roads could eat up an attacking force, as it was compelled to fight from street to street and house to house. It was a concern shared by Horrocks, who was anxious to avoid further casualties in a war that was virtually over. But we knew that the Germans would make us fight for the place and there was a rumour that the burgomeister had been shot by the SS for wanting to declare Bremen as an open city, to spare its inhabitants from destruction. On 22 April, shells carrying 4000 leaflets were fired over the city urging its garrison to surrender, but the German commander, General Fritz Becker, refused. Later that night, the RAF flew a more deadly mission over the city. We heard the air-raid sirens wailing as the bombers approached and we watched them fly in low as they headed towards their target, where the beams of searchlights and flak reached up into the sky to meet them. Bomber Command made further sorties against the city and a pall of black smoke still hung over Bremen as our tanks rumbled on to the start line and married up with the infantry two days later.

XXX Corps launched the final attack on Bremen with three infantry divisions and the tanks of 8th Armoured Brigade. As the Sherwood Rangers attacked with 43rd Division from the southeast, the 52nd and 3rd Divisions attacked from the south and north. The city was a scene of utter devastation. The latest air attacks had come at the end of over four years of bombing, which included several thousand bomber raids. Hardly a building in the centre was left standing and those that had not been flattened were empty shells. My Sherman was the first tank to enter the city and I was shocked by the extent of the damage, although I felt no sympathy for the Germans, as I thought of our own cities like London and Coventry that had suffered during the Blitz. There were plenty of die-hards from the Hitler Youth, naval marines and a stiffening of SS detachments that were prepared to defend the rubble of their city. They engaged us with volleys of Panzerfausts and machine guns from barricades, slit trenches and the shattered remains of upper-storey buildings. But it was a futile effort that would achieve nothing more than increasing casualties and would just delay their inevitable defeat. We kept asking ourselves why they continued to fight and why they didn't give up. The answer, of course, lay in a mixture of motivations. Totalitarian obedience, indoctrination into the cult of Adolf Hitler, fear of the Allied demands for unconditional surrender and state terror, which had already brought about the execution of thousands of combatants and civilians for even the slightest trace of defeatism or an unwillingness to fight; all played their part. But we knew or cared little for abstract notions of cause. If the Germans were willing to fight it out with us, we had absolutely no inhibitions about inflicting maximum force to ensure that it was they who died and not us.

The pace of an assault against determined resistance in a built-up area is invariably slow, especially if it is made by troops keen to avoid becoming casualties when the end of a conflict is in sight. But while the majority of commanding officers, brigadiers and men like Horrocks understood this, von Thoma kept up the pressure on his brigade commanders. When one of his brigadiers explained his numerous difficulties as a reason for slow progress in the advance, von Thoma simply told the officer, who had an impressive war record that included being awarded the DSO twice, to 'fucking get on with it'. Getting on with it meant taking casualties. Initially, the infantry placed a heavy reliance on artillery fire to keep their losses down, but indirect shellfire has a much reduced effect in an urban area, so they requested us to get ahead of them and blast out a position with HE fire. We obliged, but Gartside's eyes were out on stalks as he sprayed down every doorway with .30-calibre fire in case it concealed a Panzerfaust. Meanwhile I ran the inevitable gauntlet with the snipers, while calling out targets for Martin to engage. On the other side of the breech, Mayo worked hard to keep the 75mm serviced with ammunition. Sergeant Webb supported me by staying a tactical bound behind my tank and shooting up any enemy infantry that attempted to take on my Sherman from the rear. We attempted to set as many of the buildings on fire as possible. The infantry would then close up, to clear through the rubble or join us in shooting down the enemy if they broke from cover.

The process went on building by building, block by block and street by street, slowed down by each enemy position and the piles of rubble that barred our progress. It continued until a new troop or squadron was pushed forward to take over and repeat the process, as we nudged forward less than a hundred yards at a time. Where we could, we called up the Funnies to deal with larger, well-constructed defensive bastions. The petards of the AVREs (Armoured Vehicle Royal Engineers) would demolish a troublesome building and the flamethrowing Crocodiles burned them out with belching jets of flaming petroleum liquid. Some Germans managed to slip back to depth positions to continue the fight further back, others came out with their hands above their heads or carrying their wounded. Those that didn't died where they stood. The attack continued into the night and we catnapped in the tanks as the ruined remains of Bremen burned around us. By the second day we were closing in on the final defensive position centred on the strongpoint created in Bürgerpark in the heart of the city, where General Becker had located his command bunker. A Squadron managed to get in behind the park and attacked it from the north with men of the Wiltshire Regiment. We ran into German marines who put up stiff resistance, but with C Squadron attacking from the south with a battalion of the Somersets, it was a last-ditch effort and B Squadron passed through us and managed to surround Becker's bunker and bring about his surrender and that of the city on 28 April. The final mopping up was left to the infantry, who also had to intervene against former slave labourers who ran amok in the docks in an orgy of killing, looting and rape among the local population. But by then we had received new orders to move with 43rd Division to capture the port of Bremerhaven at the mouth of the Weser, thirty miles to the north. The crew gave a collective groan when I told them that we would remain under von Thoma's command and the normal expressions regarding the inequity of life followed.

I felt it myself when we set off the next day. Each squadron was allocated to a different battalion group, which would travel on separate routes; not surprisingly the infantry CO of our group expected the tanks to lead. The country to the north of Bremen is low-lying and perennially wet, which meant that movement would be restricted to the roads, with all the risks of mines and ambushes. Surprisingly, the German officer who popped up from a ditch at the side of the road and decided to take us on with a Panzerfaust, as we advanced north, went for Sergeant Webb's tank instead of mine. It was a choice that cost the enemy his life, as Webb's Sherman had a length of spare track welded to its front. I had little faith in such measures, but it did its job in preventing the projectile from penetrating Webb's tank. Surviving the blast, Webb ran the unfortunate officer down and ground him to pieces beneath his tracks. As horrific as it may seem, the German was a combatant and had taken his chances in taking us on in an action that may well have resulted in five men being roasted alive had he been successful. However, the real horror lay only a few miles away and had nothing to do with the battlefield.

Towards the end of April, reports had begun to circulate through the army of the utterly horrifying discovery of a detention facility at a place called Belsen on Lüneburg Heath, near the city of Hamburg.

As 43rd Division advanced north, 8th Armoured Brigade discovered its own concentration camp located in the woods near the village of Sandbostel, eight miles from where the regiment leaguered in preparation for the coming attack on Bremerhaven. Apart from vague rumours of something unspeakable, I knew nothing about concentration camps. Consequently, I had no notion of what lay behind the wire and the guard posts when A Squadron motored past Stalag XB, as we headed to the leaguer location in the village of Hipstedt at the beginning of May. However, the image of the two figures that emerged from the gates and waved like listless scarecrows at us as we passed has been burned indelibly into my memory. Dressed in strange, filthy, striped uniforms, they were dreadfully thin. Their eyes and cheeks were sunk into the grey, stretched skin of their faces and lifting their arms seemed to require all their strength. I glanced at the sign over the gates and noted the meaningless German words 'Arbeit macht frei'. I later found out that it meant 'Work sets you free' and that the very same words appeared above the gates at Auschwitz.

The camp at Sandbostel had not been taken over by the British when A Squadron drove past. It was only later that we heard something of the details of what lay behind the wire. Originally designed as a POW camp to house 10,000 prisoners, the population of Sandbostel had swollen to over 30,000 inmates, including thousands of Jews and Soviet prisoners, by the time it was liberated. The place had been ravaged by typhus and chronic dysentery and 2000 bodies of the people that had already died there were spread among the slime of human excrement that littered the camp. Those that lived and were not among the population of British and French prisoners of war were packed into overcrowded, filthy, disease-ridden huts. Even after the medics of 8th Armoured Brigade's field hospital arrived, over a hundred individuals continued to die each day and the place became known as 'Little Belsen'. Thankfully, I never had to go there, but Hilda Young and Padre Skinner did. Despite all they had seen on the battlefield, it turned their stomachs and both men were relieved to get away from the indescribable awfulness of the place.

Horrocks ordered all the surrounding towns and villages to supply a quota of women to clean up the camps and look after the inmates. He later wrote that he expected them to show some indication of horror or remorse, but instead he never saw any sense of guilt or shred of pity in any of them. It was an attitude that we came across at our level as well. I never met a German who claimed to be a Nazi or showed any sense of shame for what had been done in their name. The owner of the house 5 Troop were billeted in at Hipstedt was typical, when she came to protest at the occupation of her home. The blokes told me that we had an angry frau at the door and I went to see her. The woman stood rigidly to attention and proceeded to berate me in broken English and German about her predicament, mentioning words like 'mein Haus' and 'nicht essen'. I suggested that she might proceed to the camp at Sandbostel and see if they would accommodate and feed her there. The woman immediately flew into a rage, immediately denying that she had anything to do with the Nazis or had any knowledge of such things. It was remarkable that a place that housed so much deliberately inflicted human misery could exist in such close proximity to ordinary Germans without them knowing anything about it, especially as the camp regularly sent out thousands of its inmates to work as slave labour gangs in the surrounding area. I suggested that she buggered off and bothered to find out something about it. Shutting the door on her, I could not help noticing the prominent empty picture hook on the wall. Like so many other German homes we entered, I strongly suspected that it once held a framed picture of Adolf Hitler.

The Führer that so many Germans were so quick to deny had committed suicide on 30 April, as his bunker in Berlin was about to be overrun by the Red Army. Four days later, a day after my spat with the *hausfrau* had taken place, an altogether more important Anglo-German discussion was being conducted at Montgomery's headquarters on Lüneburg Heath. At 1700 hours, a senior delegation signed the surrender of all German forces in Holland, Denmark and Northwest Germany. The order was to take effect from 0800 hours the next day, on Saturday 5 May. Earlier that day, the Sherwood Rangers had already moved into their attack positions for the assault on Bremerhaven and von Thoma had visited the CO to give him the details for the next operation. The regiment was hard at work preparing for the next day's battle when word went round that the war in Europe was over. Mayo was manning the radio and picked up the message before me. He shouted for me from inside the turret and told me it was 'bloody over'. It took me a few moments to register what he had said and then Gartside's face appeared suddenly next to mine; his repetition of the words 'Fooking hell! It's fooking over!' were ample enough confirmation of what I had just heard.

Back home the crowds went mad, as the BBC announced the news. In London they thronged the Mall demanding to see the King, in a huge outpouring of emotion. All along the British line in Germany, the night sky was filled with the red and green lights of Very flares fired off in celebration, which replaced the thunder and flashes of artillery that were now strangely absent. The crew were ecstatic; they shook my hand, slapped me on the back and immediately went off in search of booze and crumpet. Champagne from a looted stash was broken out among the officers, but I paused in the cool night air before I went to join them. In just under eleven months we had travelled far, fighting all the way from the beaches of Normandy, breaking out across the Seine and battling our way to Nijmegen and then, through the bloody months of hard winter, slogging in the mud and water of the Low Countries, before finally crossing the German frontier to take part in the last engagements in places like Lochem and Bremen. I reflected on all that we had done and thought of those that we had lost. I thought of Dixon, Sergeant Major Hutchinson and many others that now lay in makeshift cemeteries tied up in dirty army blankets. But most of all I thought of Harry Heenan. Of a best friendship made and lost, as the result of a gallant action that meant I was standing under a sky full of the fluorescent brilliance of bursting coloured light and Harry was not.

AFTERWORD

In the early hours of the morning on 7 May 1945, representatives of the German High Command signed the formal unconditional surrender of all German forces to Eisenhower at his headquarters in Reims. The next day the same terms were signed with the Soviets in Berlin. The signatures on the final capitulation documents brought the war in Europe to a close and marked the end of nearly twelve months of battle that had cost the Sherwood Rangers 153 dead and 287 wounded. Horrocks later remarked that the regiment had seen more fighting than any other unit in the British army. A week later, those of us who had survived drove past the XXX Corps commander as part of a victory parade through the shattered streets of Bremen, in highly polished tanks that only a few days before had been covered in the mud and grime of battle.

With the conflict officially over, the regiment became part of the occupying forces in the British sector of Germany. Initially stationed in Hanover, our primary duties consisted of protecting the civilian population from the large numbers of displaced persons bent on wreaking revenge on their former persecutors, safeguarding key installations and distributing domestic commodities such as food and coal to the local populace. It seemed incongruous that after five years of doing our level best to inflict the maximum damage on them and their country, we now found ourselves protecting the Germans from those whom we had liberated, sustaining them and guarding their critical infrastructure. In June the regiment moved to Magdeburg, where we met the Russians on the other side of the Elbe, who had a very different interpretation of occupation.

A structure called the 'Bridge of Friendship' had been constructed to link the two banks of the British and Soviet sectors. However, the concept of comradeship did not extend to the thousands of former Russian and Polish prisoners of war and slave labourers that we saw filing across the bridge. The Red Army troops that met them were an unruly rabble who mobbed around a T-34 tank and Cossacks mounted on ponies. The T-34 took a pot shot at us, no doubt explained away as a vodka-fuelled error. But the shooting that we heard break out as soon as most of the displaced persons had crossed the bridge had more deliberate and deadly intent, as the Soviet secret police began dispatching those who were considered traitors for having been captured or forcibly transported by the Germans from their native countries. We felt some sympathy for the local people of Magdeburg when we handed the place over to the Russians at the end of the month, as the Soviet soldiers then began systematically stripping the place of anything of value. The last sector I served in was in Einbeck, near the Harz Mountains, where we took the surrender of a company of sixteen Panthers. The German tanks were drawn up in parade order, with immaculately turned-out crews wearing their smart, well-fitting tank uniforms of black and silver. They saluted us as they handed over their tanks and stood in marked contrast to our encounters with the Red Army.

My time as an occupier was destined to be a short one. With the fighting over I had hoped to be discharged and sent back to England. But I was still not twenty-one and with eighteen months of my emergency commission still to run the War Office dictated that younger men with time left to serve should be dispatched to fight the Japanese. On 9 August a second atomic bomb was dropped on the city of Nagasaki. Six days later, Japan announced its surrender and the Second World War was over. I was already destined for the Pacific, but the advent of what were to be called nuclear weapons made the posting pointless and I was diverted to service in Egypt. Today the decision to use such weapons against two Japanese cities is surrounded by controversy, but you won't catch me marching against the bomb or criticising the decision to use it to end the war. None of us who were on our way to the Far East relished the prospect of fighting another campaign, having just survived the one in Europe. While the atom bombs inflicted terrible casualties, they ultimately saved hundreds and thousands more Allied and Japanese lives, which would have been lost if a full-scale invasion of Japan had been mounted.

I spent the next eighteen months based in Alexandria, close to sites of the former North African battles of the Sherwood Rangers. Attached to the Derbyshire Yeomanry, I took part in patrolling the desert in armoured cars to help impose post-war order on the local Arab tribes. My own regiment was not to survive for long after my departure. On 2 February 1946, Stanley Christopherson received a letter from Montgomery informing him that the Sherwood Rangers were to be placed in suspended animation, an army term designed to soften the blow of disbandment. The unit had already lost its tanks the previous summer just before I left and this added to the poignancy of an emotional farewell from the regiment that had become my home. With the war over, the army needed to reduce in size and on 1 March the Sherwood Rangers were officially removed from the order of battle.* The older men who had joined up from the

---

* The regiment was reformed in 1947 to meet the growing tension of the Cold War. Although later reduced in size to a single sub-unit, the Sherwood Rangers continue to exist today as a squadron of the Royal Yeomanry in the Army Reserves.

Territorial Army when the regiment was mobilised, or had been con-scripted earlier in the war, were discharged from service. Like many of the other younger men, who had joined later in the war, I wasn't demobbed until 1947 when I was issued with an ill-fitting suit, a hat and a pamphlet entitled 'Release and Resettlement' for my trouble.

Despite the horror that the men of the regiment had witnessed, the privations of battle and the death of friends, for most being part of the Sherwood Rangers was the most significant and formative event in their lives. For some of us, it was our only adult experience and for many the overwhelming feeling on being demobbed was of loss. Most had grown up in the Great Depression and many found it difficult to adjust to the drab outside world of post-war Britain. Not surprisingly, they missed the sense of structured purpose, belong-ing, discipline and comradeship. For some there were deeper, darker mental issues to overcome and many suffered from what has come to be recognised as PTSD, with its hypersensitivity to unfamiliar sur-roundings and loud noises and a loss of inner psychological integrity. Not all suffered from the invisible scars of war and I was fortunate to be one of them. But others, often with significant gallantry awards, did. George Dring, with his countryman's eye for ground, which made him one of the most courageous and successful tank com-manders in the regiment during the war, was badly affected by his experiences. Reticent by nature, for years after the war he refused to speak of his experiences in the army and would not watch a war film or walk on his own down a country lane at night. During one reunion after the war, Dring was invited to climb into a Sherman tank. Although in his seventies, it was a challenge that he couldn't refuse. When congratulated on his agility given his age, he retorted, 'Aye, but there'll be nightmares tonight.'

There was no counselling in those days and we were from a gener-ation where few people had not experienced something of war. Terms like 'shellshock' and 'battle fatigue' were reserved for only the most acute and obvious cases, who might receive clinical treatment. But many hundreds of thousands of wartime servicemen suffered alone and in silence, as they knuckled down and got on with their lives. John Semken went on to have a highly successful career at the Bar, becoming the senior legal adviser to the Home Office, where he was decorated for his service. For much of his life after the war, he kept many of his experiences to himself. Stanley Christopherson started a new life in South Africa, where he became a senior executive in the goldfield industry, before being offered a high-profile job in a top-notch stockbroking company in London. He lost none of his charm or gaiety, but beneath his friendly and smiling exterior he continued to harbour a deep sense of responsibility for every one of the lives of the soldiers lost under his command.

My relative youth, and the fact that I had not served as long as some members of the regiment, may have helped. I had gone to war as a kid and returned as a man, with a greater sense of inner self-confidence. Through the experiences and responsibilities of leading a troop in battle, I was also more comfortable with myself. I came home having recently been promoted to the rank of captain, although there was no fanfare when I returned, either in the form of welcoming parades or from my own parents. They loved me and were glad that I had returned safely, but their Victorian values prevented any particularly emotional outpouring. My father's first concern was my civilian employment and I joined his firm. After a year, I knew that I had to be my own man and yielded to my independent streak and the desire to forge my own path. I borrowed £2000, which was a huge sum in those days, and bought out a failing concrete manufacturing company. It took years of hard work, but by the time I sold it in 1991, it was a robust and highly profitable concern with a hundred employees, fifty cement-mixing trucks and three quarries producing 16,000 concrete blocks a day. I also built up a farm with 5000 pigs and an extensive property portfolio, which I still manage today. Becoming a successful businessman allowed me to pursue my passion for racing and rally-ing fast cars. In 1983, I won the National Brighton Speed Trials and took the record in 1985, which I held for nine years.

Most of us were busy with building our new lives, or restarting old ones, in the years that followed on immediately from the war. However, with the passage of time, many felt a great collective yearning for the comradeship and regimental pride that we had once shared in that brief and extraordinary time. As a consequence, I started to attend Sherwood Ranger reunions and travel on regi-mental pilgrimages to old battle sites in Europe. These journeys to places like Normandy, Vernon and Nijmegen later became annual events. The numbers attending grew, as we celebrated significant anniversaries such as the 50th and 60th D-Day commemorations. We visited former objectives, the battle damage long since repaired and the scarred landscape much softened by time, although seeing a particular wood or track was still poignant enough to rekindle memory-etched scenes, sounds and feelings: the crack of an 88mm, the burp of stuttering machine guns or the pungent smell of burned explosive in the nostrils and its tangy taste in the mouth. Reunions and commemorations became a time to meet old comrades in an atmosphere of mutual respect, affection and humour. Sam Gartside and Sid Martin were sometimes there and would always insist on standing up and calling me 'Sir'; the old bonds of military discipline hardly eroded as we advanced in years. We talked of a sticky time here, or a hilarious moment there, remembering good fellowship, the adrenaline of battle and sometimes its dread. We also remembered those who didn't make it home, like Harry Heenan who now lies at peace in Jonkerbos War Cemetery in Holland, which tinged every event with remembrance and sadness. My other sadness was that I never managed to keep up with Ken Mayo. I tried to make contact with him a few years after the war. He had moved to Norfolk and found employment there as a radio engineer, but he did not attend the regimental gatherings. Stanley Christopherson was a regular attendee at reunions and the collective love for him as a commander was as strong as ever at the time of his death in 1990. Similar love, like only a soldier can know, still exists for John Semken, who had lost none of his flair for meticulous preparation and attention to detail. With failing health and eyesight, in preparing for the 60th Anniversary Commemoration of D-Day he dictated his battlefield tour notes in advance. John then spent three days memorising every word, so that he could speak with accuracy about the events of seven decades before to the audience that sat in a large coach, as it toured the area where we had once fought.

John was also with us when we attended the official commemoration event on Gold Beach, but I was on my own when I slipped away from the main crowd when it had finished and wandered along the same stretch of Gold Beach where we had landed. The tide was much further out than it had been on D+4 and I found myself staring at the distant waves as they rolled and broke, to run in the last few yards towards the beach in foaming white lines of water. I was thinking about the loss of the Cromwell and then I saw it. A tidal rip in the shallows appeared several yards out from the beach, as the waves receded with the current. As they sluiced backwards they revealed a large trough in the shingle that had been excavated by the constant drag of tidal pressure. The channel was certainly big enough to swallow a tank and explained what had happed to the first Cromwell when it had dropped off the ramp seventy years before. A few feet either side of the hollow, and the tank would have been in four feet of water, but the crater carved by the constant motion of the waves was well over ten feet deep. The ramp of the LST must have been directly over it and those two young troopers didn't stand a chance. I don't think I ever knew the names of the boys that lost their lives in the Cromwell that was claimed by the peculiar oceanology of Gold Beach. I can remember that they appeared young, but I can't remember their faces. However, they were much in my thoughts as I walked along the lonely stretch of beach and the belief that their loss might have had something to do with me finally lifted.

With the passage of time the number of veterans attending commemorations has reduced. Our ranks have been wearied and depleted by age. But those of us who are still able will continue to gather in our faded tank berets, regimental ties and smart blazers or suits, with campaign medals on our chests. We will continue to celebrate and reminisce about events, the depth of comradeship forged by war and how we fought together and triumphed in adversity during that extraordinary time in northwest Europe all those years ago. We will continue to swell with pride in the regiment and the fact that we were part of it and we will continue to remember those who never made it home. While there is some sadness, I have no regrets and wouldn't have missed it for the world. I have been fortunate in life, fortunate to survive the war and find success and love after it. Despite the luck that I have had, I have always thought of myself as a soldier first and foremost. Someone once asked me what it was like the day I left the Sherwood Rangers. I replied that I never did, as that day has not yet come.

ACKNOWLEDGEMENTS

In writing this book the authors wish to express their thanks to a variety of people who were so willing to give up their time to make it possible. We are particularly grateful to James Holland, an expert on the history of the Second World War, who first made the introductions possible, as well as supplying source material and providing guidance. We would also like to thank Jonathan Hunt, former Colonel of the Sherwood Rangers and Mike Elliot, the Regimental Secretary, who were incredibly supportive of the project and generous with their time and with the advice and support that they provided. Jim Clark deserves a special mention for making the Sherman tank that he so lovingly restored available to crawl over and drive in around the Gloucestershire countryside. As does Christopher Semken, who provided incredibly helpful indirect access to his father, John Semken.

We would both like to say a big thank you to Annie and Sasha, the women in our lives who supported us throughout and put up with long hours of us being locked away in our studies, journeying to France or endlessly talking on the telephone.

It was a pleasure to work with Orion and we owe a big vote of thanks to Alan Samson and his team for having faith in publishing the story. Finally, I would like to thank Phil Patterson. Acting as our agent he was always there, constantly providing detailed advice and support and encouraging us with his enthusiasm throughout.

BIBLIOGRAPHY

PUBLISHED SOURCES

Bailey, R., *Forgotten Voices of D-Day* (Ebury 2010)

Beevor, A., *D-Day* (Viking 2009)

Bishop, G., *The Battle – A Tank Officer Remembers* (privately published, n.d.)

Buckley, J., *Monty's Men* (Yale University Press 2013)

Campbell, J.D. and Leinbaugh, H.P., *The Man of Company K* (Bantam Books 1986)

Cross, R., *Fallen Eagle* (Caxton Editions 1995)

Douglas, K., *Alamein to Zem Zem* (Faber and Faber 2008)

Ellis, J., *The Sharp End of War* (Corgi Books 1982)

Forty, G., *Companion to the British Army* (The History Press 1998)

Hastings, M., *Armageddon* (Macmillan 2004)

Hastings, M., *Overlord* (Book Club Associates 1984)

Hills, S., *By Tank into Normandy* (Cassell 2002)

Holland, J., *An Englishman at War* (Bantam Press 2014)

Horrocks, B.H., *A Full Life* (Leo Cooper 1974)

Hunt, J., *Hard Fighting: A History of the Sherwood Rangers Yeomanry 1900–1946* (Pen & Sword 2016)

Jarry, S., *18 Platoon* (Sydney Jarry 1987)

Kite, B., *Stout Hearts* (Helion 2014)

Lindsay, M., *So Few Got Through* (Pen & Sword 2000)

Lindsay, T.M., *Sherwood Rangers* (Burrup, Mathieson 1952)

McNab, C., *Hitler's Armies* (Osprey 2010)

Reddish, A., *A Tank Soldier's Story* (privately published, n.d.)

Reynolds, M., *Steel Inferno* (Spellmount 1997)

Ryan, C., *The Longest Day* (Coronet 1988)

Skinner, L., *The Man Who Worked on Sundays* (Revd. Leslie Skinner RAChd 1997)

Skinner, L., *The Sherwood Rangers Casualty Book 1944–1945* (Revd. Leslie Skinner RAChd 1997)

Trelor, G., *The Memoirs of Trooper G. Trelor* (privately published, n.d.)

Urban, M., *Tank War* (Little Brown 2013)

Whiting, C., *Bloody Bremen* (Leo Cooper 1998)

Whiting, C., *West Wall* (Pan Books 1999)

Wilmot, C., *The Struggle for Europe* (Richard Clay 1954)

Zaloga, S.J., *The Sherman Medium Tank* (Osprey 1993)

UNPUBLISHED SOURCES

8th Armoured Brigade, War Diary – WO171/4327, WO171/613 and WO171/666

43rd Infantry Division, War Diary – WO223/45

59th Infantry Division, War Diary – WO171/667

Stanley Christopherson, War Diary

The Private Letters of David Render – 1944–45

The Sherwood Rangers, War Diary

Bibliography

CITATIONS

Christopherson, Stanley (Lieutenant Colonel, DSO) – WO373/51/280
Lanes, James (Corporal, MM) – WO373/53/196
Semken, John (A/Major, MC) – WO373/49/47
Webb, Dennis (Sergeant, MM) – WO373/52/733

INDEX

Index

Index

Index

Northern Polytechnic, 29

Nottinghamshire dialect, 83

O groups, 74–6, 85, 106, 269, 275

Odon, river, 104–5, 126

Officer Training Corps, 30

Omaha Beach, 8, 10, 24

Ondefontaine, 157, 163, 167

Operation Blackwater, 168

Operation Bluecoat, 146, 156–7, 160

Operation Clipper, 227

Operation Cobra, 144–5

Operation Epsom, 104–5, 108, 126, 129

Operation Fortitude, 7

Operation Goodwood, 138, 144

Operation Grenade, 249n

Operation Market Garden, xvi, 195–6, 205–6, 212, 221, 225

Operation Martlet, 105

Operation Pepper Pot, 250, 257

Operation Plunder, 262, 266

Operation Veritable, 249–51, 255–6

O'Pray, Sergeant, 269

Orne, river, 8

Palenberg, 229, 234–5

Palestine, 79, 83

Palmer, Sergeant Robert, 21

Panther tanks, 52, 71–2, 90, 114, 123–4, 126–7, 132–4, 178, 222, 234

detection of, 133–4

fuel consumption, 180

provides Jagdpanther chassis, 157

surrender to A Squadron, 292

Panzer Lehr, 52, 55–6, 62, 87, 89–90, 131, 137

defeated, 172, 256

Panzer Mark IV tanks, 70–1, 89, 123, 188

Panzerschrecks, 154

paratroopers

Allied, 8, 195, 207–14, 220, 222, 225, 228, 263–4

German, 154–5, 196, 198, 201, 203–4, 252–3, 256, 265, 269

and Hitler cult, 203, 256

Paris, 88, 172, 174

Patton, General George, 193

Petard mortars, 9, 22, 230–1, 284

PIAT anti-tank weapons, 204

Point 102, 94–5, 101, 104, 106–7, 109–12

Point 103, 51–2, 56, 58, 62, 82

Poland, 28

Polish forces, 171

Portsmouth, 37–8, 40

promiscuity, of Allied soldiers, 226, 278–9

propaganda leaflets, 246, 282

Proussy, 168–9

Prummern, 233–4

Python leave programme, 256

radios

18 Set, 111